Eat Well
spend less

Over **250** healthy recipes
for busy cooks who want
to save money

Sarah Flower

SPRING HILL

To my wonderful sons, Orri and Tamlin

Published by Spring Hill, an imprint of How To Books Ltd.
Spring Hill House, Spring Hill Road
Begbroke, Oxford OX5 1RX United Kingdom
Tel: (01865) 375794
Fax: (01865) 379162
info@howtobooks.co.uk
www.howtobooks.co.uk

The right of Sarah Flower to be identified as author of this work has been
asserted by her in accordance with the Copyright, Designs and Patents Act 1988.

© 2010 Sarah Flower

British Library Cataloguing in Publication Data
A catalogue record of this book is available from the British Library

ISBN: 978 1 905862 39 9

Produced for How To Books by Deer Park Productions, Tavistock, Devon
Designed and typeset by Mousemat Design Ltd
Printed and bound by Bell & Bain Ltd, Glasgow

NOTE: The material contained with this book is set out in good faith for general
guidance and no liability can be accepted for loss or expense incurred as a
result of relying in particular circumstances on statements made in the book.
Laws and regulations are complex and liable to change, and readers should
check the current position with relevant authorities before making personal
arrangements.

Contents

Introduction

This book combines healthy eating ideas with budget tips for the savvy shopper. You can lead a healthy lifestyle *and* save money. Our grandparents' generation were remarkably fit during the Second World War, even though they were subject to the most stringent food rationing, so if they can do it with those restrictions, we can do it with our unlimited resources.

Although I am a nutritionist, I have tried to create recipes that will appeal to all tastes and ages. You will find plenty of family favourites, but you may notice I have tweaked some of them very subtly in order to make them slightly healthier. If your diet has so far consisted of more processed food than fresh home-cooked, these small steps will make a massive difference. By following the recipes and using fresh ingredients, you will reduce your salt intake and be on the way towards a healthier life. Depending on your previous lifestyle, you may even find some of the recipes will help you lose weight. There are tips and ideas to help you lead a healthier lifestyle in the following chapters: *We Are What We Eat*, *Tips for a Healthier You* and *Cooking Tricks for Health*.

A word about alcohol
You may notice that some recipes in this book include wine. If you are worried about giving this to children, don't be as the alcohol does burn off during cooking, leaving only the flavour. If you are still concerned, you can either omit the wine or opt for alcohol-free wines which are great if you like the flavour but want to avoid any alcohol.

The cost of recipes
Food prices are changing all the time. Since writing this book you may find that some prices have changed but, even so, the price of each recipe will give you a good idea of how much you are likely to spend. Here is a breakdown on how I have priced the recipes.

Price of the recipe

This is the price of the ingredients only – it does not include the cost of cooking, as that would depend on the individual's cooking equipment. The ingredients costs are calculated on the actual cost of what is used, not the cost of the whole packet you may have to buy. For example, if 1kg of Sainsbury's Basic long-grain rice costs 73p and the recipe needs 200g, the actual cost of the rice is rounded up to 15p.

Herbs, spices and dollops of olive oil

I grow my own herbs so I have a large amount of fresh herbs in my garden, particularly throughout the summer months. I use frozen herbs (some I do myself, others I buy). I also use dried herbs and spices which I buy in 500g or 1kg bags. To break down the cost of 1 teaspoon of herbs or spice is going to be very difficult, so as these are everyday items, I have not included them in the costs. Currently you can buy spices for as little as 50p per 20g from supermarkets or from suppliers such as Essential Trading in Bristol (www.essential-trading.co.uk), and www.redmoors.net from as little as £2 a kilo, so you can imagine how difficult it would be to price half a teaspoon! The same problem arises when trying to price a dollop of olive oil, therefore this is not included.

Fresh fruit and vegetables

I prefer to buy my fruit and vegetables locally from farmers' markets, allotment swaps and organic box schemes; however, for ease of pricing, I have compared the prices of the three leading supermarkets, Asda, Sainsbury's and Tesco, and found the best price of each single item – for example, 2 bulbs of garlic for 39p. You get roughly 8 cloves per bulb, so I have estimated that a clove of garlic costs 3p. Applying the same principle for other vegetables, an onion would cost 10p, a tomato 20p, a red pepper 50p and so on.

Optional and cheat ingredients

I have not included the price of the optional ingredients as they are what they are – optional! Using cheat ingredients, such as a ready-made jar of pasta sauce in your bolognese instead of making your own, are an option. Obviously this will push the price of the meal up. If, however, the cheat ingredient is part of the recipe (such as using ready-made puff pastry), then this will be included in the price.

We Are What We Eat

Cooking healthy meals doesn't have to be stressful

We have been led to believe that healthy food is the weird stuff you find in health food shops, but actually healthy food is plain traditional food. Over the past 30–40 years, we have to a great extent lost the ability or desire to cook meals from scratch. Together with our lack of exercise this adds up to an unhealthy lifestyle. As with most things in life, there is a scale of what is considered healthy and unhealthy. You choose where you want to be on that scale. Ready meals are moderately better for us than a fast-food diet, but a home-cooked meal is far better than either of them. So, if you simply eat the same food but cook it yourself, you will dramatically improve your diet. Add a few tweaks to traditional recipes and, without really trying, you are even further up the scale towards good health.

Why should we eat a healthy diet?

Hippocrates said, 'Let the food be thy medicine,' but how many of us follow this principle? Would you feed your dog on a diet of burgers and chips with a bowl of cola for refreshment? If you did, would you be surprised to find the dog gets sick? Would you purée a Big Mac and fries and serve it to your six-month-old baby? Perhaps you think this sounds ridiculous, but how many of us feed ourselves with poor-quality food? You can make the excuse that you are too busy, too stressed, can't afford a better diet, but I assure you, every excuse can be quashed. You owe it to your family to ensure they have the best possible start in life – and what better start than following a diet and lifestyle that provides strong building blocks and foundations for a healthy life?

The big excuse . . .

I may be a nutritionist but I was brought up on a typical 1970s diet. Spaghetti bolognese was considered adventurous; I devoured crisps, chocolate and biscuits as fast as the next child. I am still a chocoholic. If I get stressed, I crave comfort food; if I am pumped up with adrenaline, I forget to eat. I am human. What I try to do is ensure that 90% of my diet is good. That is the best we can do in our world. What really interests me is helping real people make small but meaningful changes in order to lead a healthier and hopefully longer life.

Below are some of the most common excuses for not preparing and cooking our food from scratch.

'I don't have time to cook' You know the story: home from work, tough day and the last thing you feel like doing is putting together a meal. It is easier to call for a takeaway or search in the freezer for a frozen something. Yet you could make a fresh pasta dish from start to finish in less than ten minutes, including preparation. You could, if you follow this book, have something already cooking in the slow cooker as you walk through the door. Alternatively, by following these ideas, you could have a home-made meal in the fridge or freezer ready to heat up. The secret to making life easy for yourself is preparation.

'I can't cook' Everyone can cook. If you can read, you can follow a recipe. The secret to cooking is not to get too stressed. Enjoy the experience and make the dishes your own. So what if you burn something! Next time you will remember not to have the hob on so high. You learn by trial and error and, somewhere along the way, you will find yourself making up your own recipes or even cooking without weighing the ingredients. Get your children involved at an early age; they will enjoy the experience and you will pass on to them a skill that will benefit them for the rest of their lives.

'Healthy food is too expensive' Each of my recipes gives the price of the ingredients, alongside the price per portion. You will be pleasantly surprised; you can cook a nutritious and filling soup

for four people for less than £1 – that's less than 25p per person. Healthy cooking is about giving your family pure, honest food that has not been altered, zapped, bashed, bruised and mutilated by a machine or food manufacturer. It is how our ancestors ate; it is how we are supposed to eat.

Small steps build up to success

Opting for healthier choices does not have to mean starting with huge steps. Go at the pace that suits you and makes you feel good. If you love white bread, try white with wholegrains added, or even start to make your own bread. Home-made white bread is better than processed white bread – but it is still white bread. If you love chips, why not try some home-made potato wedges; or, for real chip addicts, opt for a chip fryer that uses very little oil, such as the Tefal ActiFry.

The real cost of a poor diet

We don't need to be told that convenience food is bad for us – we all know that, deep down. What we do need is quick, easy and ultimately healthy advice, lifestyle tips and recipes to help us lead the fit, active lives we want to lead.

Childhood obesity, heart disease, diabetes and even cancer can all be attributed to poor diets. We are living in a society with rising numbers of children who are obese yet malnourished. Convenience foods tend to be loaded with salt, sugar and a cocktail of chemicals; at the same time they are devoid of essential nutrients. Children are sent to school after eating sugar-loaded breakfast cereals that are so lacking in essential nutrients, the manufacturers have to add nutrients in order to con us into thinking we are giving our children a nourishing start to the day. We then give them another sugar and salt high in their packed lunches: crisps, sugar-rich bars masquerading as healthy snacks, processed bread sandwich, with equally processed fillings. To help us feel like good parents, we may throw in an apple or a banana (which ends up rolling around the lunchbox for a few days until it is too bashed and bruised to be edible, before it eventually gets thrown away). As soon as they are back from school they have more sugary or salty snacks, before plonking themselves in front of various screens for the rest of the evening. Is it any wonder the statistics are now showing that parents will outlive their children?

The onus is very much on the family to make changes towards healthier lifestyles, but I also believe the Government should make more of an effort to change things. They could begin by tackling the food manufacturers.

I would estimate that the combined costs to the NHS of obesity, heart disease, diabetes and all the other illnesses associated with poor diets and lifestyle are probably higher than the cost of smoking-related illnesses. If food manufacturers had to place health warnings on particularly nasty junk foods, and manufacturers were not allowed to advertise them (don't get me started on junk food advertising aimed at children!), it would be a great start to the campaign for healthy eating. Instead we have the reverse: the foods that are worst for our health are the most advertised and promoted. Think about the big fast-food outlets, the confectionery companies, manufacturers of crisps, fizzy drinks, ready-made meals – then compare the marketing of these products to the marketing of fresh fruit and vegetables, healthy snacks, real food. Is it any wonder that our children recognise the golden arches of McDonald's, but will struggle to name most fruit and vegetables?

Are we getting our five a day?

The Government has spent millions trying to promote healthy eating. The Campaign4life (costing £75 million to launch), which includes advice on how to encourage children to eat five portions of fruit or vegetables a day, is slowly getting its message across to supermarkets and food manufacturers, but as ever the messages are being distorted. Amid the confusion of what actually constitutes five portions a day, we also have food manufacturers producing sugary, man-made products and claiming that they can be included as part of your five a day. Is it any wonder we are all confused?

A survey by Tropicana fruit juices in the summer of 2009 reported that over 66% of UK respondents understood the importance of eating their five a day. However, on closer inspection, over 60% were failing to meet the target. Some were including chips (potatoes do not count as part of your five a day), orange squash and, bizarrely, even herbs. Vegetables are often neglected in favour of fruit, so the balanced five-a-day message is falling far short of its target. According to the book *Statistics on Obesity, Physical Activity and Diet*, published by the NHS Information Centre in February 2009, only 19% of boys and 22% of girls eat five portions of fruit and vegetables daily. So, it appears we are listening to the message but making our own assumptions about how to execute it. Inadequate cooking techniques, too much reliance on processed foods, and an inability to decide what really does count as a portion are to blame. One teacher I worked with believed that five a day is the maximum amount of fruit and vegetables you should have – in fact, it is the minimum.

Teach your children well

I have spent time working with primary age children, helping them understand more about food and healthy eating. For the majority of children, eating fresh fruit and vegetables is an alien concept – bananas, apples and oranges are really the only fruit they seem to recognise and eat on a regular basis. Getting children to touch, taste and feel different foods is the first step to healthy eating. Over 90% of the children I have worked with love new foods once they have tried them.

Children's tastes develop according to what you feed them at a young age. I have seen mums turn their noses up at the food they are trying to push into their toddlers' mouths – is it any wonder the child rejects it? Children respond well to education, and if you can teach them about healthy food and make it fun, entertaining and lecture free, you will get the message across. Children are easy – it is the parents who are hard work!

Follow in our grandparents' footsteps

I have just read *Sucking Eggs* by Patricia Nicol. It is a fantastic insight into how our grandparents coped during the Second World

War. 'Reduce, reuse and recycle' was part of their everyday lives. They had to survive on meagre food rations but were educated and supported by the Government, headed by minister of food Lord Woolton. Children responded well to the cartoon images of Dr Carrot and Potato Pete; housewives were taught which foods offered energy, essential vitamins and minerals to their families. Throughout this terrible time, the nation managed to stay in the peak of health.

Yet they did nothing fancy. They cooked pure, honest food, using very few ingredients. They grew what they could, shopped daily for fresh food and lived by the seasons. The average number of calories consumed per day by each person during the 1940s and 1950s was actually greater then we consume today, and yet people were thinner. Obesity was unheard of and diabetes, cancer and heart disease rates were a fraction of what they are today. Can we put this all down to diet? Actually, I believe we can put it down to lifestyle and diet. We are less active now; we eat less wholefood (as in pure, unadulterated food); we use more chemicals on our foods, in our foods and in our homes. Physical exercise and home economics classes have declined dramatically in our schools, particularly secondary schools. Fingers and thumbs get the most exercise, battering away on keyboards or games consoles.

Why can home-made food help?

It is only in the past 20–30 years that we have become reliant on processed foods. I was born in 1970. I only ever ate home-made food. The nearest we got to processed was a beefburger or, as a special treat, maybe fish and chips from the chip van that visited our village once a week. I remember having Angel Delight and thinking it was a really special treat. Sundays were spent cooking our Sunday roast while preparing and baking a host of food for the following week. Cakes, pies, biscuits were all baked to fill our lunch-boxes. Shop-bought biscuits were a special treat and we were only allowed two. I remember being told, 'You are only allowed one chocolate and the other plain.' To this day, I still follow that rule!

Good health is not about calorie counting, it is about

providing a balanced, nutrient-rich diet. Nature has provided us with this in the shape of pure, wholesome food; all you have to do is prepare it. It doesn't matter if you use a little sugar, fat or even a touch of salt in home-cooked food. By comparison, processed food is oozing with salt, sugar, colourings, flavourings and a wealth of other chemicals. It's a no-brainer really.

Saving time or killing your time?

I am constantly shocked by the vast array of products available under the guise of 'saving time' or 'easy cook': fruit and vegetables cut into slices and bagged (how long does it take to cut an apple – in fact, why do we need to cut an apple – bite it!); porridge sachets, quick and easy, two minutes in a microwave (I can make porridge in two minutes in a saucepan without zapping it with microwaves or additional preservatives and additives in order to make it 'easy'). If we spend our lives taking short cuts with our food, ultimately we will be cutting time off our lives. Sounds dramatic, but think about it: you are what you eat. Our bodies are designed to consume wholesome, natural food. The human body does not recognise man-made chemicals or adulterated foods; it needs the correct fuel in order to operate efficiently. Gillian McKeith has demonstrated perfectly what a difference a wholesome diet can make to health and weight. You don't have to take the dramatic steps Gillian was advocating (unless you want to!), but start to choose your food in its purest form and cook it yourself instead of relying on processed and microwave foods.

The wonderful thing about cooking is that it can become addictive. You are creating something that your family and friends will enjoy. Revel in that glow, savour the experience and soon you will be experimenting with your own creations. If you have children, remember to include them – after all, the kitchen really is the heart of the family home.

Tips for a Healthier You

You don't have to become a fitness freak in order to lead a healthy lifestyle – it is all about moderation and small steps. Think about the tale of the tortoise and the hare – small, steady and consistent steps are far better than racing around frantically and wearing yourself out. Anyone can make a start with these small steps.

Opt for home-cooked meals

Fast food, junk food, processed food – they are all the same thing. Packed with unhealthy fats, salts, sugars and chemicals, they contain very few nutrients. They also cost more than home-cooked meals. So why do they account for approximately 60–70% of the average family food shopping? Most will argue it's because of their convenience; hopefully, this book will show you how to change your processed food habit and opt for easy-to-make, home-cooked meals.

Respect your food

Cooking and processing food can destroy nutrients, so it is certainly better to buy fresh ingredients and cook meals yourself at home. However, to gain the most benefit from food, you must learn to treat it with respect.

Nutrients, particularly vitamins, are lost when you boil vegetables. Steaming preserves more of the nutrients and the vegetables will taste better too. As well as buying a steamer, consider investing in a wok; stir-frying locks in both flavours and nutrients. Slow cookers are also a great tool, not just for convenience but also for making nourishing soups, casseroles and one-pot meals. And don't forget that food doesn't always have to be cooked at all; in its natural, raw state it is packed with vitamins, so include in your diet salads, smoothies, juices and fresh fruit or vegetable sticks.

Watch your waistline

The larger your waistline, the more at risk you are from heart disease, diabetes and strokes. Women with a waist size of over 31 inches have an increased health risk, and a greatly increased risk if it is over 35 inches. For men the figures are respectively 37 inches and 40 inches. Measure your waistline and make a note of the results. Start a new eating and exercise plan and measure again in a month. Set yourself goals and reward success – but not with food!

Keep an eye on portion sizes

When serving food, we tend to load the plate and overeat. Try using a smaller plate and you will soon be cutting down without really noticing. Use the same principle when feeding your children – they often feel intimidated by an overloaded plate. Far better to give them less and enjoy hearing them ask for more, than to watch them struggle with a large meal.

Lower the fat

Swap the fats. Choose low fat options, such as skimmed milk and, for 80% less saturated fat, replace butter with low fat spreads. Not only will this help you lose weight, it will also help lower cholesterol.

Saturated fats are the worst kind of fats to have in your diet. You will find more saturated fats in meat and dairy products, which is why health experts and nutritionists recommend eating less of these foods. If you do opt for meat, try to buy lean cuts where possible. There are plenty of low fat dairy options available, such as low fat crème fraiche, and low fat soft cheeses, including quark, mozzarella and cottage cheese.

You can include more of the 'good' fats in your diet by eating more oily fish, such as mackerel, and cooking with olive oil or omega-3-rich flax oil (though flax oil should never be heated!).

Always read labels as some products claim to be low fat when actually they are higher in fat than other regular brands. Fat levels should ideally be below 3g per 100g.

Curb the carbs

Many of you may be surprised to discover that carbohydrates are as, if not more, responsible for our weight problems than fats. Refined carbohydrates are the real baddies: white bread, white sugar, white flour and white pasta. So, limit your consumption of these and instead choose wholemeal/wholegrain options. If you are serious about weight loss, I would highly recommend *The Harcombe Diet: Stop Counting Calories and Start Losing Weight* by Zoe Harcombe. She explains in easy terms why calorie counting may not work for you, and why carbohydrates cause weight gain.

Ditch the sugar

Fluctuating blood sugar levels can lead to health problems such as diabetes and adrenal problems, so it is best to try and keep them stabilised and as normal as possible. To do this, avoid bursts of high sugar intake. Sugar, like salt, is in most of our foods, particularly processed foods. Teach yourself and your family to avoid unnecessary sugar intake, particularly refined sugars. Breakfast cereals are packed with sugar, especially those aimed at children. For instance, Kellogg's Frosties contain 37g of sugar per 100g and Morrison's Choco Crackles a whopping 38.4g per 100g. When you compare these amounts to the recommended Guideline Daily Amounts (GDA), of 90g sugar for an adult and 80g for a child, you will begin to see the problem. Choose healthier options such as Shredded Wheat or home-made porridge with fresh fruit. Alternatively, make a delicious fruit smoothie, or opt for a poached egg on wholemeal toast. They will keep you going far longer than a bowl of sugary cereal.

Cut down, and then cut out, sugar in tea and coffee. Do it gradually and you won't notice the difference. If you really can't manage without a sugar substitute, try to avoid artificial sweeteners as some research has linked them to some nasty health and emotional problems. Instead, opt for a natural sugar substitute such as Xylitol. This has a low GI (Glycaemic Index) and has been shown to reduce gum disease and cavities. It also comes under the name of Perfect Sweet and is available from health food stores and some leading supermarkets.

People have reported a reduction in sugar cravings after taking a daily supplement of Chromium as it helps balance blood sugar levels. This is an ideal supplement to take when attempting to diet.

Cut out the salt

My recipes do not contain salt – I never use it and the only salt I have in the house is for the dishwasher! Before you all shrink back in horror, consider the amount of salt (also known as sodium) that's present in everyday foods that are part of your diet. The *maximum* recommended daily allowance for an adult is 6g per day. This is just over 1 teaspoon per day, so remember this when you randomly add salt to your cooking or sprinkle it liberally over your food.

Below is a very rough average day in the life of an adult.

Food	Salt intake
Breakfast	
Cornflakes, 30g	.5g
Semi-skimmed milk, 200ml	.11g
Toast, butter and marmalade, 2 slices	1.4g
Mid-morning snack	
Chocolate muffin	.3g
Lunch	
Subway 6-inch Meatball Marinara	4.7g
Cheese and Onion Crisps, 25g packet	1g
Snickers Bar	1.3g
Dinner	
Chicken Tikka Masala Meal with Pilau Rice	4.5g
Apple pie and custard	.20g
TOTAL	**12.75g**

The total comes to over double the amount of sodium we should have in our diet and that does not include any other snacks or salt added to the food before eating. The figures are much worse for children. The table below gives the maximum recommended daily sodium allowance for children

Children 7 to 12 months	1g a day
Children 1 to 3 years	2g a day
Children 4 to 6 years	3g a day
Children 7 to 10 years	5g a day
Children over 11 years	6g a day

If you add up the average child's daily intake, the results are quite shocking. Below is a typical daily diet for a school age child, but does not include additional snacks or salt added to the food when cooking or serving it.

Food	Estimated salt intake
Breakfast	
Coco Pops cereal, 30g	.5g
Semi-skimmed milk, 200ml	.11g
Mid-morning snack	
Apple	trace
Lunch	
Dairylea Lunchable Ham and Cheese Crackers	1.8g
Cheese and onion crisps, 25g packet	.5g
Penguin chocolate bar	.1g
Muller Crunch Corner Snack, Vanilla and Banana	.5g
After-school snack	
Wotsits Crisps	.14g
Dinner	
Oven chips	.1g
2 x Bernard Matthews Turkey Dinosaurs	.6g
C&B Sponge Bob Pasta Shapes, 213g	.8g
Tomato ketchup, 15ml serving	.5g
Chocolate Arctic Roll Slice	1g
TOTAL	**6.65g**

If this were the diet of a six-year-old child, they would already be consuming double their recommended maximum salt intake per day, which would seriously affect their health.

Manufacturers defend the high salt levels in their products by saying it is what consumers want. Actually, it is what consumers will eat. Take out the salt and you will realise the meal is pretty tasteless. This is not because salt tastes great, but because it masks the bland taste of junk food (or non-food as a fellow nutritionist says). Manufacturers also use salt to entice people to eat more. Think of crisps – once you start you can't stop, can you? If you eat fresh, instead of processed, food on a daily basis you will not only lower your sodium intake, you will also start to enjoy the real taste of food.

Always read the labels on packaged food as salt is added to most everyday foods – even biscuits. According to research compiled by *Which?* magazine, 16 out of 100 breakfast cereals tested contained more salt per portion than a packet of salt and vinegar crisps. Morrison's Honey Nut Cornflakes contain the same amount of salt per serving as a 50g bag of salted peanuts!

Some food labels give the sodium content, some the salt and some state both. The sodium content is 2.5 times less than the equivalent salt content, so if your label states sodium, multiply this by 2.5 to get the right salt level. I have noticed that the higher the salt level in processed foods, the less likely the manufacturer seems to be to use the word salt in the labelling – opting instead for sodium. A cynic might say that this is in order to fool the consumer into believing the food contains less salt than it really does.

If you do have a 'salt tooth', you will be surprised how quickly this will go if you stop adding it to your food. Within three to four days you will start to taste the real flavour of food instead of the salty overkill. If you would like to start reducing your salt gradually, opt for something like Solo Low Salt which contains 60% less salt but is packed with other minerals such as magnesium.

Get moving

Dump the remote, hide the car keys and do all you can to keep moving. Not only are you burning calories, you're also increasing your heart rate, expanding your lungs and moving your muscles. Aim for at least 20 minutes of exercise a day. Try swimming, walking, cycling, or join a dance class. Whatever you choose, make sure you have fun.

Get hydrated

Many people confuse thirst signals for hunger pangs. Drink plenty of plain, still water (not fizzy drinks, tea or coffee) throughout the day. This will help rehydrate you and will also keep hunger and headaches at bay.

Throw out the frying pan

Grill or oven bake instead of frying your foods. If you love chips, try baking potato wedges coated with paprika and spray them with olive oil for a healthier option. I fill a spray container with light olive oil, ready to spray food or pans, as this works well and reduces the oil content.

Be creative with colour

You can tell at a glance whether a meal is healthy or not. Healthy food is full of colour and vibrancy; junk food is biscuit coloured. Fill your plate with a variety of colours for a healthy and nutritious meal; for example, you could opt for green cabbage, vibrant orange carrots and yellow sweetcorn. Get creative with your food colour palate.

Eat regular meals

Eat three nourishing meals a day. It is a complete myth that you will lose weight if you skip meals. All you will do is experience a slump in your blood sugar level, which will lead to a headache and make you feel generally groggy. You will then be more likely to grab the nearest chocolate bar in search of a quick fix. Instead, eat more, but choose your food with care. Pack all your meals with nutritious wholegrains to avoid sugar slumps and cravings. Organisations such as Slimming World and WeightWatchers include foods in their diets that may be eaten freely. These are usually fruits, vegetables and wholegrains, so there is no excuse, even when you are trying to lose weight, to go hungry.

Chew them over carefully

Chewing is the start of the digestive process, so give your body a helping hand; eat slowly and chew each mouthful thoroughly before you swallow.

Avoid pre-packed sandwiches

According to statistics, we spend a whopping £5.3 billion a year on pre-packed sandwiches. Not only is this costing us money, it is also costing our health. In spring 2009, *Which?* magazine reviewed many ready-made lunches and the results are quite shocking. A Pret A Manger chicken sandwich contained 23g of fat (5.5g of saturated fat) and 2.1g of salt. Sainsbury's Taste the Difference chicken sandwich contained 20.9g of fat, of which 4.9g was saturated fat, and 1.9g of salt.

It only takes a few minutes every day to make yourself a tasty, nutritious packed lunch. It's also much cheaper to make your own. Alternatively, try asking your employer if they will give you facilities to make your own food. We had a stockpot in our office. We all put money into a kitty and every morning we would take it in turns to make soup. By lunchtime, the smell of home-made soup was so appetising no one wanted to go to the sandwich bar.

Give up smoking

This will dramatically improve both your health and your bank balance, as you can see from the following benefits.

- Twenty minutes after having your last cigarette, your blood pressure and pulse return to normal.
- Within 24 hours your lungs start to clear out mucus and other smoking debris.
- Within 48 hours, taste and smell are greatly improved.
- Within three to six months, your lung function has increased by 10%.
- Within five years, your risk of heart attack is halved; after 10, it is as if you have never smoked.
- Giving up a 30-a-day habit will save you over £3,000 a year.

For more help and information. register with www.smokefree.nhs.uk or call 0800 022 4 332

Go green

Cut out caffeine and opt for healthier substitutes. You can start by switching to decaffeinated tea and coffee but, for ultimate health, cut down or ditch them altogether. Green tea is packed with powerful antioxidants which can help lower cholesterol, boost your immune system and lower blood pressure.

Cut the fizz

Fizzy drinks are packed with sugars and chemicals – even diet/sugar-free drinks are bad for you. If you like the fizz, try sparkling water mixed with fruit juice or natural cordial or, even better, a slice of lemon.

Go for the omega factor

Take fish oil supplements (or flaxseed oil if you are a vegetarian) daily. Rich in omega-3 essential fatty acids (EFA), they help protect against heart disease and joint problems, boost the immune system, aid brain function and speed up healing. Try to buy the best quality you can. I would recommend Nutrigold (www.nutrigold.co.uk) or, for a high street product, opt for Solgar or Viridian ranges. You will pay more for these, but you will gain more from them than the cheaper alternatives. Try also to include plenty of oily fish in your diet, such as mackerel, sardines, salmon and halibut.

Manage your stress levels

One of the commonest reasons for overeating is emotional stress (the other big reason is boredom!). An unhealthy diet, particularly one heavily reliant on processed foods, can upset your natural balance and can often lead to emotional health problems. Changing to a nutrient-rich diet, while perhaps adding some interim supplementation, should help. Vitamin B and St John's Wort supplements can help ease stress and depression.

Smile!

The act of smiling or laughing increases production of your feel-good endorphins. Not only will you feel better and more positive, but those around you will also benefit as smiling is contagious.

Cooking Tricks for Health

You can eat the food you love but change the way you cook. The simple suggestions in this chapter could help you lose weight, lower cholesterol and improve your family's overall health. It comes as no real surprise that the main problem areas are with meat and dairy products – either in preparation or actual product. Bear this in mind and try to include more wholefoods, oily fish and fruit and vegetables in your diet. Dispel the myth that your meal should comprise meat and two veg every single day. Not only is meat the least healthy of our foods, it is also the most expensive.

Healthier ways to fry

Dry fry
This may sound a bit, well, dry, but honestly it really does work. You can dry fry a number of foods. It's best to use a non-stick pan for dry frying. Just add the ingredients to a hot pan and cook as normal.

Use water
I have successfully made roast potatoes, oven-baked chips and stir-fry using water. You need a non-stick pan. Use enough water to come just less than halfway up the potatoes, sprinkle them with paprika and herbs, and cook as normal until the potatoes start to crisp. Turn them over and cook the other half of the potatoes without adding more water – they should all then crisp as normal.

Mix lemon juice, garlic and ginger
This combination makes delicious stir-fry meals. Simply heat some lemon juice, crushed garlic and ginger in a wok, before adding the stir-fry ingredients. Delicious!

Opt for olive oil
Olive oil is a monounsaturated fat which is known to help guard against heart disease and cholesterol. Use the best quality you can

afford and, when frying, use sparingly – you really don't need to fry an egg in an inch of oil – a drop or two is enough.

Spray away

Oil sprays are a perfect way to get a small amount of oil onto your food. Supermarkets sell these in their own spray bottles, but it is an expensive way to buy. Instead, pour some olive oil into a disused spray container. Use this spray to coat pans, baking trays or even food with a light spray of oil.

Alternatives to frying

Baking, grilling, steaming, poaching or boiling are all healthier alternatives to frying. If the food looks dry, you can always coat it with a brush of olive oil or marinate.

Healthier ways to roast

Use oil sparingly

It really is true that a little bit of oil goes a long way. If you are roasting meat, let the meat juices enhance the flavour. When roasting vegetables, place a small amount of oil, garlic and herbs in a bowl and toss the vegetables in this before transferring them to the roasting pan.

I am a huge fan of roast potatoes. As the recipes below demonstrate, you don't have to use gallons of oil to create delicious, crisp roast potatoes.

Delicious Roast Potatoes

Large potatoes
Oil of your choice (I use light olive oil)
Semolina
Paprika

1. Preheat the oven to 200°C/gas mark 6.
2. Peel and cut the potatoes ready to roast.
3. Steam or boil the potatoes for 10 minutes.
4. While the potatoes are cooking, add oil to roasting tin (no more

than 1cm in depth) and place in a very hot oven.
5. Drain the potatoes and replace in the saucepan.
6. Sprinkle 2–3 teaspoons paprika and 3–4 teaspoons semolina onto the potatoes.
7. Put the lid on the pan and shake the potatoes for a few seconds.
8. Add the potatoes to the hot roasting oil, being careful not to splash.
9. Roast for 1–1½ hours, turning regularly to ensure even, crisp coating. When you turn the potatoes, add more paprika.

Mini Roast Potatoes

1kg new potatoes, washed but not peeled
1 tablespoon olive oil
1–2 teaspoons mixed herbs (or herbs of your choice)
2 teaspoons paprika
Chillies, garlic or other spices of your choice

1. Preheat the oven to 200°C/gas mark 6.
2. Place the potatoes in a bowl with the oil and all the other ingredients and mix well to ensure the potatoes are evenly coated with oil and herbs/spices.
3. Spread the potatoes on a baking tray and bake in the oven for 30–35 minutes until golden.

Give food the brush-off
Instead of pouring oil over food, brush it on using a pastry brush. This ensures the oil goes where you want it but does not saturate the food. Alternatively, use your home-made olive oil spray bottle.

Rack and go
Roast your joint on a rack to enable the fat to drain from the meat.

Choose leaner cuts of meat
The following guidelines will help you make healthier choices.

- Opt for the leanest pieces.
- Ask your butcher to help you find the best cuts to suit your budget and health.

- Choose low fat meats such as turkey and chicken.
- Trim off excess fat before cooking.
- Even if you are cooking with lean mince, drain off the fat before adding other ingredients.
- Try to eat fish at least twice a week. Oily fish has great health benefits, so try to include some in your diet.

Lighten up

Butters and spreads
Butter and margarine are used a lot in cooking. There are some recipes where only pure butter will do, but increasing numbers of low fat and light spreads are filling our supermarket shelves, so experiment with some of these. Clover, Country Life and Anchor all have lighter buttery spreads in their ranges. Benecol and Flora also both make spreads with a buttery taste. However, some of the purest and lightest of low fat spreads may not react in the same way as butter when cooking or baking.

Milk
Skimmed and semi-skimmed milk can be used in most recipes. If you want to go dairy free, choose something like soya milk, oat milk or rice milk. I use soya milk all the time and only have a problem with hot drinks, particularly coffee, as it can curdle.

Cheese
You can buy cheese that is half fat or promoted as lighter than regular. I haven't noticed much difference in taste, so why not give these a go? I buy mature cheese, particularly for cooking, as you need less of it to achieve a good flavour.

Marigold Nutritional Yeast Flakes, available from health food stores, are packed with nutrients, including B vitamins. I sprinkle a handful of flakes into my cheese sauce as it gives a nice cheesy flavour and means I can use less cheese. You can mix flakes with tofu to make a vegan cheesy scrambled egg, or mix tofu, onion, flakes and some cheese to make a great cheese and onion tart.

Yoghurt

Yoghurt is delicious and such a versatile ingredient to have in the kitchen. I buy large pots of supermarket own brand natural yoghurt for less than 50p. My sons love a bowlful of chopped banana, natural yoghurt, a drizzle of honey and covering of granola – an excellent start to the day that beats nasty, sugar-laden breakfast cereals. Buy low fat natural yoghurt, crème fraiche and fromage frais – you won't taste any difference but your waistline and your heart will appreciate it.

I use Greek yoghurt in food – Total 0% Fat Greek Yoghurt is really good in hot food. It keeps its creamy texture and does not curdle like some thinner yoghurt. I also use quark, which is a virtually fat free soft cheese. It doesn't taste particularly good on its own, but if you mix it with some creamy yoghurt or fruit, it is actually quite nice. It is also great to cook with.

Being a Savvy Shopper

Whether you are aiming to save money, or to live a healthy lifestyle, or both, you will first need to learn to be a savvy shopper. Most people walk around supermarkets in a trance, picking up items from habit rather than need or desire. Break that mould! Be proud of your desire to save and be healthy. Revel in the challenge and enjoy hunting for those great bargains.

Be prepared

Always, always make a list before shopping. This will help keep you focused so that you're less likely to buy unwanted or doubled-up items. I cannot emphasise this enough. You can save pounds every week by being organised and following your list. If you only take one thing from this book, please let it be the list making! If all that seems like hard work, you can shop online. The beauty of this is that those magic gremlins actually store your information every time you shop, so when you place your next order, you will be able to check off all your favourite purchases – you will have an automatic list!

Beware of BOGOF/B2GOF / deals

These may seem like a good deal, but only if you were intending to buy the product in the first place. Sadly, most of these amazing offers are for the unhealthiest foods, so proceed with caution. Before you buy, remember to compare the price. You may find you are paying more than double when compared to other brands. Don't be fooled into thinking that the manufacturers or supermarkets are offering a free item out of the goodness of their hearts. This is purely a marketing tool to lure us into buying products we might not normally buy, or to help launch a new range. So, follow the golden rule: **only buy if it saves you money, is something you need, and something you will use.**

Be guided by your head, not your stomach

Never go shopping when you are hungry. It is a sure-fire way to spend more money. You will get to the checkout and discover your trolley is heaving with crisps, chocolate and biscuits. Have you ever wondered why the supermarkets have started baking bread on the premises? Not to give us the freshest bread (most is just reheated anyway), but simply to create that mouth-watering smell to tempt us into buying.

Experiment with organic

Organic food is not much more expensive if you shop wisely. I buy from local sources such as farmers' markets and an organic delivery company. I am also a member of an organic wholefood co-op. Growing your own produce means you can be sure organic principles have been followed – and don't be afraid to barter and swap produce with friends and neighbours. Above all, it is better to opt for fresh fruit and vegetables rather than processed food – organic or not. So do the best you can and be a savvy thinker.

Shift to lower range products

Downshifting does not necessarily mean jumping from a premium brand straight to a no frills product; look at the middle-of-the-range goods on the shelf. I have noticed no difference in quality for a number of value items, such as dried pasta, flour, butter and even some biscuits.

If you are concerned about your health, read the labels. Some lower range products are actually healthier options than premium brands. Sainsbury's offer some great fruit and vegetables in their Basics range.

Store Cupboard Know-How

The vast majority of us are unaware of what we have in our store cupboards, fridges and freezers. So how can we possibly budget for food when we are not sure what we already have? You can save money and time if you keep a well-stocked store cupboard and replace things as you use them. Keep a list.

Just as in *Ready, Steady, Cook*, with a few key ingredients you can put together a great meal. Here is a list of foods I *always* have in my kitchen – just to give you some ideas.

Fruit and vegetables

Onions – I buy red and brown onions as they give different flavours (red onions are nutritionally superior to brown onions).

Garlic – I am not very good at remembering to use fresh garlic, so I confess to buying cheat ready-crushed garlic as a standby.

Potatoes – I keep large and new potatoes and I store them in potato sacks from Lakeland as they keep better.

Peppers – I always have a selection of red, yellow and green peppers in my fridge.

Carrots – I buy organic carrots or from our farmers' market as the taste is superior.

Ginger – I am a big fan of fresh ginger – it can really lift a meal. I buy it fresh and if I have any left over, I slice it into thin slices and place it in a jar, topped up with white wine vinegar. It is always on hand for recipes. You can also store ginger in the freezer.

Herbs and spices

You don't have to go mad and buy the entire shelf of herbs and spices. I use the following a lot in cooking so I make sure they are always in my store cupboard. I buy from a local warehouse or my co-operative as they sell 500g bags for less than I would pay for one small pot in the supermarket.

Herbs are unbeatable when used fresh. If you have a windowsill or garden, you can grow your own herbs. Don't buy fresh from the supermarket as you may be paying a premium. If you can't grow your own, or it is the wrong time of year, try frozen (see the following chapter, 'Make the Most of Your Freezer').

Paprika – this rich red spice has a very delicate flavour. I use it on my roast potatoes and also in soups and casseroles – even sprinkled on cheese on toast.

Garam masala – this is a blend of herbs and spices traditionally used in Indian cookery.

Sweet curry powder – this is a mild curry flavour which is perfect for a child's dahl or a quick and easy curry sauce to have with your potato wedges.

Curry paste – this can add an instant zing to a meal.

Chilli powder or freeze-dried chillies – great to add a bit of spice to your dishes. Try mixing some chilli powder with grated cheese before toasting – delicious! I grow my own chilli plants in the summer. Any leftover chillies I bottle in oil or freeze whole until I need them.

Ground cinnamon – lovely in biscuits, apple cakes or apple pies. I use cinnamon powder as it is less expensive than the sticks and less hassle.

Ground coriander – this is lovely in savoury dishes, but I also use it in cakes as it has a surprising flavour.

Ground ginger – don't mistake this for fresh ginger as the tastes are quite different. Ground ginger is good in savoury dishes and excellent for baking.

Nutmeg – I have a few whole nutmegs in a jar and use a fine grater to add a bit of nutmeg magic to my food. Great in baking, but also very comforting sprinkled on milky drinks and puddings.

Mixed spice – optional but good if you love baking.

Turmeric – some call this the poor man's saffron, but nutritionally it is a very good product. Add to savoury dishes or use to colour rice that lovely vibrant yellow.

Mixed herbs – this is a good safe option for newbie cooks. Add to savoury dishes, salad dressing and even sprinkle on pizzas if you don't have any oregano.

Dried bay leaves – don't underestimate a bay leaf – they can really lift a savoury dish, particularly soups.

Store cupboard basics

Baked beans – a great standby and good for you.

Rice – I buy my rice in bulk and store it in a large metal container. We eat rice at least three times a week. I also buy pudding rice to make creamy rice puddings – a lovely comfort food.

Pasta – you can always make a meal with pasta. Again, I buy in bulk as it is much cheaper and ensures I always have plenty to hand. I stock spaghetti, penne pasta and macaroni and I also love wheat-free spelt, vegetable, rice and corn pasta.

Flour, plain and self-raising – you can buy white flour for less than 30p a bag (own brands), and wholemeal for less than £1 a bag. Perfect for baking, making pastry and sauces. I also buy multigrain flour as this makes a wonderful savoury pastry. Wholemeal flour is available as both self-raising and plain. It gives cakes a slightly heavier texture, but is so much better for your health. Try combining white and wholemeal flour to help ease you into the new flavour and texture.

Sugar – I always buy unrefined brown or golden sugar and, again, I buy in bulk to save money. Xylitol (also known as Perfect Sweet) is a healthy sugar alternative (not to be confused with unhealthy artificial sweeteners). It is more expensive than ordinary sugar so don't waste it!

Tomato Purée – you can buy tubes or tins of tomato purée for less than 30p. Tubes tend to be less wasteful (I normally find a half-empty tin growing mould in the back of my fridge!). I also like the flavour of sun-dried tomato paste.

Tinned tomatoes – not as tasty as fresh tomatoes, but a fraction of the price and a good standby for all sorts of dishes. Sun-dried tomatoes are also useful to have on standby – adding a few pieces to a tomato soup really enhances the flavour. If I have a load of ripe tomatoes that need using up, I bake them (see the recipe for Slow-Baked Tomatoes in the chapter, 'Ooh, Saucy!') and store them in a jar covered in light olive oil until they are needed.

Red lentils – a real must-have. If you are new to pulses, these are perfect as they don't need to be soaked. I use them in soups, casseroles and even rice dishes. They also make a great dahl. They are cheap and an excellent source of nutrients – what could be better!

Soup mix – you can buy dried pulse mixes known as soup mix. They normally contain a variety of pulses such as lentils, split peas and aduki beans, plus pearl barley and barley flakes. You simply add the mix to your soup or casserole – no need to soak. You can buy 500g mixes for as little as 60p. With the price of meat rising, this is the perfect way to make that meal stretch a little bit further, and add essential nutrients at the same time.

Oats – porridge oats are very versatile, cheap to buy and full of goodness. Use them in home-made burgers, topping for crumbles, flapjacks and biscuits, and of course in wholesome porridge or muesli for breakfast.

Long-life or fresh (frozen) milk – you can freeze fresh milk or buy long-life for emergencies. I use soya milk which has a long shelf life until opened.

Olive oil – buy the best quality you can afford. You only need small amounts when cooking, so a little goes a long way. I place oil in a spray container for spraying potato wedges, pans and baking trays.

Stock cubes – I never use stock cubes, so this really is not part of my essential list, but I know many people do. However, a word of warning – they are full of salt so try to use sparingly. If you do use them, don't add more salt to the dish. I have included recipes for making your own stock – this is a good way of using up a wide variety of foods you may have lurking in your fridge. (See the chapter, 'Ooh, Saucy!').

Dried fruit – mixed dried fruit is essential if you love baking cakes or biscuits. I also add a sprinkle to apple pies. You can even add a handful of sultanas to your sweet curry sauce.

Chocolate, cocoa and chocolate chips – having children, and a sweet tooth myself, I always make sure I have the ingredients to make cakes, biscuits and desserts. I only buy plain chocolate. I also buy as a special treat (and it lasts for ages) Willie Harcourt-Cooze's Pure Cacao (£5.99 from Waitrose, or visit www.williescacao.com) as it's great in savoury and sweet recipes. It is actually a very healthy product. Chocolate and healthy – my type of food!

Balsamic vinegar, lemon juice and soy sauce – I could not do without these three gems.

White and Red wine and wine vinegar – wine enhances certain dishes, so I always have cooking wine on hand.

Optional extras

Ready-made pasta or curry sauces (bought on offer!) – these are handy if you want a quick and easy meal. Better still, why not make your own and store or freeze until needed?

Bread flour and dried yeast – there's very little to beat the smell and taste of fresh bread. Bread makers are great and you can make a fresh loaf for less than 50p. Alternatively, you can bulk buy your favourite bread and store it in the freezer. Not only will you have bread when you need it, but you will also improve the efficiency of your freezer as they use less energy when full.

Tinned tuna – a good standby for creating some quick and easy dishes.

Passata (sieved tomatoes) – you can buy these in cartons now for less than 50p. Use instead of tinned tomatoes in soups, casseroles, or even for making your own pasta sauces.

Foods to store in the fridge

Cheese – I buy mature Cheddar, especially for cooking, as you need to use less. I also use mozzarella, goat's cheese, ricotta and Parmesan regularly.

Eggs – you can always make a meal with an egg! Great for cooking, baking and snacks.

Milk – you can also store milk in the freezer or opt for long-life milk in your store cupboard for emergencies.

Butter or margarine – an essential for cooking and baking.

Natural yoghurt – you can buy 500g pots for less than 50p. Use instead of cream or add to fruit to make delicious smoothies. I also buy Greek yoghurt (my favourite is 0% Total Greek Yoghurt as it can be used in cooking and as a dessert topping).

Low fat crème fraiche – as with yoghurt, use in cooking or instead of cream with your favourite dessert.

Quark – this is a very low fat soft cheese. It tastes quite bitter by itself, but you can use it in cooking or mix it with some Greek yoghurt and fresh fruit and you have a yummy dessert.

Foods to store in the freezer

Peas and other vegetables – useful as a standby but remember that fresh is better than frozen, so try to include some fresh for your five a day!

Puff pastry – this is a real cheat ingredient but if you buy supermarket own brands at approximately 90p a block, it is worth some corner cutting. For quick and easy meals, I use puff pastry to make delicious sweet or savoury tarts in minutes.

Mince – whether this is beef, lamb, turkey or even veggie mince, it is a versatile ingredient to have at your fingertips. Quorn mince is delicious and lower fat than meat, so even if you are not veggie, why not give it a try? Mince is ideal for bolognese, lasagne, shepherd's pie and home-made burgers.

Bread and bread rolls – as stated above, keeping bread or bread rolls in your freezer is not only convenient, it also helps your freezer run more efficiently.

Chicken – you can do so much with chicken. Chefs believe that the meat from thighs gives more flavour. I would advise fresh is best but, for standby, if you like chicken, it may be worth including some frozen for backup.

Sausages – there are times when all you fancy is deliciously comforting bangers and mash, or maybe you feel like having a cooked breakfast one Sunday morning.

Frozen herbs – as mentioned above, these have a superior taste to dried herbs, so, if you can't grow your own, this is a good alternative.

I always make sure that I keep these items topped up. From the above list I could, in an emergency, make several meals.

Storing fresh produce

Now you have your store cupboard sorted, you need to work out how to get the best out of your food. Think about where you are storing your fresh fruit and vegetables. Traditionally, homes would have a cool pantry or larder, which kept things fresh. Apples would be stored to last the whole winter, yet we struggle to get them to last a week. Supermarkets may have had the produce for weeks before it reaches you, thereby shortening its life, so it is always best to buy from your local farmers' market, pannier market or greengrocer.

Bananas
If you want them to last, buy green. Never store bananas in the fridge, but do try to keep them in a cool place, and not touching other fruit, as they omit a gas that speeds up the ripening process. Lakeland sells a handy banana storage bag at £4.98. Amazingly, the fruit will stay just as it should for around a fortnight – twice its normal lifespan. You can also freeze bananas. I freeze bananas that are starting to brown (knowing my boys won't touch them!). I keep them in the skin – they are ideal to use in smoothies, cakes or baked banana puddings.

Mushrooms
Although most supermarkets sell mushrooms in those horrible plastic containers, they should be placed in paper bags and stored in the fridge. Plastic bags produce moisture and the mushrooms will start to decay and rot very quickly. As with bananas you can buy bags for mushrooms which do work well. They are worth the investment if you regularly buy and store mushrooms.

Root vegetables
Keep these in a dry, cool, dark place. If you do not have an area suitable, store in your fridge, but not in the plastic packaging. Placing an old tea towel on the fridge shelf will avoid moisture. Potatoes love dark, cool places. Never leave them in plastic, though paper bags are fine.

Salad produce

Bagged salads are very expensive as well as damaging to the environment. Out of season, buy lettuce whole (iceberg seems to be the longest lasting). Store all salad items in your fridge, out of plastic and away from moisture. Again, you can use the tea towel trick. Why not grow your own lettuce or tomatoes? Lettuce can be grown in window boxes or grow your own tomatoes in growbags on your patio. Cucumbers and tomatoes should be firm. If you like tomatoes with lots of flavour, place them in a bowl at room temperature. They will only last three to four days but will be very tasty.

Fruit

Store all fruit and vegetables in a cool, dry place. This sounds obvious, but I have walked into houses with fruit bowls next to radiators, or in front of windows. If in doubt, store in the fridge.

Strawberries

These never taste the same out of season. Don't buy punnets that contain mouldy fruit, as these will speed up the ripening process of the other fruits. Store strawberries in the fridge until you are ready to eat them, but remember to take them out at least an hour before serving, as this improves the flavour.

Cheese

According to experts, cheese should be stored wrapped in waxed paper and not in plastic bags or packaging.

Make the Most of Your Freezer

Years ago people chose large chest freezers in a bid to save as much time and money as possible. Over the past 25 years, we have seen a decline in the need for these large freezers as more and more families opted for fresh food, processed and takeaways. We have however, seen a rise in waste. Currently almost a third of our weekly food ends up in the dustbin. With a bit of savvy and a more frugal head, you can make the most of your freezer, fridge and store cupboard, avoid waste and save pounds.

If you are planning to save money, a freezer is a huge asset. You can fill it with bargains, food grown from your allotment and with home-made ready meals. Remember, they work more efficiently when filled to capacity, but do make a note of what is going in. If you are storing home-produced items, label them with contents and date. Remember, the bigger the freezer, the easier it is to lose track of its contents, so keep a list! If you are buying a new freezer, make sure you buy one with the best energy efficiency grading.

Opinion is split on the nutritional value of frozen food. I believe it is all about balance and like to look at the bigger picture. Most busy families rely heavily on processed or takeaway food. For them, opting instead to utilise a freezer packed with freshly frozen home-made food is by far the better and healthier option.

The big freeze

To help your fridge or freezer run more efficiently:

- Replace your plug with a gadget such as the SavaPlug, which will help reduce electricity consumption by up to 20%.
- Defrost your fridge and freezer regularly.
- Keep your fridge and freezer at least three-quarters full. If you have a large chest freezer and cannot fill it with food, place cardboard boxes or rolled up newspaper inside to help fill it up.

- Do not leave the fridge or freezer door open longer than necessary.
- Make sure the door seals are working correctly.
- Do not place warm or hot food into the fridge or freezer – allow the food to cool first.
- Allow enough room for air to circulate around the fridge or freezer, particularly around the condenser coils at the back. Clear the condensers of dust regularly as dust can reduce efficiency by up to 25%.

Think ahead

Start saving your old containers. I use margarine/butter containers, small milk cartons, yoghurt pots and ice cube trays (preferably silicon as the food 'pops' out more easily). I have sets of Tupperware and plastic containers picked up from boot sales and when discounted in shops.

Foods to freeze

Herbs
If you love cooking, you probably buy fresh herbs. For the same price as fresh, you can buy a large container of freshly frozen herbs that can last you months and offer a superior taste to dried varieties. Waitrose sell 75g resealable bags of herbs and seasonings. Simply use what you want and pop the rest back into the freezer. If you grow your own and have a surplus, you can freeze herbs yourself. Some herbs go limp when frozen but will still maintain their flavour. Herbs that freeze well are basil, oregano, sage, dill, rosemary, mint, lemongrass, chives, tarragon and thyme. I also freeze fresh chillies, garlic and ginger.

Leftovers
It is really frustrating to throw away half-empty jars, tubes, tins or loaves of bread. Well, now you don't have to. Here are some tips to reduce waste and make the most of those odds and ends we all usually discard.

Bread

Stale or leftover bread can be turned into breadcrumbs. Spread the breadcrumbs on a tray first to stop them clumping together, then freeze. When frozen, place them into a container or freezer bag. French sticks or speciality breads and bread rolls can go stale very quickly. Revitalise with a few splashes of water and bake in the oven for 2–3 minutes.

Cheese

This is an ideal tip for leftover cheeses, especially those we don't buy very often, such as blue cheese. You can grate them and, as with breadcrumbs above, to avoid clumping, place on a tray and freeze before placing into a container or freezer bag. This is also ideal for Parmesan as it lasts for ever and avoids the smelly fridge scenario.

Pesto, pastes and purées

If, like me, you love spicy pastes and herb purées or pesto, place any leftovers in silicon ice cube trays. This makes it easy to pop out portion-sized dollops and avoids cluttering the back of your fridge with mouldy jars. You can also use this tip to freeze herb butters.

Ripe avocados

Scoop the flesh from ripe avocados and mix with a touch of lemon or lime juice before freezing. Once defrosted, use to make tasty dips.

Sweet potato

I sometimes have sweet potato in my vegetable tray that needs using up. To avoid waste, I chop usable chunks and coat them with lemon juice to prevent discoloration, before placing them in a freezer bag to freeze. They are ideal for adding to casseroles when I don't have any fresh to hand.

Lemons

Sometimes recipes ask for the zest and juice of half a lemon. You can squeeze the lemon juice from the remaining half and place in ice cube trays until needed. A friend of mine slices lemons into wedges, freezes them and uses them in her gin and tonic – she says it saves adding ice!

Pastry

Bought pastry does not have to be the only pastry in your freezer. Why not double up your batch of home-made pastry and place the leftovers in the freezer for another day? Alternatively, think of some extra ways to use up the pastry – you could make mini tarts or pies and place them in the freezer, ready as delicious nibbles for an impromptu drinks party, or to fill your packed lunch.

Salsa

Leftover salsa? Simply freeze until needed. I love using salsa to spice up tomato pasta dishes.

Peppers

Chop and place in a freezer bag until needed.

Swede

Sometimes a swede can be too large for your immediate needs. Slice the unwanted swede into chunks and place in the freezer until needed.

Bananas

Freeze bananas whole in the skins, or in slices in a container – ideal for smoothies or cakes.

Curry, casseroles or pasta sauces

Leftover curry, casserole or pasta sauces can be frozen ready to be transformed into a new dish later on.

Ripe tomatoes

Ripe tomatoes can be chopped and stored in a container ready to use in tomato or pasta sauces. I prefer to slow bake them in the oven with garlic and herbs (see the recipe for Slow-Baked Tomatoes in the chapter, 'Ooh, Saucy!'), then place in jars with some olive oil.

Berries

I absolutely love berries. My freezer is always well stocked with a variety of fruit berries ready for smoothies or delicious desserts. To freeze your own berries, place them on a baking try so they are not touching each other and freeze. Once frozen, you can then scoop them up and place in a freezer bag or container.

Vegetables

You can freeze most vegetables. The ideal way to freeze is to blanch the veg in boiling water for 1–2 minutes, then place in iced water to cool. Drain and pat dry before placing in freezer bags. (Remember to use the leftover water as a base for your home-made stock!) Alternatively, if you have any leftover vegetables, make a delicious soup or casserole, and then place in the freezer as a nutritious home-made ready meal.

Pulses

Pulses are so useful and you can store them in their dried form for months. I have lots of glass Kilner jars around my kitchen and pantry, filled with a variety of pulses. However, cooking pulses can be a bit of a faff. You can, of course, buy tinned, but this does cost more. Instead, cook them in bulk and then freeze, ready to add to your favourite recipe.

Wine

If you have any wine left in the bottom of a bottle, you can freeze it in small portions ready to add to casseroles or pasta sauces.

Onion

Chopped onion can be frozen in a freezer bag and added to dishes when needed. This is also a good way to use up onions that are starting to turn.

Coconut milk

I love curries but find a whole can of coconut milk is not only fattening but also too rich to add to one dish. Instead I freeze it in large ice cube trays and just pop out a couple of cubes as and when I need them.

Tortilla wraps

My eldest son is the only one in our family who loves wraps, so there is inevitably some wastage from a bag of ten. I now freeze the wraps and he defrosts them for 30 seconds under the grill before filling them to his heart's content!

Juices
Kids (and adults) love lollipops and ice creams. I have some silicon ice cream moulds which are easy to fill and form the perfect twirled ice lollies. Fill these with leftover juices, smoothies, or even custard!

Bake one, make one free
If you are baking or being creative in the kitchen, why not double up? You can then freeze one item for another day, saving you time, energy and money. As long as you have space in your freezer, this makes sense for everyone, whether you are cooking for one or for a family of four.

- When baking a pastry dish, I double up the recipe and place one uncooked pie or pastry tart in the freezer. Christmas is a great time to get ahead with a whole host of savoury and sweet pastry delights, making the most of your puff, filo and standard pastry.
- Cakes and biscuits do freeze well. If you are freezing a decorated cake or gateau, to avoid damaging the decoration, place it in the freezer unwrapped until it is frozen, before putting it into a freezer bag or container.
- Don't only freeze your baking. You can also freeze meals, so learn to double up recipes. Meat, fish, poultry and vegetarian meals can all be frozen, though be aware of the correct defrosting and reheating procedures with meat, poultry and fish.
- When parboiling potatoes prior to roasting, double up and place leftovers in the freezer until needed another day. Simply defrost the potatoes gently, coat with your oil/paprika mix and place in a preheated oven. Some people coat the potatoes in the oil or herb mixture before freezing.

Freezers aren't the only way to store food. Get into the habit of using your larder, pantry or store cupboard more. I would recommend reading *The New Home Larder – The Essential Storecupboard Makeover* by Judith Wills.

The Soup Kitchen

Soups are bursting with nutrients. They can be used as a quick snack or a nutritious meal. And they're economical too!

Kids can be tempted with a side helping of toasted soldiers, hot pitta bread with hummus or even healthy potato wedges. If you or your child has a packed lunch, why not invest in a small flask and fill it with your home-made soup – satisfying and warming, especially during the winter months.

Tips for making soup

Stock – try to avoid using stock cubes. They are far too salty and overpower the natural flavours. I just add water or home-made vegetable stock.

Puréeing soups – some people like a chunky soup, others prefer a smooth one. It is purely a matter of personal taste. When puréeing a soup, I use an electric hand blender (or some call it a stick blender). It is simple to use and saves on washing up and messy transfer to a liquidiser (though make sure the end of the blender is fully submerged in the soup or you will end up with it everywhere!). Electric hand blenders are available from as little as £4. For a really fine soup, you can filter it through a sieve.

Slow cookers – I make my soups in a slow cooker unless I am in a hurry and have forgotten to prepare something earlier. Slow cookers are designed to cook the food at a lower temperature – therefore they need to cook longer. The beauty of a slow cooker is that they retain the food's nutrients (boiling destroys many essential nutrients). If you don't have a slow cooker, try to get into the habit of cooking your food slowly on a low heat. This not only preserves the nutrients but also avoids you burning anything!

Chunky soups – some chunky soups may benefit from a thicker stock/sauce. To thicken the sauce, simply remove about a quarter of the soup and purée, and then return it to the pan.

Liquid – you may need to add more water or stock to your soup depending on your personal preference and how you cook the soup. The higher the temperature when cooking, the more liquid evaporates.

Meat and fish – although there are soup recipes that include meat and fish, many are vegetarian. You can add meat to a soup to create more of a broth/casserole. When adding meat or fish to a recipe, make sure it is well cooked or reheated (if applicable) before serving.

Red Pepper and Tomato Soup with Pesto Swirl

SERVES 4 • COST OF INGREDIENTS: £1.80 • COST PER SERVING: 45p

1 teaspoon olive oil
1 large onion, chopped
1–2 cloves garlic
4 red peppers, deseeded and chopped
1 teaspoon mild chilli powder (optional)
4–6 fresh tomatoes, peeled and chopped
1 teaspoon paprika
500–750ml water (or home-made stock)
Seasoning to taste
Half a jar of pesto

1. Heat the olive oil and cook the onion, garlic and peppers together until soft and the onions are translucent. Add the chilli powder to the pan and stir well.
2. Add the tomatoes and cook for 2 minutes, then add the paprika and water and cook slowly on a low heat for 1 hour. If using a slow cooker, cook on a low heat for approximately 4 hours.
3. Cool slightly. Use an electric hand blender to purée the mixture. Season to taste and return it to the pan until ready to serve.
4. Serve, adding a spoonful of pesto to the centre of each bowl. Using a sharp knife, swirl the pesto from the centre of each bowl.

Mint and Green Pea Soup

SERVES 4 • COST OF INGREDIENTS: £1.50 • COST PER SERVING: 38p

1 teaspoon butter or olive oil
4–6 spring onions, chopped to include most of the green stalks
400g fresh peas (or frozen if not in season)
A small handful of fresh pea pods, chopped finely (unless you are using frozen peas)
500ml water
2–3 sprigs of fresh mint
Black pepper to season
A swirl of low fat crème fraiche and a sprig of fresh mint to garnish

1. Heat the oil in a pan and fry the spring onions for 2 minutes. Add the pea pods and cook for a further 2 minutes.
2. Add water, peas, mint and black pepper and cook gently on a low heat for 45 minutes to 1 hour.
3. Cool slightly. Use an electric hand blender to purée the soup, then return it to the pan until ready to serve. Alternatively, you can place the soup in the fridge to serve chilled.
4. Serve with a dollop of low fat crème fraiche to each bowl and swirl from the centre. Garnish with a sprig of fresh mint.

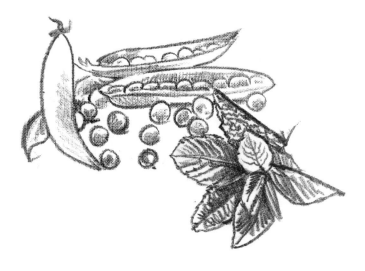

Cream-free Broccoli and Stilton Soup

This recipe is lower in fat than most recipes. It's great for using up leftover potatoes.

SERVES 4–6 • COST OF INGREDIENTS; £2.45 • COST PER SERVING; 40p

1 teaspoon olive oil
1 onion, chopped
1 small leek, finely chopped
2 cooked potatoes, chopped
2 heads of broccoli
900ml water or stock
120g Stilton cheese, crumbled
Black pepper to taste

1. Add the oil to the pan and cook the onions and leeks until soft and translucent.
2. Add the potatoes, broccoli and water and cook for 30 minutes on a low heat until tender.
3. Cool slightly. Use an electric hand blender to purée, then return the soup to the pan until ready to serve.
4. Add the cheese and cook for a couple of minutes prior to serving, until the cheese has melted. Season to taste with black pepper.

Note: If you prefer the soup with a creamier flavour, add a few spoonfuls of low fat crème fraiche when you add the Stilton.

Tomato Soup

SERVES 4 • COST OF INGREDIENTS: £2.20 • COST PER SERVING: 55p

1 teaspoon olive oil
1 onion, finely chopped
1 clove garlic, crushed
800g fresh tomatoes, peeled and finely chopped
2 teaspoons sun-dried tomato purée
50g sun-dried tomatoes
½ stick of celery, finely chopped
450ml water
1 teaspoon paprika
Black pepper to taste
A few basil leaves to garnish

1. Heat the oil in a pan and fry the onion and garlic gently until translucent.
2. Add all the remaining ingredients to the pan or slow cooker and leave to cook slowly on a low heat for 45 minutes to 1 hour.
3. Cool slightly. Use an electric hand blender to purée, then return the soup to the pan until ready to serve.
4. Serve garnished with basil leaves.

Minestrone Soup

SERVES 4–6 • COST OF INGREDIENTS: £2.50 • COST PER SERVING: 42p

A drizzle or spray of olive oil
1 large onion, chopped
1 clove garlic, crushed
1 red pepper, finely chopped
1 carrot, diced
1–2 sticks of celery, finely chopped
3–4 fresh tomatoes, peeled and chopped
50g red kidney beans, cooked
50g fresh green beans, chopped
500ml water or fresh stock
3 teaspoons pure tomato purée
½ teaspoon cayenne pepper
1 teaspoon paprika
2 bay leaves
50g cabbage, shredded
40g dried spaghetti, broken into pieces
1 tablespoon of fresh basil
Seasoning to taste

1. Heat the oil in the base of a slow cooker or heavy saucepan. Cook the onion and garlic until translucent and soft. Add the pepper and cook for another 2 minutes.
2. Place all the remaining ingredients except the cabbage and basil into the pan and cook slowly on a low heat for 45 minutes to 1 hour (or longer if cooking in a slow cooker).
3. 20 minutes before serving, add the cabbage, spaghetti and basil.
4. Serve with crusty bread and hummus for a hearty meal.

Rich Vegetable Soup

This also makes a hearty casserole if left chunky.

SERVES 4 • COST OF INGREDIENTS: £2.50 • COST PER SERVING: 63p

1 teaspoon olive oil
1 medium onion, coarsely chopped
1–2 cloves garlic, crushed
1 quarter swede, finely chopped
1 parsnip, finely chopped
3 medium tomatoes, chopped
2 small carrots, chopped
1 small stalk celery with leaves, chopped
1 small apple, chopped
500–750ml stock or water
100ml apple juice
2 bay leaves
2 teaspoons paprika
A dash of cayenne pepper
Seasoning to taste
½ teaspoon dill
2 teaspoons chopped parsley, plus extra to garnish

1. Heat the oil in the base of a slow cooker or heavy saucepan. Cook the onion and garlic until translucent and soft.
2. Place all the remaining ingredients into your pan, except the dill and parsley.
3. Cook on a low heat for 1½–2 hours on the hob, or 4–6 hours in a slow cooker.
4. Add the herbs 20 minutes before serving.
5. If you want a smooth soup, allow it to cool slightly, use an electric hand blender to purée and then return it to the pan until ready to serve. Alternatively, leave the soup chunky.
6. Garnish with chopped parsley.

Cream of Split Pea Soup

SERVES 4 • COST OF INGREDIENTS: 75p • COST PER SERVING: 19p

100g yellow split peas
Olive oil
1 medium onion, chopped
1–2 cloves garlic, crushed
I large potato, diced
1 stick of celery
1 teaspoon caraway seeds
¼ teaspoon ground mace
1 bay leaf
750–900ml water or stock
Seasoning to taste

1. Soak the split peas in hot water for an hour and drain.
2. Heat the oil in the base of a slow cooker or heavy saucepan. Cook the onion and garlic until translucent and soft.
3. Add all the remaining ingredients and cook for 1 hour on a low heat, or 4–6 hours in a slow cooker.
4. Allow the soup to cool slightly, then use an electric hand blender to purée and return it to the pan until ready to serve.

Carrot and Coriander Soup

SERVES 4 • COST OF INGREDIENTS: 90p • COST PER SERVING: 23p

A drizzle or spray of olive oil
2 teaspoons ground coriander
1 teaspoon ground cumin
1 onion, chopped
1 clove garlic, crushed
3 carrots, diced
2 celery sticks, finely chopped
500ml water or stock
Seasoning to taste
1 teaspoon coriander leaves, finely chopped (optional)

1. Heat the oil in the base of a slow cooker or heavy saucepan. Cook the spices for no more than 1 minute.
2. Add all the remaining ingredients and leave to cook for 1 hour on a low heat or 4–6 hours in a slow cooker.
3. Cool slightly. Use an electric hand blender to purée and return the soup to the pan until ready to serve.
4. Season to taste and reheat gently. Serve hot, garnished with the chopped coriander leaves.

Country Vegetable Broth

Anything goes with this soup! It is excellent for using up leftover vegetables.

SERVES 4 • COST OF INGREDIENTS: £1.50 • COST PER SERVING: 38p

A drizzle or spray of olive oil
1 onion, chopped
1 clove garlic, crushed
25g green split peas
25g red lentils
1 medium parsnip, diced
1 sweet potato, diced
1 medium potato, diced
1 carrot
700–900ml vegetable stock or water
2 teaspoons tomato purée (optional)
1–2 bay leaves
1–2 teaspoons paprika
2 teaspoons rosemary, freshly chopped
1 teaspoon thyme, finely chopped
Seasoning to taste

1. Heat the oil in the base of a slow cooker or heavy saucepan. Cook the onion and garlic until translucent and soft.
2. Add all the remaining ingredients except the herbs to the pan and leave to cook for 1½ hours on a low heat or 4–6 hours in a slow cooker.
3. Stir in the herbs and season to taste. You can serve the soup immediately, just as it is, or for a smoother texture, blend it briefly in a liquidiser or with a hand blender. Do not liquidise the soup completely or it will lose its character.

Note: You can substitute 50g dried soup mix (containing a range of pulses and barley) for the lentils and split peas.

Roasted Pumpkin Soup

This makes a delicious treat for Halloween or, for an all-year treat, you can use other squash.

SERVES 4 • COST OF INGREDIENTS: £1.20 • COST PER SERVING: 30p

1 small pumpkin
Olive oil
1 onion
1 garlic clove, crushed
1 teaspoon grated root ginger
1 teaspoon grated nutmeg
½ teaspoon ground coriander
1–2 carrots, chopped
1 medium sweet potato
2 sticks of celery
4 tomatoes, peeled and chopped
2 teaspoons of tomato purée (optional)
300–425ml water or stock
15ml lemon juice
Seasoning to taste

1. Preheat the oven to 160°C/gas mark 3.
2. Cut the pumpkin into wedges, lightly brush with oil and place in the oven for 20 minutes.
3. Meanwhile, prepare the vegetables. Cook the onion, garlic and spices together in a saucepan until soft and the onions are translucent.
4. Remove the flesh from the pumpkin wedges and add to the pan with the spices. Add all the remaining ingredients.
5. Cook slowly on a low heat for 1 hour or, if using a slow cooker, for 4–6 hours.
6. Cool slightly, use an electric hand blender to purée and return the soup to the pan until ready to serve.
7. Season as required. For impressive presentation, use hollowed out pumpkins as serving dishes.

Carrot, Tomato and Lentil Soup

SERVES 4 • COST OF INGREDIENTS: £2.20 • COST PER SERVING: 55p

A drizzle or spray of olive oil
1 large onion
1–2 cloves garlic
2 teaspoons paprika
6–8 tomatoes, chopped
2 carrots, chopped
½ red pepper, chopped
1 teaspoon dried basil or 1 bunch fresh basil, chopped
570ml water or stock
1–2 teaspoons sun-dried tomato paste
125g lentils, washed
2 dessertspoons tomato purée (optional)
1 bay leaf

1. Fry the onion and garlic together in the oil in a saucepan until soft and the onions are translucent. Chop all the remaining vegetables and add to the pan with the herbs.
2. Cover with water or stock. Add all the remaining ingredients and cook slowly on a low heat for 1 hour or, if using a slow cooker, for 4–6 hours.
3. Cool slightly, use an electric hand blender to purée and return the soup to the pan until ready to serve.
4. Serve garnished with chopped basil.

Butter Bean and Vegetable Soup

SERVES 4 • COST OF INGREDIENTS: £2.20 • COST PER SERVING: 55p

225g dried butter beans (or 1 x 410g can)
500–900ml water or stock
Olive oil
25g butter
2 leeks, finely sliced
2 carrots, chopped
1 parsnip, chopped
¼ teaspoon dried thyme
Black pepper to taste

1. If you are using dried butter beans, soak them overnight in lots of water.
2. Rinse the beans well and cook in the stock or water until soft, adding more water if the liquid is evaporating. When cooked, place to one side. Alternatively, you can use canned butter beans.
3. Put the leeks in a saucepan with the butter and a dash of oil, and cook until they are soft. Add the carrots and parsnip and cook for a further 2 minutes before adding the thyme and black pepper.
4. Cook slowly on a low heat for 1 hour or, if using a slow cooker, for 4–6 hours.
5. Season to taste before serving.

Carrot and Courgette Soup

SERVES 4 • COST OF INGREDIENTS: £1.60 • COST PER SERVING: 40p

Olive oil
1 onion, chopped
2–3 carrots, diced
1 sweet potato, diced
1–2 teaspoons grated fresh ginger
900ml water or stock
1 teaspoon dried or fresh thyme
2–3 courgettes, diced

1. Add a dash of olive oil to a saucepan and fry the onion until soft and translucent.

2. Add the carrots and sweet potato and cook for a further couple of minutes to help soften. Add fresh ginger and cook for another minute.

3. Add all the remaining ingredients and cook slowly on a low heat for 1 hour or, if using a slow cooker, for 4–6 hours.

4. You can leave the soup chunky but, if you prefer a smooth texture, cool slightly, use an electric hand blender to purée and return the soup to the pan until ready to serve.

Mulligatawny Soup

Serves 4 • COST OF INGREDIENTS: £4 or £1.75 without chicken
COST PER SERVING: £1 or 43p without chicken

Olive oil
1 large onion, chopped
1–2 cloves garlic, crushed
1 tablespoon garam masala or curry powder
2 carrots, diced
1 sweet potato, diced
1 parsnip, diced
1 cooking apple, sliced
1 litre water or stock
Seasoning to taste
2 bay leaves
1 tablespoon lemon juice
75g long-grain rice
1 chicken breast fillet, cubed (omit if vegetarian)
Fresh coriander leaves or parsley

1. Add olive oil to a saucepan and fry the onion, garlic and spices together until soft and the onions are translucent. Add the carrots, sweet potato, parsnip and apple and sweat together for 5 minutes.
2. Add the water or stock, seasoning and bay leaves. Cover and cook for 15 minutes on a medium heat.
3. Add lemon juice and check seasoning, adding a little more garam masala if required.
4. Add the rice and chicken. Cover and cook for a further 15–20 minutes until the chicken is cooked.
5. Serve garnished with chopped coriander leaves or parsley.

Nettle Soup

SERVES 4 • COST OF INGREDIENTS: £1.50 • COST PER SERVING: 38p

500g young organic nettles (wear gloves when picking!)
1 large onion, chopped
1 clove garlic, crushed
25g butter or dash of olive oil
1 potato, chopped
1 leek, chopped
750ml water
Black pepper to taste
2–3 tablespoons low fat crème fraiche

1. Wash and chop the nettles thoroughly (you may want to wear gloves for this).
2. Fry the onion and garlic in the butter or oil until soft. Add the potato and leek and cook for a further 5 minutes.
3. Add the water and black pepper to the pan. Cook gently on a low heat for 1 hour or, if using a slow cooker, for 4–6 hours.
4. Allow to cool slightly. Use an electric hand blender to purée and return the soup to the pan until ready to serve.
5. Gently reheat, then add the crème fraiche. Check the seasoning.
6. Serve garnished with chopped fresh sage or parsley.

Variation
Instead of nettles, you can use the green tops of red radishes.

Watercress Soup

SERVES 4 • COST OF INGREDIENTS: £3 • COST PER SERVING: 75p

1 onion, chopped
A drizzle or spray of olive oil
2 potatoes, chopped
500ml water or stock
150–200g watercress, chopped
300ml semi-skimmed milk
Seasoning as required

1. Heat the oil in a saucepan and fry the onion until soft and translucent. Add the potatoes and cook for a further 5 minutes.
2. Add the water or stock and the watercress. Cook slowly on a low heat for 30–45 minutes or, if using a slow cooker, for 4–6 hours, until the potatoes are tender. .
3. Cool slightly. Use an electric hand blender to purée the soup and return it to the pan. Add the milk and season to taste.
4. Reheat gently when ready to serve.

Sweet Potato, Carrot and Parsnip Soup

SERVES 4 • COST OF INGREDIENTS: £2.70 • COST PER SERVING: 68p

25g butter
1 large leek, sliced
2 celery sticks, chopped
3–4 sweet potatoes, cubed
2–3 carrots, cubed
1 large parsnip, cubed
750ml water or stock
15ml fresh chopped parsley
Freshly ground black pepper to taste

1. Melt the butter in a large saucepan and fry the leek until soft. Add the remaining vegetables to the pan and sweat for another 5 minutes.
2. Add water or stock, and herbs. Cook slowly on a low heat for 45 minutes or, if using a slow cooker, for 4–6 hours, until the vegetables are tender.
3. Season as required.
4. If you want to thicken the soup, allow it to cool, remove about a quarter of the soup and the liquid, and liquidise until smooth. Return it to the main pan and reheat the soup before serving.
5. Serve garnished with parsley.

Leek and Potato Soup

SERVES 4 • COST OF INGREDIENTS: £3.20 • COST PER SERVING: 80p

25g butter (or a drizzle of olive oil if you prefer)
2–3 leeks, sliced or chopped
1–2 potatoes, cubed
700ml water or stock
300ml semi-skimmed milk
3 tablespoons low fat crème fraiche
½ tablespoon parsley
1 tablespoon fresh sage
 Black pepper to taste
½ tablespoon chives

1. Melt the butter (or heat the oil) in a saucepan and fry the leeks until soft. Add the potatoes and cook for a further 5 minutes.
2. Cover with water or stock. Cook slowly on a low heat for 30–45 minutes or, if using a slow cooker, 4–6 hours. Add the milk, crème fraiche, parsley, and sage. Season to taste and cook for a further 5 minutes.
3. Cool slightly. Use an electric hand blender to purée the soup and return it to the pan until ready to serve.
4. Serve garnished with chopped chives.

Sweet Potato and Butternut Squash Soup

I am very fond of sweet potatoes – they are such a vibrant colour and packed full of goodness.

SERVES 4 • COST OF INGREDIENTS: £1.70 • COST PER SERVING: 42p

Olive oil
1 onion, chopped
1–2 cloves garlic, crushed
1 teaspoon coriander seeds
1–2 teaspoons freshly grated ginger
2 sweet potatoes
1 stick of celery, diced
1 small carrot, diced
½ small butternut squash, peeled and cubed
1 litre water or stock
1–2 teaspoons ground coriander
Seasoning to taste

1. Heat the oil in a saucepan and fry the onion, garlic and coriander seeds until soft and the onions are translucent. Add the grated ginger and cook for a further minute.
2. Add the potatoes, celery, carrot and squash and a little of the water or stock and cook for another 5 minutes to help soften them.
3. Add the remaining water or stock plus the ground coriander. Cook slowly on a low heat for 45 minutes or, if using a slow cooker, for 4–6 hours. Add more liquid if necessary.
4. Cool slightly. Use an electric hand blender to purée the soup and return it to the pan until ready to serve.
5. Season to taste before serving.

Scotch Broth

SERVES 4 • COST OF INGREDIENTS: £4 or £1.40 without beef
COST PER SERVING: £1 or 35p without beef

Olive oil
1 onion
1 leek, finely chopped
1–2 carrots, cubed
1 parsnip, cubed
400g beef skirt, thinly sliced
75g soup mix
¼ of a small cabbage
1 litre water or stock
1 bay leaf
Seasoning to taste

1. Heat the oil and fry the onion and leek together in a saucepan until soft and the onions are translucent.
2. Add the carrot and parsnip and cook for a further 5 minutes.
3. Add the beef skirt slices and cook for 2 minutes before adding all the remaining ingredients.
4. Cook slowly on a low heat for 1 hour or, if using a slow cooker, for 4–6 hours.
5. Season to taste before serving.

Sweet Potato, Apple and Ginger Soup

SERVES 4 • COST OF INGREDIENTS: £2 • COST PER SERVING: 50p

Olive oil
1 onion
2 sweet potatoes, chopped
2 sticks of celery, chopped
2 cooking apples, chopped
2–3 teaspoons grated fresh ginger (depending on desired strength)
700ml water or stock
Seasoning to taste
Lemon juice
Coriander leaves to garnish

1. Heat the oil in a saucepan and fry the onion until translucent. Add the sweet potatoes, celery and apples and sweat for another 5 minutes.
2. Add the grated ginger and cook for 2 more minutes. If the mixture is too dry you can add a dash of water.
3. Add the water or stock, cover the pan with a lid and cook slowly on a low heat for 30–45 minutes or, if using a slow cooker, for 4–6 hours.
4. Cool slightly. Use an electric hand blender to purée the soup and return it to the pan. Add seasoning and lemon juice to taste.
5. Reheat gently before serving. Serve garnished with coriander leaves.

Pea Soup

SERVES 4 • COST OF INGREDIENTS: £1.70 • COST PER SERVING: 43p

25g butter
1 onion, finely chopped
1–2 cloves garlic, crushed
1 medium potato, diced
700ml water or stock
400g peas (fresh peas give a richer taste)
2 tablespoons fresh chopped mint
Seasoning to taste
1 tablespoon crème fraiche

1. Melt the butter in a saucepan and fry the onion and garlic for 2 minutes.
2. Add the potato and cook for a further 3–4 minutes.
3. Add the water or stock and cook for 10 minutes, or until the potato is tender.
4. Add the peas and mint, and cook for a further 10 minutes.
5. Cool slightly. Use an electric hand blender to purée the soup and return it to the pan. Season to taste and add the crème fraiche. Stir well and reheat gently.
6. Serve warm with a spoonful of crème fraiche and garnished with mint leaves.

Sweetcorn and Haddock Chowder

SERVES 4 • COST OF INGREDIENTS: £3.20 • COST PER SERVING: 80p

25g butter
1 onion
2 potatoes, cubed
2 sticks of celery, chopped
2–3 lean smoked bacon rashers, chopped (optional)
500ml water or stock
2 smoked haddock fillets, chopped
200ml semi-skimmed milk
2 teaspoons chopped parsley
Seasoning to taste

1. Melt the butter in a large saucepan and fry the onion until translucent.
2. Add the potatoes and sweat for 5 minutes, then add the celery and bacon and cook for another 2 minutes.
3. Add half the water or stock and continue cooking for 5 more minutes to help soften the potatoes slightly.
4. Add all the remaining ingredients to the pan and cook for 10 minutes.
5. Test the haddock to make sure it is cooked – it should flake if pressed with a knife or fork.
6. Reheat the soup gently and season to taste. Serve garnished with parsley.

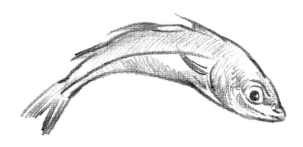

Chinese-style Beef Broth

SERVES 4 • COST OF INGREDIENTS: £4 • COST PER SERVING: £1

Olive oil
1 onion
1–2 cloves garlic, crushed
200g beef steak, thinly sliced
½ red pepper, sliced
1–2 red chillies
4–5 button mushrooms, finely sliced
5cm (2in) knuckle of ginger, chopped
100ml dry sherry
1–2 teaspoons soy sauce
500–750ml water or stock
100g fine noodles
30g bean sprouts
Seasoning to taste

1. Heat the olive oil in a pan and fry the onion and garlic for 2 minutes.
2. Add the beef steak, pepper, chilli, mushrooms and ginger and cook until the beef is brown.
3. Add the sherry and soy sauce and cook for 1 minute before adding the water, noodles and bean sprouts.
4. Season to taste. Cook for a further 10 minutes before serving.

Fast Food That's Good For You

If your family love junk food, why not give them what they crave but in a quick, easy and healthy way? You could create your own little fast food outlet, and serve your food in paper bags – sounds crazy, but kids love it!

Old McBurger

Burgers are shockingly easy to make. All you need is a chopping board and a mixing bowl. Kids can get involved and create their own McBurger. Below I have some ideas, but feel free to create your own special recipe.

Tasty Beefburgers

SERVES 4 • COST OF INGREDIENTS: from £1.30 • COST PER SERVING: 33p

- **Can be frozen**
- **Can be cooked in advance**
- **Make 2, keep 1**

1 onion, finely chopped
1 clove garlic, crushed
400g lean beef mince
1 tablespoon home-prepared wholemeal breadcrumbs
1 egg, beaten
1 teaspoon coriander
1 teaspoon cumin
1 teaspoon yellow mustard
2 teaspoons tomato purée
Seasoning to taste

1. Put the onion and garlic into a large bowl and stir well. Add the beef and breadcrumbs and mix thoroughly.
2. Add the beaten egg, coriander, cumin, mustard and tomato purée. Season to taste.
3. Mix thoroughly and form into balls – these should be firm but moist.
4. Use the palm of your hand to flatten the balls into burger shapes.
5. You can place them in the fridge until you are ready to use them, or freeze them in layers (separate the layers with parchment to prevent the burgers sticking together).
6. When you are ready, grill or light fry the burgers in olive oil. Cook them for 4–5 minutes on each side until golden.
7. Garnish with salad and serve with wholemeal baps.

Fishburgers

This recipe is priced for supermarket fresh haddock at £7.96 per kg and white fish fillets at £3.73 per kg, which makes the total price of the fish £2.34. Ask your fishmonger for fish pieces as this will also help to reduce the price. Some supermarkets offer a fish pie mix (at the time of writing this was £2.99 for 320g and contained haddock, pollock and salmon). Although slightly below weight, this would be suitable for this recipe.

SERVES 4 • COST OF INGREDIENTS: £3.11 • COST PER SERVING: 78p

- **Can be frozen**
- **Can be cooked in advance**
- **Make 2, keep 1**

½ bunch of spring onions, finely chopped
200g haddock fillet, finely chopped
200g white fish fillet, finely chopped
1 teaspoon tarragon
Juice of ½ a lemon
1 egg, beaten
1 tablespoon home-prepared wholemeal breadcrumbs
1 tablespoon flour
Seasoning to taste

1. In a large bowl, thoroughly mix together the spring onions, fish fillets, tarragon and lemon juice.
2. Season and then add the egg. Mix thoroughly.
3. Gradually add the breadcrumbs and flour until you have a firm but moist mixture.
4. Form the mixture into balls – again these should be firm but moist.
5. Use the palm of your hand to flatten the balls into burger shapes.
6. You can place them in the fridge until you are ready to use them, or freeze them in layers (separate each layer with parchment to prevent them sticking together).
7. When you are ready, grill or light fry the burgers in olive oil. Cook for 4–5 minutes on each side until golden.
8. Serve with wholemeal baps and a salad garnish, or chunky chips and peas for a variation on fish and chips.

Beef and Bacon Burgers

SERVES 4 • COST OF INGREDIENTS: £2.20 • COST PER SERVING: 55p

- **Can be frozen**
- **Can be cooked in advance**
- **Make 2, keep 1**

1 onion, finely chopped
1 clove garlic, crushed
400g beef mince
2–3 rashers of lean bacon, finely chopped
2 teaspoons tomato purée
1 tablespoon home-prepared wholemeal breadcrumbs
1 egg, beaten
1 teaspoon mixed herbs
2–3 teaspoons Cajun seasoning

1. In a large bowl, mix together the onion and garlic and stir well. Add the beef, bacon, tomato purée and breadcrumbs and mix thoroughly.
2. Add the egg, herbs and seasoning.
3. Mix thoroughly and form into balls – these should be firm but moist.
4. Use the palm of your hand to flatten the balls into burger shapes.
5. You can place them in the fridge until you are ready to use them, or freeze them in layers (separate each layer with parchment to prevent them sticking together).
6. When you are ready, grill or light fry the burgers in olive oil. Cook for 4–5 minutes on each side until golden.
7. Garnish with salad and serve with wholemeal baps.

Turkey Burgers

SERVES 4 • COST OF INGREDIENTS: £1.77 • COST PER SERVING: 44p

- **Can be frozen**
- **Can be cooked in advance**
- **Make 2, keep 1**

1 onion, finely chopped
1 clove garlic, crushed
400g lean turkey mince
1 tablespoon home-prepared wholemeal breadcrumbs
1 egg, beaten
1 teaspoon dried basil (or 2–3 teaspoons fresh, chopped)
A small handful of fresh parsley, chopped
2 teaspoons tomato purée
Seasoning to taste

1. In a large bowl, mix together the onion and garlic and stir well. Add the turkey and breadcrumbs and mix thoroughly.
2. Add the egg, herbs, purée and seasoning.
3. Mix thoroughly and form into balls – these should be firm but moist.
4. Use the palm of your hand to flatten the balls into burger shapes.
5. You can place them in the fridge until you are ready to use them, or freeze them in layers (separate each layer with parchment to prevent them sticking together).
6. When you are ready, grill or light fry the burgers in olive oil. Cook for 4–5 minutes on each side until golden.
7. Garnish with salad and serve with wholemeal baps.

Chicken Burgers

SERVES 4 • COST OF INGREDIENTS: £2.87 • COST PER SERVING: 72p

- **Can be frozen**
- **Can be cooked in advance**
- **Make 2, keep 1**

1 onion, chopped
1–2 cloves garlic, crushed
1 stick of celery, chopped
½ yellow pepper, chopped
500g chicken mince
30g pine nuts
1 tablespoon home-prepared wholemeal breadcrumbs

1. Place all the ingredients in a food processor and mix thoroughly.
2. When mixed, form into balls – these should be firm but moist. If the mixture is dry, add some beaten egg.
3. Use the palm of your hand to flatten the balls into burger shapes.
4. You can place them the fridge until you are ready to use them, or freeze them in layers (separate each layer with parchment to prevent them sticking together).
5. When you are ready, grill or light fry the burgers in olive oil. Cook for 4–5 minutes on each side until golden.
6. Serve with wholemeal baps, a salad garnish and a dollop of mayonnaise.

Spicy Beefburgers

SERVES 4 • COST OF INGREDIENTS: £1.50 • COST PER SERVING: 38p

- **Can be frozen**
- **Can be cooked in advance**
- **Make 2, keep 1**

1 onion, finely chopped
1 clove garlic, crushed
1 chilli, finely chopped
400g minced beef
1 egg, beaten
A splash of Worcestershire sauce

1. In a large bowl, mix together the onion, garlic and chilli and stir well. Add the beef and mix thoroughly.
2. Add the egg and Worcestershire sauce.
3. Mix thoroughly and form into balls – these should be firm but moist.
4. Use the palm of your hand to flatten the balls into burger shapes.
5. You can place them in the fridge until you are ready to use them, or freeze them in layers (line each layer with parchment to prevent them sticking together).
6. When you are ready, grill or light fry the burgers in olive oil. Cook for 4–5 minutes on each side until golden.
7. Garnish with salad and serve with wholemeal baps.

Lamb and Bulgur Burgers

SERVES 4 • COST OF INGREDIENTS: £2.01 • COST PER SERVING: 50p

- **Can be frozen**
- **Can be cooked in advance**
- **Make 2, keep 1**

75g bulgur wheat
150ml hot water or hot stock
1 onion, chopped finely
1 garlic clove, crushed
1 large carrot, grated
300–400g lean minced lamb
1 egg, beaten
Splash of Worcestershire Sauce
2 teaspoons dried mixed herbs
Seasoning to taste

1. Put the bulgur wheat into a large bowl, pour over the hot water or stock and leave for 20 minutes until the bulgur wheat is soft and tender. Drain off any excess fluid.
2. Add the onion, garlic and carrot and stir well. Add the lamb and mix thoroughly.
3. Add the egg, Worcestershire sauce, herbs and seasoning.
4. Mix thoroughly and form into balls – these should be firm but moist.
5. Use the palm of your hand to flatten the balls into burger shapes.
6. You can place them in the fridge until you are ready to use them, or freeze them in layers (separate each layer with parchment to prevent them sticking together).
7. When you are ready, grill or light fry the burgers in olive oil. Cook for 4–5 minutes on each side until golden.
8. Garnish with salad and serve with wholemeal baps.

Spicy Tofu Burgers

SERVES 4 • COST OF INGREDIENTS: £2.50 • COST PER SERVING: 63p

- **Suitable for vegetarians**
- **Can be frozen**
- **Can be cooked in advance**
- **Make 2, keep 1**

1 tin chickpeas, drained
250g or 1 pack firm tofu
1 onion, finely chopped
1–2 cloves garlic, crushed
1 chilli, finely chopped
1 celery stick, finely chopped
1 teaspoon tomato purée
1 teaspoon garam masala
Splash of soy sauce
Seasoning to taste
1 tablespoon home-prepared wholemeal breadcrumbs
1 tablespoon oats

1. Put the chickpeas in a large bowl and mash until soft. Add the tofu and continue to mash until the two are thoroughly mixed together.
2. Meanwhile, fry the onion, garlic, chilli and celery until soft. Add to the chickpea and tofu mixture.
3. Add the tomato purée, garam masala, soy sauce and seasoning. Stir well before adding the breadcrumbs and oats.
4. Mix thoroughly and form into balls (on a floured surface if the mixture is sticky) – the balls should be firm but moist.
5. Use the palm of your hand to flatten the balls into burger shapes.
6. You can place them in the fridge until you are ready to use them, or freeze them in layers (separate each layer with parchment to prevent them sticking together).
7. When you are ready, grill or light fry the burgers in olive oil. Cook for 4–5 minutes on each side until golden.
8. Garnish with salad and serve with wholemeal baps.

Chickpea and Cashew Nut Burgers

Serves 4 • COST OF INGREDIENTS: £2.50 • COST PER SERVING: 63p

- **Suitable for vegetarians**
- **Can be frozen**
- **Can be cooked in advance**
- **Make 2, keep 1**

1 tablespoon home-prepared wholemeal breadcrumbs
1 tablespoon oats
400g cooked chickpeas (or 1 tin, drained)
1 onion, finely chopped
1–2 cloves garlic, crushed
1 large or 2 medium carrots, grated
2 tablespoons tomato purée
100g cashew nuts, chopped
1 egg, beaten
2–3 teaspoons Worcestershire sauce
Seasoning to taste

1. In a small bowl, mix the breadcrumbs and oats together and leave to one side.
2. Meanwhile, in a large mixing bowl, mash the chickpeas until broken and softened. Add the onion, garlic and carrots and stir well.
3. Add the tomato purée and mix thoroughly before adding the cashew nuts.
4. Add the egg, Worcestershire sauce and seasoning.
5. Mix thoroughly and form the mixture into balls – these should be firm but moist. If the mixture is too wet, add a sprinkle of oats. If too dry, add a small amount of olive oil.
6. Use the palm of your hand and flatten the balls into burger shapes.
7. Dip the burgers into the breadcrumb mixture, thoroughly coating each one. You can place them in the fridge until you are ready to use them, or freeze them in layers (separate each layer with parchment to prevent them sticking together).

8. When you are ready, grill or light fry the burgers in olive oil. Cook for 4–5 minutes on each side until golden.
9. Garnish with salad and serve with wholemeal baps.

Fish and Chips

This is a real British favourite. Use white fish such as cod or pollock, or ask your fishmonger for some cheap but tasty suggestions. And, to complement the fish, try the recipe for home-made chunky chips, below.

SERVES 4 • COST OF INGREDIENTS: £2.54 • COST PER SERVING: 64p

225g plain flour
3 teaspoons baking powder
285ml cold beer
4–6 boneless fish fillets
Flour for dusting

1. Mix the flour, baking powder and beer together to form a batter. This should be the consistency of double cream.
2. Coat the fish fillets in flour on both sides; this will help the batter adhere to the fillets.
3. Coat the floured fillets in batter, drop them into hot oil and deep-fry for 4–6 minutes.
4. Serve with chunky chips (see the following recipe).

Chunky Chips

I am a big fan of chunky chips, but I do make them myself. I don't own a deep-fat fryer – I can't stand the smell of fat. Instead I get the best of both worlds – chips made with very little fat and very little effort, that taste divine!

SERVES 4 • COST OF INGREDIENTS: £1.20 • COST PER SERVING: 30p

4–6 larger potatoes
2 tablespoons olive oil (or spray with light oil)
2–3 teaspoons paprika
Herbs (optional)
Coarse sea salt

1. Preheat the oven to 200°C/gas mark 6.
2. Slice the potatoes into thick chunks, leaving the skins on.
3. Boil for 10 minutes, strain and place in a large bowl with the oil and paprika. If you are watching your oil consumption, put the olive oil in an old spray container and lightly spray the potatoes until coated, then sprinkle with paprika.
4. Stir well, ensuring that the oil has coated the potato thoroughly.
5. Place potatoes on a greased baking tray. Sprinkle with herbs if desired. Bake for 10 minutes, then turn. Cook for another 10–15 minutes until golden.
6. Serve sprinkled with sea salt.

Note: You can use sweet potatoes instead of white potatoes to make healthy chips with a wonderful orange colour. Spice them up with some crushed chillies or serve with a salsa dip.

Pizza Piazza

If I have children over for a play date, I normally get them to make their own pizzas. They have a great time making the dough. I place a large piece of foil or baking parchment in front of each child. They can roll their dough straight onto the foil, which saves mess and avoids using baking trays. I normally put a variety of topping ingredients in small bowls so they can choose whatever they want to make their own creation. When the pizzas are finished, I simply pick them up and place them straight into the oven to bake for 10–15 minutes.

To save time, you could make your own dough in advance. Roll it out and place each piece on greased foil or a parchment sheet. Stack the pizza bases on top of each other, cover in cling film or foil and refrigerate until ready to use.

Basic Dough Recipe

- **Suitable for vegetarians**
- **Can be frozen**
- **Can be cooked in advance**
- **Make 2, keep 1**

500g strong bread flour
325ml warm water
1 sachet of dried yeast
1 teaspoon brown sugar
2 tablespoons olive oil

1. Sift the flour into a bowl.
2. Mix the water, yeast, sugar and oil together. Make sure the sugar is dissolved. Make a well in the middle of the flour and pour in.
3. Mix thoroughly before transferring the dough onto a floured board. Knead well until the dough springs back when pulled.
4. Place the dough in a floured bowl and cover with cling film or a warm, damp cloth until it has doubled in size. This takes about 1 hour.
5. Knead again, and divide into individual pizza bases or as preferred.
6. This dough can be stored in the fridge or freezer until needed.

Basic Pizza Topping

Pizza topping can be made using your own home-made pasta sauce (see the recipe for Tomato and Herb Sauce on page 181 in 'Ooh, Saucy!') or even simple tomato purée mixed with olive oil and herbs. There are no hard and fast rules for pizza toppings so experiment with whatever you fancy and have fun.

Below are some suggestions to help you but, really, anything goes!

Tomato and cheese;
Pepperoni, mushrooms, red onions and cheese;
Ham and mushroom;
Ham, pineapple and cheese;
Chorizo, jalapenos, tomato and cheese;
Red onions, black olives, tomatoes, cheese and red peppers;
Cheese and chilli.

Chick, Chick, Chicken

Chicken is one of the most popular meats in the UK. It is versatile, cheap, and kids don't turn their noses up at it! It is easier to digest than red meats and is lower in fat. As with most foods, a lot depends on how you cook it. Chicken skin is higher in fat than the flesh, so try to avoid this if you are concerned about your fat intake. Chicken, like lots of our food today, can be tampered with. It is quite common for the flesh to be injected with water to give a 'plump' appearance. In addition, there are serious questions to be answered concerning the welfare of chickens, particularly those in battery farms. If this is a concern for you, read the labels and buy from sources you are happy with.

Chicken Chow Mein

SERVES 4 • COST OF INGREDIENTS: £6.59 • COST PER SERVING: £1.65

4 chicken pieces, thinly sliced (you can use cooked chicken pieces)
2–3 teaspoons Chinese five-spice
Olive or sesame oil
2.5cm knuckle of ginger, finely sliced
1 chilli, finely cut
3–4 cloves garlic, crushed
2 carrots, finely chopped into thin slices
4–5 broccoli florets
4–6 spring onions, diagonally sliced
1 pepper, sliced
½ small spring cabbage, shredded
A handful of bean sprouts (optional)
50g mushrooms, sliced
300g noodles
3 tablespoons sherry or rice wine
2–3 teaspoons soy sauce
Juice of ½ a lemon
3 tablespoons sweet chilli sauce

1. Mix the chicken with the Chinese spices. If you are using fresh chicken, heat a splash of olive oil in a wok and fry for a few minutes until browned, then leave to one side until needed.
2. Add more oil to the wok and fry the ginger, chilli and garlic. Next add your chopped vegetables (apart from the mushrooms) and cook for another 2 minutes, until the vegetables start to wilt slightly, but not go soft.
3. Add the chicken, bean sprouts, mushrooms and noodles and cook for 1 more minute.
4. Add the sherry or rice wine, soy sauce, lemon juice and sweet chilli sauce and stir well for 1 minute. Serve immediately.

Chicken in Red Wine Sauce

My mum used to make this when we were children and it was always a big favourite of ours. She served with it with mini roast or sauté potatoes and vegetables. You can also make a veggie version of this by substituting Quorn fillets for the chicken.

SERVES 4 • COST OF INGREDIENTS: £6.51 • COST PER SERVING: £1.63

• **Can be cooked in advance**

Olive oil
1 onion
2–3 cloves garlic, crushed
1 red pepper, diced
4 chicken fillets or pieces
2 teaspoons paprika
1 tin chopped tomatoes
200ml red wine
350ml stock or water
150g button mushrooms
1 teaspoon tarragon
Seasoning to taste

1. In a large sauté pan or ovenproof pan, fry the onion and garlic in a dash of olive oil for 2 minutes. Add the pepper and cook for another 2 minutes.
2. Add the chicken fillets and paprika. Stir, cooking gently for 5 minutes.
3. Add all the remaining ingredients. Cover the pan with a lid and cook on a moderate heat for 45 minutes, until the chicken is tender and the sauce has thickened.
4. Serve with small roast or sauté potatoes and vegetables.

Sweet and Sticky Glazed Chicken

This is a very simple dish recommended by a friend of mine – not sure where she got it from! It takes minutes to prepare but the preparation must be done the evening before you need it, to make good use of the flavours.

SERVES 4 • COST OF INGREDIENTS: £4 • COST PER SERVING: £1

• **Can be cooked in advance**

4 chicken breast fillets
3 tablespoons maple syrup or honey
1 tablespoon mustard
1 tablespoon Worcestershire sauce
1 tablespoon soy sauce
2 teaspoons paprika

1. Place all the ingredients apart from the chicken in a bowl and mix well.
2. Meanwhile, score the fillets with a sharp knife to give the marinade something to hold on to.
3. Have a large freezer bag ready as this can get messy! Dip the fillets into the marinade and ensure they are evenly coated, then pop each fillet into the bag.
4. Leave in the fridge until the following day. When you are ready to cook, as a precaution, line your grill pan with foil to collect any sticky drips. Grill the chicken gently on both sides, adding marinade as you go.
5. Serve with salad.

Hearty Chicken Casserole

This is a great standby to use up any leftovers, whether chicken or vegetables.

SERVES 4 • COST OF INGREDIENTS: £4.82 • COST PER SERVING: £1.21

- **Can be frozen**
- **Can be cooked in advance**
- **Use up your leftovers**
- **Make 2, keep 1**

Olive oil
1 onion, finely chopped
1–2 cloves of garlic, crushed
1 stalk of celery, chopped
1 leek, chopped
1 large carrot, sliced
1 large potato, cubed
300g chicken (use fillets, breast, thighs or chicken pieces – all boneless)
1 tin of tomatoes (or 4–6 ripe fresh tomatoes)
200ml white or red wine (optional)
700ml chicken stock
2 teaspoons paprika
1 bay leaf

1. Heat the olive oil in a large ovenproof casserole dish (or slow cooker) and fry the onion and garlic for 2 minutes. Add the celery, leek, carrots and potato and cook for 3–4 minutes, stirring occasionally to prevent the mixture from sticking.
2. Add the chicken followed by all the remaining ingredients. Cover with a lid and cook on a very low heat for 1–2 hours or, if you are using a slow cooker, for 4–6 hours.
3. Serve with mini jacket potatoes.

Chicken and Mushroom Casserole

SERVES 4 • COST OF INGREDIENTS: £6.19 • COST PER SERVING: £1.55

- **Can be frozen**
- **Can be cooked in advance**
- **Use up your leftovers**
- **Make 2, keep 1**

A drizzle or spray of olive oil
1–2 cloves garlic
2 leeks, finely chopped
6 spring onions, finely chopped
300g chicken pieces (you can use cooked chicken)
175g mushrooms
200ml white wine
300ml chicken stock
1 teaspoon cornflour
1 teaspoon paprika
100g French beans
1 teaspoon dried tarragon (or a handful of fresh tarragon)

1. Heat a little olive oil in an ovenproof casserole dish or slow cooker and sauté the garlic, leeks and spring onions for 2–3 minutes. Add the chicken and cook for a further 5 minutes.
2. Add the mushrooms, wine and chicken stock. Mix the cornflour with 10ml of water in a cup to form a smooth paste. Stir well then add to the chicken pot.
3. Add all the remaining ingredients. If you are using fresh tarragon, add half now and retain half to add in the last 10 minutes of cooking.
4. Cook gently on a low heat for 45 minutes.

Note: If you prefer a creamier sauce, add some low fat Greek yoghurt or low fat crème fraiche 5 minutes before serving.

Home-made Chicken Nuggets

These are great served with home-made potato wedges (see instructions below).

SERVES 4 • COST OF INGREDIENTS: £4.03 • COST PER SERVING: £1.01

• **Can be cooked in advance**

For the chicken nuggets
4 skinless and boneless chicken fillets
4 tablespoons plain flour
3–4 teaspoons chicken seasoning
2 teaspoons paprika
2 eggs, beaten
100g breadcrumbs (made from leftover bread)
A spray of olive oil

For the potato wedges
Potatoes, cut into chunks
1 tablespoon olive oil
1–2 teaspoons paprika

1. Preheat the oven to 200°C/gas mark 6.
2. Cut the fillets into the required size for nuggets.
3. You will need three bowls. In the first bowl mix the flour, seasoning and paprika, in the second put the beaten eggs, and in the third the breadcrumbs.
4. Dip the chicken fillets into the first bowl, ensuring all sides are covered, then into the second, again ensuring all sides are covered, and finally into the third bowl.
5. Place the dipped chicken onto a greased baking tray, spray with olive oil and bake in the oven for 20 minutes until golden. Serve with home-made potato wedges.

To make the potato wedges
1. Place the potato chunks in a bowl with the olive oil and paprika. Ensure all the potatoes are evenly covered with the oil and paprika mixture.
2. Transfer onto a baking tray and cook in the oven at 200°C/gas mark 6 until golden.

Variations
Add chopped garlic, chillies and herbs of your choice for extra spice.

Leftover Chicken Pie

This is another of my mum's recipes. Now we have grown up and flown the nest, Mum and Dad have had to adapt to cooking for two instead of four. This meal is made from the leftovers of Mum's Sunday roast, so they usually tuck into it early in the week.

SERVES 4

COST OF INGREDIENTS: £1.43 if using leftover chicken; £3.82 if using fresh chicken pieces

COST PER SERVING: 36p if using leftover chicken; 95p if using fresh chicken pieces

- **Can be frozen**
- **Can be cooked in advance**
- **Use up your leftovers**
- **Make 2, keep 1**

A drizzle or spray of olive oil
1 onion, chopped
2 sticks of celery, chopped
75g mushrooms, quartered
200–300g cooked chicken (removed from bone)
100g cooked ham (optional)
1 can chicken or mushroom condensed soup
½ pack of ready-made puff pastry

1. Preheat the oven to 200°C/gas mark 6.
2. Heat the oil and fry the onion in a pan, add the celery, mushrooms, cooked chicken, and ham if using, and cook for 3–4 minutes.
3. Add the soup and heat for a further 3 minutes.
4. Put the mixture in a pie dish and cover with pastry (if you are short of time, use ready-made puff pastry).
5. Bake for 30 minutes until the pie crust is golden.

Creamy Chicken, Leek and Ham Pie

This is a similar recipe to the above, but it is made with a combination of Greek yoghurt and quark. This gives the pie a rather decadent feel, but without the extra calories you would gain by adding cream. If you are nervous about using quark, you can opt for the more calorific double cream.

SERVES 4
COST OF INGREDIENTS: £7.83 but much less if you use leftover chicken)
COST PER SERVING: £1.96

- **Can be frozen**
- **Can be cooked in advance**
- **Use up your leftovers**
- **Make 2, keep 1**

300g cooked chicken (chunky breast or thigh is good)
100g thick ham, cut into chunks
2 leeks, finely sliced
200ml Greek yoghurt (Total is good as it holds its consistency)
100ml quark (or double cream, if preferred)
1–2 tablespoons wholegrain mustard
Seasoning to taste
2 tablespoons chives, chopped
1 teaspoon dried tarragon
½ a 500g pack of puff pastry

1. Preheat the oven to 180°C/gas mark 4.
2. Place all the ingredients for the filling together in a bowl (or you can layer them in your pie dish) and stir well to ensure the quark or cream and yoghurt thoroughly coat all the food.
3. Season to taste.
4. Cover with your puff pastry and brush with milk.
5. Bake in the oven for 30 minutes until the pastry is golden.

Mary had a little lamb

In this chapter you will find a selection of lamb recipes. You can find more ideas for using lamb mince in the chapters 'A Load of Meatballs' and 'Don't Mince About'.

- Lamb is expensive so opt for cheaper cuts of meat. Speak to your local butcher, who should be able to advise you on the best offers available and give you some tips on how to cook the meat.

- If you are making a stew or casserole, cheaper cuts such as neck fillet, boneless loin, brisket, shanks or even shoulder are ideal. The long, slow cooking time can produce a flavoursome and tender result. At the time of writing, supermarket prices for diced lamb are approximately £4 for 400g.

- Make the most of your purchase. For example, roast a whole joint for one meal, use leftovers in a pie for another, and thereafter any remaining meat can be used cold in sandwiches or to accompany salad. Choose rack of lamb, leg or boneless loin.

Lamb and Apricot Casserole

This is a lovely wholesome dish. You can use lesser cuts of lamb as the cooking will make it nice and tender – cook slowly for longer periods to tenderise the meat. Why not make double and freeze one portion ready for another meal?

SERVES 4–6 • COST OF INGREDIENTS: £6.38 • COST PER SERVING: £1.60

- **Can be frozen**
- **Can be cooked in advance**
- **Make 2, keep 1**

A drizzle or spray of olive oil
1 onion, chopped
2–3 cloves garlic, crushed
400g lamb, diced
3 teaspoons harissa paste or hot chilli paste
2 teaspoons ground cinnamon powder
200ml red wine
1 tin chopped tomatoes
200ml water or stock
1 tin chickpeas, drained
100g dried apricots, chopped
Fresh coriander leaves for garnish

1. Heat the oil in a large casserole dish, cook the onion, garlic and lamb for 2–3 minutes.
2. Add the harissa paste and stir well for 2 minutes.
3. Add all the remaining ingredients and cook slowly for 1 hour on a low heat setting on the hob, or in the oven at 180°C/gas mark 4, or for longer if you are using a slow cooker.
4. Serve garnished with coriander leaves.

Spicy Moroccan-style Lamb Cutlets

SERVES 4 • COST OF INGREDIENTS: £6.01 • COST PER SERVING: £1.50

• **Can be cooked in advance**

100ml pomegranate molasses (buy in a bottle or see 'Ooh, Saucy!' for recipe)
2 lemons
2–3 cloves garlic, crushed
2 teaspoons chilli powder
2 teaspoons paprika
Black pepper to taste
4 lamb chops
4 tablespoons Greek yoghurt

1. Place the molasses, juice and zest of the lemons, garlic, chilli and paprika into a bowl. Season with black pepper.
2. Place the chops in the liquid and leave for 2–3 hours to marinate.
3. When ready to cook, remove the chops from the marinade. Mix the yoghurt with the marinade and place in a pan over a very low heat.
4. Grill the chops evenly on both sides, brushing some of the marinade sauce over them as you cook.
5. When the chops are cooked, transfer to plates, drizzle with the warm marinade and serve with couscous and salad or, for a more traditional meal, new potatoes and vegetables.

Lamb and Almond Tagine

This is a lovely rich recipe. You can cheat by adding a spicy tagine sauce instead of the individual spices. I have used Al'Fez Honey and Almond Tagine Sauce (£1.99 a jar) which has a very authentic flavour and is great when you are in a hurry. For more information visit www.alfez.com

SERVES 4 • COST OF INGREDIENTS: £6.89 • COST PER SERVING: £1.72

- **Can be frozen**
- **Can be cooked in advance**
- **Make 2, keep 1**

Olive oil
1 large onion, chopped
2–3 garlic cloves, crushed
1 teaspoon coriander seeds
1 teaspoon cumin seeds
2 teaspoons chilli powder
3–4 teaspoons paprika
3–4 teaspoons turmeric
3–4 teaspoons cinnamon powder
400g lamb, diced
8 shallots, halved
1 carrot, diced
1 sweet potato, diced
1 tablespoon honey
600ml water or stock
200ml red wine
50g almond flakes
Seasoning to taste
Fresh coriander to garnish

1. In a large ovenproof dish or slow cooker, sauté the onions and garlic in a little olive oil.
2. Add the herbs and spices and the lamb. Continue to cook for 2–3 minutes.
3. Add the shallots, carrot and sweet potato and sweat for another minute or two before adding the remaining ingredients.
4. Cook slowly on a low heat for 1 hour or, if using a slow cooker, for 6–8 hours. If you are using one of the cheaper cuts of lamb, cook on a very low heat for longer as this will help tenderise the meat.
5. Stir occasionally and add more liquid if necessary; it may evaporate as you cook.
6. Sprinkle over a few more almond slices and chopped fresh coriander and serve with couscous or rice.

Lamb Hotpot

This is a real winter warmer. The price of this hotpot could be reduced. I have priced the leeks at 50p each, as this is the average price if you buy them loose. However, at the time of writing, supermarkets are reducing the price of vegetables in a bid to encourage healthy eating. Prices also depend on whether or not the fruit and vegetables are in season. For example, Asda currently offer a pack of 4-5 leeks for 50p, so if you hunt around, you will get deals which will reduce the cost.

SERVES 4 • COST OF INGREDIENTS: £7.11 • COST PER SERVING: £1.78

- **Can be frozen**
- **Can be cooked in advance**
- **Make 2, keep 1**

400g lamb, cubed
50g plain flour
2–3 teaspoons paprika
3–4 leeks, sliced
2 cloves of garlic, crushed
Olive oil
1–2 carrots, chopped
Knob of butter
500ml lamb stock
1 teaspoon mixed herbs
2–3 sprigs of thyme (or cube of frozen fresh thyme)
6–8 potatoes, thinly sliced
25g mature Cheddar, grated

1. Preheat the oven to 180°C/gas mark 4.
2. In a bowl mix the lamb with the flour and paprika, ensuring the lamb is evenly coated all over.
3. Heat a little olive oil in a large sauté pan and fry the leeks and garlic for 2–3 minutes. Add the meat, carrots and butter and cook for a further 2–3 minutes to help brown the meat.
4. Pour on the stock, dried herbs and thyme and cook for 10 minutes.
5. Place a layer of potato slices in the bottom of a greased ovenproof dish. Cover with a layer of meat mixture and continue alternating layers of meat and potato, finishing with a final layer of potato slices.

6. Cook in the oven for 1 hour.
7. Remove from the oven and sprinkle over the grated cheese before returning the hotpot to the oven for a final 20–30 minutes.

Lamb Moussaka

SERVES 4 • COST OF INGREDIENTS: £7.57 • COST PER SERVING: £1.89

- **Can be frozen**
- **Can be cooked in advance**
- **Make 2, keep 1**

2–3 aubergines, sliced
1 onion
2 cloves garlic, crushed
Olive oil
400g lamb mince
1 tin chopped tomatoes
2 teaspoons tomato purée
1 teaspoon dried mint
2 teaspoons cinnamon powder
Seasoning to taste
300ml low fat crème fraiche
50g mature Cheddar or Parmesan cheese, grated

1. Preheat the oven to 180°C/gas mark 4.
2. Place the aubergines in a pan of boiling water for 2 minutes. Remove and pat dry. Leave to one side.
3. Meanwhile, heat a little olive oil in a sauté pan and fry the onion and garlic. Add the lamb mince and cook until brown.
4. Add the tomatoes, tomato purée, mint, cinnamon and seasoning and cook for another 2–3 minutes.
5. Place a layer of mince in an ovenproof dish, followed by a layer of aubergine. Continue alternating mince and aubergine, finishing with a layer of mince.
6. Mix the crème fraiche with the grated cheese and pour over the final layer of mince. Garnish with a sprinkle of Parmesan before placing in the oven for 30–40 minutes.

You Can't Beat A Bit of Bully

Beef is a perennial British favourite. You can find more beef recipes in 'A load of Meatballs' and 'Don't Mince About', and ideas for pasties in 'Roll out the Pastry'.

- Your butcher will be able to advise you about cheaper cuts of meat and how to cook them.

- Rib of beef, sirloin, rump and topside are all good for roasting. And, as with any joint, use leftovers to make a pie for another meal, or cut slices of cold meat for sandwiches or salads.

- Mince is great for a number of family favourites, including spaghetti bolognese, shepherd's pie and chilli con carne. Choose lean mince and, before adding the meat to your dish, drain off any fat after cooking.

- Steak is best for frying – you can ask for feather steak, fillet or sirloin, frying steak or rib steak. Ask your butcher for advice and, again, always opt for the leanest choice.

- Cheaper cuts of meat are ideal for stews or casseroles. Feather steak, brisket, silverside, oxtail, diced steak, shin and leg are all perfect for slow cooking, which tenderises the meat and brings out the flavours.

- Cook double the amount of stews and casseroles to make two meals. Serve one with dumplings and make the other into a hotpot by adding a topping of sliced potato sprinkled with grated cheese.

I have priced the stewing steak in the following recipes based on a price of £3.49 per 500g.

Beef Casserole

You can make a vegetarian version of this if you like, either without the beef or substituting Quorn chunks for the beef (Quorn pieces cost £1.75). The casserole can be cooked in the oven, on the hob or in a slow cooker.

SERVES 4
COST OF INGREDIENTS: £5.80 or £2.31 for a vegetarian version without beef
COST PER SERVING: £1.45 or 58p without beef

- **Can be frozen**
- **Can be cooked in advance**
- **Make 2, keep 1**

A dash of olive oil
1 onion, chopped
1–2 cloves garlic
300–400g beef stewing steak, chopped into chunks
2 sticks of celery, chopped
2 leeks, sliced
2 carrots, sliced
2 potatoes, chopped
100ml red wine
750ml water or beef stock
3 teaspoons paprika
2–3 bay leaves
50–75g pearl barley
2–3 teaspoons tomato purée
Seasoning to taste

1. Preheat the oven to 180°C/gas mark 4 (if cooking this in the oven).
2. Heat the olive oil in a large sauté pan, casserole dish or slow cooker and fry the onion, garlic and beef for 2–3 minutes before adding the other vegetables. Stir gently for 3–4 minutes to help soften the veg.
3. Add all the remaining ingredients and heat gently.
4. If using a slow cooker, place on a low heat and cook for 6–8 hours. You may need to add more liquid if it starts to evaporate. If you are cooking in a casserole dish in the oven or on the hob, cook slowly on a low heat for 1–1½ hours. Stir occasionally and add more liquid if necessary.

Beef and Mushrooms in Red Wine

You can cook this in the oven, on the hob or in a slow cooker. Again, you can make a vegetarian version without beef if you prefer, or substitute Quorn pieces (£1.75 a pack) for the beef.

SERVES 4
COST OF INGREDIENTS: £7.54 or £4.05 for a vegetarian version without beef
COST PER SERVING: £1.89 or £1.02 without beef

- **Can be frozen**
- **Can be cooked in advance**
- **Make 2, keep 1**

450g stewing steak, cut into cubes
50g plain flour
3 teaspoons paprika
Olive oil
1 onion
2 leeks, sliced
2 carrots, sliced
1 parsnip, sliced
2 tablespoons redcurrant jelly
200ml red wine
550ml beef stock
125g button mushrooms

1. Preheat the oven to 180°C/gas mark 4 (if cooking this in the oven).
2. Place beef steak in a bowl and coat with the flour and paprika.
3. Heat the olive oil in an ovenproof casserole dish, sauté pan or slow cooker and cook the onion and leeks for 2 minutes.
4. Add the beef and cook for a further 3–4 minutes, stirring well to avoid sticking. Add the carrots and parsnip and sweat the mixture for another 3–4 minutes with the lid on.
5. Add the redcurrant jelly and stir well. Gradually add the wine, beef stock and button mushrooms.
6. Cover and place on a low heat on the hob or in a preheated oven and cook gently for 1–1½ hours (4–6 hours if using a slow cooker). The lower the heat and the longer this cooks, the tenderer the beef will be. However, you may have to add more liquid as this will evaporate.

Beef Stroganoff

This tastes really special yet is so quick and easy to make. The fromage frais gives a lovely creamy sauce and is a healthier option than cream.

SERVES 4 • COST OF INGREDIENTS: £5.31 • COST PER SERVING: £1.33

• **Can be cooked in advance**

Olive oil
1 onion, finely chopped
2–3 cloves of garlic, crushed
500g lean beef steak chunks
300g mushrooms, sliced
2–3 teaspoons paprika
2–3 teaspoons Dijon mustard
200ml white wine
2 teaspoons fresh tarragon
150ml fromage frais

1. Heat the oil in a large sauté pan and fry the onion and garlic for 1 minute. Add the beef and cook for 3–4 minutes, ensuring it is evenly browned.
2. Add the mushrooms, paprika and mustard; stir well, before adding the wine. Some of this will evaporate as you continue to cook for a couple of minutes.
3. Add the tarragon and cook for 2–3 minutes more.
4. Just before serving, remove from the heat and stir in the fromage frais to form a creamy sauce. Serve on a bed of white rice.

Beef and Stout Stew
Another hearty and comforting winter warmer.

SERVES 4 • COST OF INGREDIENTS: £5.05 • COST PER SERVING: £1.26

• Can be cooked in advance

500g stewing beef
3 tablespoons olive oil (plus extra for frying)
2 tablespoons plain flour
1 onion, chopped
2 cloves of garlic, crushed
2 carrots, sliced
2 potatoes, cubed
350ml stout or Guinness
200ml water or beef stock
4 sprigs of thyme
Pinch of cayenne pepper
Seasoning to taste

1. Dip the beef in olive oil then roll it in the flour. Leave to one side.
2. Heat a little more oil in a large casserole dish and fry the onion and garlic for 2 minutes.
3. Add the carrots and potatoes and cook for a further 5 minutes, stirring occasionally to prevent the vegetables from sticking.
4. Add the floured beef and cook for a further 2 minutes, stirring continuously. Add the stout, water or stock, thyme, cayenne pepper and seasoning.
5. Cover with a lid and cook gently on a low heat on the hob for 1–3 hours depending on taste, or in a slow cooker for 4–6 hours. The longer you cook this dish the tenderer the meat. You may need to add more liquid when you are cooking for longer periods.

Piggy in the Middle

This chapter contains a selection of pork, ham and bacon recipes. The chapters 'A Load of Meatballs' and 'Don't Mince About' will give you more ideas for using pork mince and 'Roll out the Pastry' has some great recipe ideas for bacon.

- Ask your butcher for advice about cheaper cuts of pork and how to cook them.

- If you roast a joint for one meal, use the leftovers to make a pie for another day or cut slices of cold meat for sandwiches or salads.

- Boiling ham gammon slipper or shoulder is cheaper than gammon and still lean. Cook for 20 minutes per pound. Boil, bake or slow cook for tender meat. Serve with ham, egg and chips, or with parsley sauce and sauté or mash potatoes. Again, any leftovers can be used to make sandwiches, pies or a quiche.

Toad in the Hole

This is a very filling dish and is good for using up odds and ends in the fridge. The batter mix is really just the typical pancake mix (eggs, flour and milk). You can use any variety of sausages, but for the healthier option, make sure you choose good-quality low fat ones, preferably organic, as they usually contain a higher proportion of meat and are less likely to include some of the more unpleasant ingredients that can be found in cheaper sausages. If you are using a plain sausage, try adding some chopped onion and herbs to the batter mix. Vegetarians can also make this dish using veggie sausages.

SERVES 4 • COST OF INGREDIENTS: £2.56 • COST PER SERVING: 64p

- **Can be frozen**
- **Can be cooked in advance**
- **Make 2, keep 1**

100g plain flour
300ml milk
1 egg
1 onion, chopped
8 lean sausages
A handful of fresh herbs such as thyme, oregano, rosemary, or two
    teaspoons of dried
Seasoning to taste

1. Preheat the oven to 180°C/gas mark 4.
2. Using a blender with a balloon whisk, blend the flour, milk and egg together to form a batter. Mix thoroughly and leave to settle.
3. Meanwhile place the onion and sausages in a deep ovenproof dish and cook in the oven for 10 minutes, turning occasionally.
4. Just before the 10 minutes is up, give the batter mix a quick whizz with your balloon whisk, adding the herbs and seasoning before a final whizz.
5. Remove the sausages from the oven and immediately pour over the batter, ensuring that all the sausages are covered.
6. Return to the oven and cook for 20–30 minutes until golden.
7. Serve with onion gravy and steamed vegetables.

Pork Stroganoff

SERVES 4 • COST OF INGREDIENTS: £6.26 • COST PER SERVING: £1.57

- **Can be frozen**
- **Can be cooked in advance**
- **Make 2, keep 1**

Olive oil
1 onion, finely chopped
2–3 cloves garlic, crushed
4 pork chops or 500g leftover roast pork
300g mushrooms, sliced
2–3 teaspoons paprika
2–3 teaspoons Dijon mustard
100ml white wine
2 teaspoons fresh tarragon
100ml pork stock (or chicken, if you can't get pork)
150ml low fat crème fraiche

1. Heat the oil in a large sauté pan and fry the onion and garlic for 1 minute. Add the pork and cook for 3–4 minutes, ensuring it is evenly browned.
2. Add the mushrooms, paprika and mustard; stir well, before adding the wine. Some of this will evaporate as you continue to cook for a couple of minutes.
3. Add the tarragon and stock and cook on a low heat for 45 minutes.
4. Just before serving, remove from the heat and stir in the crème fraiche to form a creamy sauce. Serve on a bed of white rice.

Ham and Leek Mornay

SERVES 4 • COST OF INGREDIENTS: £5.50 • COST PER SERVING: £1.38

- **Can be frozen**
- **Can be cooked in advance**
- **Make 2, keep 1**

4 leeks, trimmed top and tail
25g butter
1 tablespoon plain flour or cornflour
500–750ml milk
2 tablespoons nutritional yeast flakes (optional)
75g mature cheese
½ teaspoon mustard
Black pepper to taste
8 slices of lean ham or bacon
2–3 tablespoons home-prepared wholemeal breadcrumbs

1. Cut the leeks to about 10–12.5cm (4–5in) in length and steam for 5–8 minutes until tender.
2. Meanwhile, melt the butter gently in a saucepan on medium heat (not high!). Add the flour or cornflour and stir well with a wooden spoon. Add the milk, a little at a time, continuing to stir to avoid lumps.
3. Switch to a balloon whisk and continue to stir over a medium heat until the sauce begins to thicken. The balloon whisk will also help eradicate any lumps that may have materialised. Add more milk as necessary to get the desired thickness. The sauce should be the thickness of custard.
4. If you are using nutritional yeast flakes, add these first as they will reduce the amount of cheese you may need – taste as you go! Then add the cheese and mustard, and stir well.
5. Season with black pepper.
6. Remove the leeks from the steamer and wrap a slice of ham or bacon around each leek. Lay them in the base of an ovenproof dish – lasagne dishes are good for this.
7. Pour over the cheese sauce and sprinkle with grated cheese and wholemeal breadcrumbs.
8. Grill for 5 minutes until the cheese is bubbling.

Sweet and Sour Pork

SERVES 4 • COST OF INGREDIENTS: £5.35 • COST PER SERVING: £1.38

- **Can be frozen**
- **Can be cooked in advance**
- **Make 2, keep 1**

2 teaspoons sesame oil
2 tablespoons light soy sauce
2 tablespoons rice wine or white wine vinegar
2 tablespoons tomato purée
1 tablespoon brown sugar
1 400g tin of pineapple chunks in natural juice
2 teaspoons cornflour
150ml stock
A spray of olive oil
400g pork, trimmed and cubed
2 cloves of garlic, crushed
2 peppers, sliced
2.5–5cm (1–2in) knuckle of ginger, thinly sliced
6 spring onions, sliced

1. Place the sesame oil, soy sauce, rice wine or white wine vinegar, tomato purée, sugar, pineapple chunks and juice, cornflour and stock in a bowl.
2. Heat a little olive oil in a wok or sauté pan and fry the pork for 5 minutes, until coloured.
3. Add the garlic, peppers, ginger and spring onions and cook for another 5 minutes.
4. Pour on the sauce and continue to cook for a further 2–3 minutes.
5. Serve on a bed of rice or noodles.

Tenderloins Stuffed with Goats' Cheese

This is the most expensive dish in the book! However, it's a very simple one and can be prepared in advance. Take out any frustrations by bashing the tenderloins into thinner pieces before stuffing them, wrapping them in Parma ham and tying them with string.

SERVES 4 • COST OF INGREDIENTS: £10 • COST PER SERVING: £2.50

• **Can be cooked in advance**

2 tenderloin fillets
125g goats' cheese
8–10 sun-dried tomatoes (or use cherry tomatoes)
2 teaspoons oregano
12 slices Parma ham

1. Bash the tenderloin fillets to help soften and thin them.
2. In the meantime, mix the goats' cheese with the tomatoes and oregano.
3. When you are happy with the tenderloins, cover one with the goats' cheese mixture and place the second on top to form a 'sandwich'.
4. Wrap the ham around the tenderloin parcel and secure with string.
5. Place in a greased ovenproof dish in the oven for 45 minutes to 1 hour. Before serving, allow to rest for 15 minutes in a warm spot.
6. Slice the tenderloins and serve with potatoes and green vegetables.

Sausage and Tomato Casserole

SERVES 4 • COST OF INGREDIENTS: £3.60 • COST PER SERVING: 90p

• **Can be cooked in advance**

8 lean pork sausages
Olive oil
1 onion, sliced
1–2 cloves garlic, crushed
1 red pepper, sliced
100ml red wine
2 teaspoons cornflour, mixed with a little cold water
4–5 teaspoons paprika
400g tin chopped tomatoes
2–3 teaspoons sun-dried tomato purée
250ml stock or water
Handful of fresh parsley

1. Fry the sausages in olive oil (or grill them) until brown. Set aside until later.
2. Heat a little olive oil in a pan and add the onion, garlic and peppers. Cook for 3–4 minutes until they start to soften.
3. Add the red wine, cornflour and paprika and stir for another minute before adding all the remaining ingredients, apart from the parsley.
4. Add the sausages. Cover with a lid and cook on the lowest heat for 45 minutes to 1 hour. Add the fresh parsley 5 minutes before serving.

Don't Mince About

It's a good idea to cook a large batch of minced meat with onions, garlic, tinned tomatoes and red wine and keep it in the fridge or freezer until needed. It can form the basis of a variety of dishes such as lasagne, spaghetti bolognese, shepherd's pie or chilli con carne. If you have time, go a step further and spend a few hours listening to your favourite music while making up a collection of mince dishes for the freezer. You will then have your own home-made meals ready whenever you need them. Remember to label and date all items before storing them in the freezer.

I have priced the mince according to supermarket basic or value ranges. At the time of writing, this sells at 97p for 400g. If you do opt for a value range of mince, make sure you drain off any additional fat when cooking.

Spaghetti Bolognese

This recipe can be made using a 'cheat' ingredient of ready-made bolognese or pasta sauce instead of the tin of tomatoes.

SERVES 4 • COST OF INGREDIENTS: £2.26 • COST PER SERVING: 57p

- **Can be frozen**
- **Can be cooked in advance**
- **Make 2, keep 1**

1 onion, finely chopped
2–3 cloves garlic, finely chopped
A spray of olive oil
1 pepper, finely chopped (optional)
400g lean minced meat or, for vegetarians, veggie mince
150ml red wine
75g mushrooms, finely chopped (optional)
3–4 fresh tomatoes, chopped, or 1 tin chopped tomatoes
Mixed herbs to taste
Seasoning to taste

1. Fry the onion and garlic in a little olive oil until soft and translucent. Add the pepper if using one.
2. Add the mince and cook until brown, followed by the wine and mushrooms if using them, and cook for 2 more minutes.
3. Add the tinned or fresh tomatoes (or 'cheat' pasta sauce), stirring well. Finally, add the herbs and season to taste. Leave to simmer for 5 minutes.
4. Serve on a bed of cooked spaghetti and garnish with grated Parmesan.

Traditional lasagne

Below is a basic recipe for lasagne. You can use the same recipe to make cannelloni. Simply fill tubes of dried cannelloni with the main bolognese sauce filling, cover with the white sauce and grated cheese and bake as you do the lasagne. If you would like a variation of the minced meat lasagne, check out more recipes in the chapter 'Bellissimo Pasta'.

SERVES 4 • COST OF INGREDIENTS: £3.30 • COST PER SERVING: 83p

- **Can be frozen**
- **Can be cooked in advance**
- **Make 2, keep 1**

For the bolognese sauce
1 onion finely chopped
2–3 cloves garlic, finely chopped
A spray of olive oil
1 pepper, finely chopped (optional)
400g lean minced meat or, for vegetarians, veggie mince
150ml red wine
75g mushrooms, finely chopped (optional)
3–4 fresh tomatoes, chopped, or 1 tin chopped tomatoes
Mixed herbs to taste
Seasoning to taste

For the white sauce
25g butter
1 tablespoon plain flour or cornflour
500–750ml milk
¼ teaspoon mustard (optional)
Black pepper to taste

Sheets of lasagne (ensure the pack says 'no precooking required')
Grated cheese to garnish

1. Preheat the oven to 200°C/gas mark 6.
2. Make the bolognese sauce as for Spaghetti Bolognese above.
3. While the bolognese mix is simmering, make the white sauce.

Melt the butter gently in a saucepan on a medium heat (not high!). Add the flour or cornflour and stir well with a wooden spoon. Add the milk, a little at a time, continuing to stir to avoid lumps.

4. Switch now to a balloon whisk. Continue to stir over a medium heat until the sauce begins to thicken. The balloon whisk will also help eradicate any lumps that may have materialised. Add more milk as necessary to get the desired thickness. The sauce should be the thickness of custard.

5. Add the mustard and season with black pepper.

6. Spoon a layer of bolognese mix into the bottom of your lasagne dish, and then pour over a thin layer of white sauce, followed by a layer of lasagne sheets. Continue alternating the layers, finishing with the white sauce. Don't overfill the dish as the lasagne may spill out during cooking.

7. Sprinkle grated cheese over the sauce before placing the lasagne in the oven for 30–40 minutes.

8. Serve with salad and garlic bread.

Chilli Con Carne

SERVES 4 • COST OF INGREDIENTS: £3.57 • COST PER SERVING: 89p

- **Can be frozen**
- **Can be cooked in advance**
- **Make 2, keep 1**

A spray of olive oil
1 onion, finely chopped
1 red pepper, chopped
100g mushrooms, quartered
1–2 cloves garlic, crushed
1–2 chopped chillies (depending on desired flavour)
400g lean mince (or pre-drained of fat)
200ml red wine
1 tin chopped tomatoes
1 tin red kidney beans
1 teaspoon paprika
1 teaspoon chilli powder
1 teaspoon mixed herbs (optional)
Seasoning to taste

1. Heat a little olive oil in a large sauté pan and fry the onion, pepper, mushrooms and garlic for 1–2 minutes. Add the chillies and cook for 1 more minute. Add the mince and cook until brown. The mixture should be cooking in its own liquid, but if it is a little dry add a small amount of the wine.
2. Add the wine, tomatoes, red kidney beans, paprika, chilli powder and mixed herbs, if using. Allow the mixture to simmer gently for 20 minutes. The longer this is cooked, the thicker it will become. Season to taste.
3. Serve on a bed of rice or use in wraps, tortilla dishes or even as a topping for jacket potatoes.

Shepherd's and Cottage Pie

*The only real difference between shepherd's pie and cottage pie is
the meat. Shepherd's pie traditionally is made with lamb mince
and cottage pie with beef. Nowadays you can make these dishes
using a variety of minced meat or vegetarian mince if you prefer.*

SERVES 4
COST OF INGREDIENTS: £3.60 if using beef, £5.49 if using fresh lamb mince,
 £4.07 if using frozen lamb
COST PER SERVING: from 90p

- **Can be frozen**
- **Can be cooked in advance**
- **Make 2, keep 1**

800g potatoes, cut into rough chunks
4 carrots, 2 roughly chopped, 2 cut into small cubes
A spray of olive oil
1 onion, chopped
400g lean mince (or pre-drained of fat)
75g mushrooms, sliced (optional)
100ml red wine
1 teaspoon yeast extract (Marmite or similar)
200ml meat gravy or vegetable gravy if using veggie mince
Seasoning to taste
Worcestershire sauce
25g butter
75g mature Cheddar
Paprika for sprinkling

1. Preheat the oven to 180°C/gas mark 4.
2. Place the potatoes and the 2 chopped carrots in a steamer and
cook until soft.
3. Meanwhile, heat the oil in a large sauté pan and fry the onion
for 1–2 minutes before adding the mince.
4. Cook until brown before adding the 2 cubed carrots, the
mushrooms and the wine.
5. Dissolve the yeast extract in the hot stock before adding to the
mince. Cook for 20 minutes until tender and reduced to the

desired consistency. Season to taste and add Worcestershire sauce.

6. Mash the steamed potato and carrots together. Add the butter and two thirds of the Cheddar. Mix thoroughly.

7. Place the mince in a deep baking dish and spoon the mash over the top. Be careful not to overfill the dish. Press the mash down gently with a fork. Top with the remaining grated cheese and a sprinkle of paprika.

8. Cook in the oven for 30 minutes.

A Load of Meatballs

Kids love meatballs and they are so simple to make they can even prepare their own. Serve them covered in pasta sauce (see 'Ooh, Saucy!' for recipe ideas) on a bed of spaghetti, or alone on a bed of spicy Savoy cabbage. They can be prepared in advance and either frozen or stored, covered, in the fridge. Here are a few recipe suggestions.

Spicy Meatballs

SERVES 4 • COST OF INGREDIENTS: £1.10 • COST PER SERVING: 28p

- **Can be frozen**
- **Can be cooked in advance**
- **Make 2, keep 1**

400g beef mince
1 small onion, finely chopped
1 teaspoon paprika
½ teaspoon chilli powder (or more if you like a spicy flavour!)
2 teaspoons Worcestershire sauce
1 teaspoon parsley

1. Combine all the ingredients together in a bowl and mix thoroughly.
2. Form the mixture into small balls and place on a baking sheet. Cover the balls with a sheet of cling film and store in the fridge for 30 minutes.
3. Alternatively, you can freeze the meatballs. I normally place them, still on the baking tray, in the freezer until they are firm, before removing them from the tray and placing in a freezer bag. This way they won't stick together and you can pull out the required number of meatballs as and when you need them.
4. When you are ready, fry the meatballs in a little olive oil for 4–6

minutes or, if you are serving them with pasta sauce, just add them to the sauce and simmer for 10–15 minutes until they are cooked.

Note: Some people like to add an egg to the mixture as they feel the meatballs stick together better. I don't think this is necessary but, if you prefer, just add a beaten egg to the above recipe. If the mixture is too wet, add some oats or breadcrumbs.

Turkey Meatballs

SERVES 4 • COST OF INGREDIENTS: £1.60 • COST PER SERVING: 40p

- **Can be frozen**
- **Can be cooked in advance**
- **Make 2, keep 1**

1 small onion, finely chopped
400g turkey mince
1–2 crushed garlic cloves
1 teaspoon ground cumin
1 teaspoon paprika
1 teaspoon olive oil

1. Combine all the ingredients together in a bowl and mix thoroughly.
2. Form the mixture into small balls and place on a baking sheet. Cover the balls with a sheet of cling film and store in the fridge for 30 minutes.
3. Alternatively, you can freeze the meatballs. I normally place them, still on the baking tray, in the freezer until they are firm, before removing them from the tray and placing in a freezer bag. This way they won't stick together and you can pull out the required number of meatballs as and when you need them.
4. When you are ready, fry the meatballs in a little olive oil for 4–6 minutes or, if you are serving them with pasta sauce, just add them to the sauce and simmer for 10–15 minutes until they are cooked.

Pork Meatballs

SERVES 4 • COST OF INGREDIENTS: £2.26 • COST PER SERVING: 57p

- **Can be frozen**
- **Can be cooked in advance**
- **Make 2, keep 1**

400g pork mince
2 tablespoons basil, chopped
2 cloves garlic, crushed
2–3 sun-dried tomatoes, chopped
1 teaspoon olive oil
1 teaspoon soy sauce

1. Combine all the ingredients together in a bowl and mix thoroughly.
2. Form the mixture into small balls and place on a baking sheet. Cover the balls with a sheet of cling film and store in the fridge for 30 minutes.
3. Alternatively, you can freeze the meatballs. I normally place them, still on the baking tray, in the freezer until they are firm, before removing them from the tray and placing in a freezer bag. This way they won't stick together and you can pull out the required number of meatballs as and when you need them.
4. When you are ready, fry the meatballs in a little olive oil for 4–6 minutes or, if you are serving them with pasta sauce, just add them to the sauce and simmer for 10–15 minutes until they are cooked.

Curry in a Hurry

Curry is now regarded as one of Britain's national dishes – with Chicken Korma as the nation's favourite. It's very versatile too: when I am making curry, I try to prepare at least two different dishes as I love the different flavours you can create. And of course curries are great for using up any bits of leftover food you may have in the fridge. A dahl is a cheap and simple dish and surprisingly nutritious as long as you keep the fat and salt content in check. I have lots of wonderful Asian friends who make the most amazing dishes, though they tend to be a bit heavy-handed with the salt. For the sake of your health it's better to avoid salt and try to let the ingredients speak for themselves. The simple recipes in this chapter will give you lots of ideas for creating your own curry dishes.

Chicken Korma

This is a very easy Chicken Korma. You can use fresh chicken or leftover chicken from your sunday roast. Make sure you cook the chicken thoroughly if you are reheating. I have made this version with natural yoghurt instead of high-fat coconut milk. If you like a coconut taste, you could add some grated coconut from a block or try reduced-fat coconut milk.

SERVES 4 • COST OF INGREDIENTS: £3.94 • COST PER SERVING: 99p

- **Can be frozen**
- **Can be cooked in advance**
- **Use up your leftovers**
- **Make 2, keep 1**

Olive oil
1 onion
1–2 cloves of garlic, crushed
2.5cm (1in) piece of ginger, finely chopped
½ fresh chilli, chopped (or ½ – 1 teaspoon freeze-dried chillies)
1–2 teaspoons mild curry powder or paste
1 teaspoon turmeric
300g chicken fillet pieces
100ml white wine
200ml water or chicken stock
300ml low fat natural yoghurt
50g almond slices

1. Heat the oil in a large sauté pan and fry the onion, garlic and ginger for 2 minutes. Add the fresh chilli, curry powder or paste and turmeric and cook for 1 more minute.
2. Add the chicken pieces and cook for 3–4 minutes, turning well.
3. Pour on the wine, water or stock and the yoghurt and add the almond slices. Mix well. Cook gently on a medium heat for 30 minutes until the chicken becomes tender and the sauce starts to thicken.
4. Serve on a bed of rice.

Tandoori Chicken

You can cheat with this recipe and use a tandoori paste. However, I prefer to make this myself – there is something deeply satisfying about flinging around herbs and spices when cooking, and it is a great way to get the family's attention as the flavours start to waft around the house.

SERVES 4 • COST OF INGREDIENTS: £3.18 • COST PER SERVING: 80p

- **Can be frozen**
- **Can be cooked in advance**
- **Use up your leftovers**
- **Make 2, keep 1**

1 onion, finely chopped
2–3 cloves garlic, crushed
1 teaspoon coriander powder
1 teaspoon cayenne pepper
1 teaspoon chilli powder (or fresh chillies, finely chopped)
1 teaspoon curry powder
2 teaspoons turmeric
2–3 teaspoons paprika
2.5cm knuckle of ginger, grated
Juice and zest of 1 lemon
A dash of olive oil
100g low fat natural yoghurt
4 large pieces of chicken (or you can use any leftover chicken)

1. In an ovenproof dish, mix the onion, garlic, herbs and spices with the lemon juice, zest, olive oil and yoghurt.
2. Add the chicken pieces and combine thoroughly. For best flavour, leave to marinate for a few hours.
3. When you are ready, preheat the oven to 200°C/gas mark 6.
4. Cook the chicken in the oven for 30 minutes.
5. Serve on a bed of rice.

Note: If you are planning a barbecue, you can marinate for up to 24 hours in a plastic bag until needed. Remove the chicken from the marinade, brush with oil and place on the barbecue to cook. You can reheat the marinade gently and your guests can use it as a dressing.

Lamb and Green Lentil Curry

The green lentils help bulk out the curry so you don't need to use as much lamb. I have made this with a medium curry powder, but you can opt for hot or mild depending on your personal taste.

SERVES 4 • COST OF INGREDIENTS: £5.79 • COST PER SERVING: £1.45

- **Can be cooked in advance**
- **Use up your leftovers**

Olive oil
1 onion, sliced
2–3 cloves of garlic, crushed
2.5cm knuckle of fresh ginger, sliced
400g lamb, cut into chunks
1–2 chillies, finely cut
1 teaspoon cinnamon powder
1 tablespoon medium curry powder
Juice of ½ a lemon
1 tin chopped tomatoes
150g green lentils
500ml water or lamb stock
Small handful chopped fresh coriander
150g low fat yoghurt or quark

1. Heat the oil in a pan and cook the onion, garlic and ginger for 1 minute.
2. Add the lamb, chilli, cinnamon and curry powder and stir well for 3–4 minutes.
3. Add the lemon juice, tomatoes, lentils, water or stock and half the coriander. Cover with a lid and cook for 1 hour until the lamb is tender.
4. Just prior to serving, stir in the yoghurt and the remaining coriander.

Spicy Spinach and Potato

*I love this dish and it is perfect for using up any cooked potatoes from the night before. Use as a side dish to create some extra colour and taste. Alternatively, you could make delicious **Spicy Spinach and Potato Pasties** by covering the potato mixture in light wholemeal pastry – great for packed lunches or quick snacks – or **Spicy Spinach and Potato Samosa**, by wrapping any leftovers in filo pastry.*

SERVES 4 • COST OF INGREDIENTS: £2.50 • COST PER SERVING: 63p

- **Suitable for vegetarians**
- **Can be frozen**
- **Can be cooked in advance**
- **Use up your leftovers**
- **Make 2, keep 1**

Olive oil
1 onion, chopped
2 cloves garlic, crushed
2 teaspoons turmeric
2–3 teaspoons curry paste
4–5 potatoes, cooked and diced
A dash of water
300g spinach leaves

1. Heat the oil in a pan and cook the onion and garlic until soft. Add the spices and cook for another minute.

2. Add the cooked potato. If the mixture is too dry, add a dash of water. Ensure the potato is well coated in the spices.

3. Quickly rinse the fresh spinach leaves in a colander under warm/hot water to soften the leaves. Add to the potato mixture and stir well. If you are using frozen spinach, simply add to the mixture and stir until soft.

4. Mix well to ensure the potato is thoroughly coated in the spices. Serve hot.

Variation

Try adding a tin of chickpeas to this recipe to make delicious **Spicy Chickpea, Spinach and Potato Curry**. You can serve this as a side dish or a complete meal.

Note: If you like a creamy sauce, add 2–3 tablespoons of natural yoghurt or low fat coconut milk – though this mixture cannot be used to make the pasties.

Lentil Dahl

This is so easy to make and costs very little. You can make it mild and creamy by adding some Greek yoghurt – ideal for children – or spice it up to suit your taste.

SERVES 4 • COST OF INGREDIENTS: £1.10 • COST PER SERVING: 28p

- **Suitable for vegetarians**
- **Can be frozen**
- **Can be cooked in advance**
- **Make 2, keep 1**

Olive oil
1 onion, chopped
2 cloves garlic, crushed
2.5cm knuckle of fresh ginger
1 pepper, chopped
2–3 teaspoons sweet or mild curry powder or paste
1–2 teaspoons turmeric
1–2 tomatoes, finely chopped
1 teaspoon tomato purée
100g red lentils
300–400ml water
A little coconut to garnish

1. Heat the oil in a large pan and fry the onion, garlic, ginger and pepper until soft.
2. Add the curry paste, turmeric, tomatoes and tomato purée and cook for another 2 minutes.
3. Add the lentils and cover with water. Simmer gently. Add more water if necessary.
4. Sprinkle with coconut before serving.

Vegetable Curry

SERVES 4 • COST OF INGREDIENTS: £3.09 • COST PER SERVING: 77p

- **Suitable for vegetarians**
- **Can be frozen**
- **Can be cooked in advance**
- **Make 2, keep 1**

Olive oil
1 large onion, finely chopped
2.5cm (1in) piece of fresh ginger, thinly sliced
2–3 cloves garlic, crushed
2 tablespoons mild or medium curry powder (depending on taste)
1 chilli (optional)
1 red pepper, chopped
4 ripe tomatoes, finely chopped
1 sweet potato, cubed
1 large white potato, cubed
150g yellow split peas
500ml water
2 handfuls baby leaf spinach
Handful fresh coriander, roughly shredded

1. Heat the oil in a large casserole or deep sauté pan and cook the onion, ginger and garlic for 1 minute before adding the curry powder and chilli. This can give off quite a fierce aroma so don't have your head right over the pan! If the mixture is too dry, add a touch of water.

2. Add the pepper, tomatoes and potatoes. Stir together, cooking gently for 5 minutes.

3. Add the split peas and water. Cover with a lid and cook gently for 20 minutes or until tender.

4. Add the spinach and coriander and cook for a further 5 minutes before serving.

Fish Biryani

SERVES 4 • COST OF INGREDIENTS: £4.20 • COST PER SERVING: £1.05

Olive oil
1 small onion, finely chopped
2–3 cloves garlic, crushed
1–2 chillies, finely chopped
1–2 teaspoons grated ginger
1 teaspoon cumin seeds
2 teaspoons garam masala
1 tablespoon coriander powder
1 teaspoon turmeric powder
400g fish pieces or fillets, cubed
3–4 tablespoons yoghurt
Freshly chopped coriander to garnish

For the rice
Olive oil
4 cloves
4 peppercorns
1 cinnamon stick
4 green cardamoms
3–4 spring onions
300g basmati rice
2 bay leaves

1. Cook the rice first. Heat the oil in a deep pan and cook the cloves, peppercorns, cinnamon, cardamoms and spring onions for 2 minutes. Add the rice and stir well.
2. Pour over 600ml water and add the bay leaves. Bring to the boil and cook for 5 minutes.
3. Cover the pan with a lid and leave to one side.
4. Meanwhile, cook the fish dish. Heat the oil in a pan and fry the onion, garlic, chillies and ginger for 2–3 minutes before adding the remaining spices and the fish.
5. Cook until the fish is done – this should take approximately 6–7 minutes.
6. Add the yoghurt and stir well.
7. Combine the rice and the fish dish together before serving. Garnish with freshly chopped coriander.

You Shall Have a Fishy

The recipes in this chapter are all very economical but ask your fishmonger for fish pieces as this will also help to cut costs. Some supermarkets offer a fish pie mix (at the time of writing this was £2.99 for 320g and contained haddock, pollock and salmon).

Creamy Fish Pie

SERVES 4 • COST OF INGREDIENTS: £2.80 • COST PER SERVING: 70p

1kg potatoes
500g fish fillets, or ask your fishmonger for pieces of flaky white fish
200g salmon pieces (optional)
100g prawns (optional)
250ml milk
25g butter
25g flour
1 teaspoon mustard
Seasoning to taste
A little grated cheese for topping

1. Preheat the oven to 180°C/gas mark 4.
2. Boil or steam the potatoes until tender. Once cooked, mash ready for use.
3. Meanwhile place the fish and milk in a pan and bring the milk to the boil. Reduce the heat and cook gently for 10 minutes or until the fish is cooked through.
4. Drain the fish and reserve the liquid for making the sauce.
5. Shred the fish and place in your pie dish.
6. Melt the butter in a pan and add the flour. Stir in the reserved milk stock and heat gently until the sauce thickens.
7. Add the mustard, season to taste and stir well. Pour the sauce over the fish.
8. Cover with mashed potato and top with a bit of grated cheese.
9. Bake in the oven for 30 minutes.

Fish Stew

SERVES 4 • COST OF INGREDIENTS: £5.20 • COST PER SERVING: £1.30

Olive oil
1 onion, finely chopped
2 cloves garlic, crushed
1 red pepper, deseeded and diced
1 tin of chopped tomatoes, or 6 ripe tomatoes
300ml fish stock
300ml white wine
500g fish fillets or pieces
12 prawns
2 bay leaves
A handful of fresh parsley, chopped
Seasoning to taste

1. Heat the oil in a casserole dish and fry the onion, garlic and pepper for 2–3 minutes.
2. Add all the remaining ingredients, cover and cook on a medium heat for 30–40 minutes.
3. Season before serving.

Salmon Fish Cakes

SERVES 4 • COST OF INGREDIENTS: £3.80 • COST PER SERVING: 95p

400g fresh or tinned salmon
400g potatoes, cooked and mashed
2 teaspoons lemon juice
1–2 teaspoons each of fresh dill and tarragon (or 1 teaspoon each of dried)
2 eggs, beaten
Plain flour

1. Mix the fish, potato, lemon juice and herbs together in a bowl. Add almost all of the egg to bind, retaining a very small amount for brushing over the cakes later.
2. Form the mixture into cakes, place on baking parchment and chill in the fridge for 5 minutes.
3. Remove from the fridge, brush the reserved egg onto the cakes and dust with flour to coat.
4. Fry the fish cakes gently on both sides until golden.

Seared Salmon with Sauté of Peas and Asparagus, with Chive Cream

This recipe was featured in a wonderful booklet which is packed with delicious and inspiring recipes for peas. It is available free from from www.peas.org

SERVES 4 • COST OF INGREDIENTS: £8.95 • COST PER SERVING: £2.24

2 tablespoons olive oil
30g butter
10 spring onions, finely chopped
1 bunch asparagus, trimmed and cut into rings
200g fresh or frozen peas
50ml water
Seasoning to taste
1 tablespoon fresh parsley, chopped
2 tablespoons chives, chopped
4 x 180g salmon fillets

275ml double cream
1 teaspoon white wine vinegar

1. Heat the oil and butter in a sauté pan and fry the spring onions and asparagus for 4–5 minutes until just soft.
2. Add the peas and water, season and simmer for a few minutes until cooked. Add the parsley and half the chives.
3. Meanwhile heat a griddle pan or grill and cook the salmon fillets for 2–3 minutes on each side or to your liking.
4. Heat the cream to just below boiling point, add the white wine vinegar and the cream will start to thicken. Season and add the remaining chopped chives.
5. Serve the salmon on a bed of the asparagus and pea mixture, and pour over the cream and chive sauce.

Lemon and Herb Pan-Fried Cod

SERVES 4 • COST OF INGREDIENTS: £2.40 • COST PER SERVING: 60p

50g home-made wholemeal breadcrumbs
2 tablespoons chopped parsley
1 teaspoon dill
Black pepper
Juice and rind of 1 lemon
Olive oil
4 fillets of cod
50g butter

1. Mix together the breadcrumbs, herbs, black pepper and lemon rind in a bowl and put to one side.
2. Heat the olive oil in a pan and fry the cod fillets for 3–4 minutes on each side until tender.
3. Sprinkle the breadcrumb mixture onto the fillets.
4. Place the pan under the grill and brown the fillets for 3 minutes.
5. Add the butter and lemon juice to the pan and melt for 1 minute.
6. Spoon the butter and lemon juice over the fillets and serve immediately with new potatoes and Green Snap Salad (see page 204 in 'Sumptuous Salads').

Italian Cod Parcels

I have chosen cod for this dish, but you can substitute any other fillet fish for the cod. Ask your fishmonger for more suggestions.

SERVES 4 • COST OF INGREDIENTS: £2.65 • COST PER SERVING: 66p

4 cod fillets
4 rashers of pancetta
1–2 tablespoons pesto
1 red onion, sliced into rings
Fresh thyme
Olive oil
Black pepper

1. Preheat the oven to 200°C/gas mark 6.
2. Wrap a rasher of pancetta around each fillet and place each fillet on a square of greased baking parchment or foil, large enough to secure.
3. Cover each fillet with a layer of pesto, add some onion rings and fresh thyme. Drizzle with a dash of olive oil and season with black pepper.
4. Seal the parcels and place them on a baking tray.
5. Cook in the oven for 15–20 minutes until the fish is tender and flaking.
6. Serve with new potatoes and green vegetables.

Note: You can use this technique to cook any fish. Salmon is great cooked this way – simply add herb butter (see 'Ooh, Saucy!') for delicious **Salmon and Herb Butter Parcels.** Try experimenting with your own variations.

Breaded Fish Fillets

You can use any fish fillet for this. Your fishmonger will be able to advise you of the best deals.

SERVES 4 • COST OF INGREDIENTS: £3.52 • COST PER SERVING: 88p

50g home-prepared breadcrumbs
1 tablespoon oats
1 tablespoon chives
1 tablespoon parsley
1 tablespoon grated Parmesan cheese
Zest of 1 lemon
4 fish fillets
4–5 teaspoons low fat cream cheese

1. Preheat the oven to 180°C/gas mark 4.
2. Place the breadcrumbs, oats, chives, parsley, Parmesan and lemon zest in a bowl and combine well.
3. Cover the fillets in cream cheese (or just the top if you don't want to get too messy!).
4. Dip the fillets into the breaded mixture ensuring they are well covered and then place on a greased or lined baking tray.
5. Bake in the oven for 10–15 minutes.
6. Serve with salad and new potatoes.

Mediterranean Fish Pot

This is a very simple dish. You can use any white fish, either fillets or fish pieces from your fishmonger, which are often cheaper. You can cook this in a slow cooker, on a low heat in a saucepan or in the oven.

SERVES 4 • COST OF INGREDIENTS: £4.58 • COST PER SERVING: £1.15

Olive oil
2–3 cloves garlic
1 red onion, finely chopped
2 sticks of celery, chopped
30g sun-dried tomatoes
1 tin of chopped tomatoes
2 teaspoons fresh basil (or 1 frozen cube if you don't have any fresh)
2 teaspoons oregano
Juice of 1 lemon
200ml red wine
500g white fish (fillets or pieces)

1. If you are using a slow cooker put all the ingredients into the cooker and cook for 4–6 hours. You may need to add more liquid if you are cooking for longer periods. Alternatively, if you are cooking on a low heat on the hob, you may prefer to do things the traditional way.
2. Heat the oil and fry the garlic and onion until translucent before adding the celery.
3. Add all the remaining ingredients. Cover and cook on a very low heat for 1 hour.
4. Serve with new potatoes and green vegetables.

Smoked Haddock with Leek and Parsley Sauce

SERVES 4 • COST OF INGREDIENTS: £6.60 • COST PER SERVING: £1.65

4 smoked haddock fillets
4 leeks
A knob of butter

For the parsley sauce
25g butter
1 tablespoon plain flour or cornflour
500–750ml milk
A handful of fresh parsley, finely chopped
Seasoning to taste

1. First make the parsley sauce. Melt the butter gently in a saucepan on medium heat (not high!). Add the flour or cornflour and stir well with a wooden spoon. Add the milk a little at a time, continuing to stir to avoid lumps.
2. Switch now to a balloon whisk. Continue to stir over a medium heat until the sauce begins to thicken. The balloon whisk will also help to eradicate any lumps that may have materialised. Add more milk as necessary to get the desired thickness. The sauce should be the thickness of custard.
3. Add the parsley and season with black pepper.
4. Melt a knob of butter in a large pan and fry the leeks for 2–3 minutes. Cover with a lid and sweat for 5–10 minutes until they soften. Add to the parsley sauce.
5. Five minutes before serving, place the fillets in a large pan of simmering water and poach for 5 minutes, until the flesh flakes easily.
6. Place the fillets on serving plates and cover with a spoonful of leek and parsley sauce. Serve with new potatoes and green beans.

Mackerel Pâté

This is a very easy recipe that can be prepared in seconds.

SERVES 4 • COST OF INGREDIENTS: £5.00 • COST PER SERVING: £1.25

4 mackerel fillets, boned and *ready to eat*
1 small tub of low fat cream cheese
Juice and zest of 1 lemon
A handful of fresh parsley, chopped

1. Make sure your mackerel fillets are free from bones and skin. If you are not sure about this, ask your fishmonger to do it for you.
2. Place all the ingredients in a liquidiser or small food processor. Whizz for a few seconds until the ingredients have blended well.
3. Season to taste.
4. Allow to settle for at least 20 minutes for the flavours to infuse before serving.

Mackerel Salad

You can use fresh or tinned mackerel for this recipe. If using fresh, fry in a shallow pan for 3–4 minutes each side.

SERVES 4 • COST OF INGREDIENTS: £6.29 • COST PER SERVING: £1.58

1 tin of mackerel or 4 fillets, boned and *ready to eat*, in chunks
6–8 cherry tomatoes, halved
½ cucumber, diced
4–6 spring onions, chopped
A handful of basil leaves, lightly torn
Seasoning to taste
1 cos lettuce, washed
3 hard-boiled eggs, halved

1. Place the mackerel chunks in a bowl and mix with the cherry tomatoes, cucumber, spring onions and half of the basil. Season to taste.

2. Line a large serving dish with a bed of cos lettuce. Add the mackerel mix and cover with the eggs. Sprinkle with the remaining basil leaves.
3. Drizzle with a dressing made with 30ml olive oil, 15ml lemon juice and 10 ml balsamic vinegar, seasoned to taste.

Pan-Fried Mackerel in Tomato Sauce

You can use sardines or even pilchards for this recipe if you prefer. As with all fish, ensure that they are free from bones before cooking and serving.

SERVES 4 • COST OF INGREDIENTS: £5.50 • COST PER SERVING: £1.38

Olive oil
1 onion, finely chopped
1–2 cloves garlic, crushed
4–8 tomatoes, diced (or 1 tin of chopped tomatoes)
1 teaspoon sun-dried tomato purée
150ml red wine
1 teaspoon mixed herbs
4 mackerel fillets, boned
25g plain flour
Knob of butter

1. Heat the olive oil in a saucepan and fry the onion and garlic until the onion is translucent.
2. Add the chopped tomatoes, tomato purée, wine and herbs and simmer gently until reduced slightly.
3. Coat the fillets on both sides with flour. Melt the butter in a pan and add the mackerel, frying gently for 3–4 minutes on each side until cooked.
4. Pour over the tomato sauce and heat for 1 minute before serving.
5. Serve with new potatoes and Green Snap Salad (see page 204 in 'Sumptuous Salads').

Lemon and Ginger Mackerel

Serve the mackerel on a bed of salad – I love the flavour of rocket, watercress and freshly cut lettuce topped with grated carrot.

SERVES 4 • COST OF INGREDIENTS: £4.25 • COST PER SERVING: £1.06

2.5–5cm knuckle of ginger, grated
Zest and juice of 1 large lemon
2 cloves garlic, crushed
1 tablespoon olive oil
Seasoning to taste
4 mackerel fillets

1. Mix the ginger, lemon, garlic and olive oil together. Season.
2. With a sharp knife, lightly score the skin of each mackerel. Rub the ginger mixture over the mackerel, paying particular attention to the scored areas.
3. Place the mackerel under a preheated grill and cook for 3–4 minutes on each side.
4. Serve on a bed of salad leaves. Before serving, drizzle any remaining ginger dressing over the fillets.

Give Peas a Chance – Lovely Veggie Meals

You don't have to be a vegetarian to enjoy tasty vegetable dishes. And vegetarian food is often cheaper and healthier than meat-based dishes so it is worth including a selection of vegetable delights among your weekly meals. Here are some recipes that will tempt the most committed carnivore.

Mushroom and Cashew Nut Roast

This is so much easier if you have a food processor that chops food. If so you can make it in minutes; otherwise you will drive yourself nuts (excuse the pun!) with all that chopping. I have many friends who are meat eaters and they all love this recipe.

SERVES 4 • COST OF INGREDIENTS: £3.36 • COST PER SERVING: 84p

- **Suitable for vegetarians**
- **Can be frozen (before baking)**
- **Can be cooked in advance**
- **Make 2, keep 1**

Olive oil
1 onion, finely chopped
250g mushrooms, finely chopped (I prefer chestnut but choose whatever works for you)
200g cashew nuts, finely chopped
2 teaspoons yeast extract
50g home-made breadcrumbs

1. Preheat the oven to 180°C/gas mark 4.
2. Heat the oil in a pan and fry the onion until translucent
3. Add the mushrooms and nuts and cook for 5 minutes.
4. Add the yeast extract, followed by the breadcrumbs, and stir well.

5. Spoon the mixture into a lined loaf tin and press down to form a firm base.

6. At this stage you can freeze the dish if you like and use when needed.

7. If you are using the dish immediately, bake in the oven for 30–40 minutes.

Variation

Wrap the mixture in half a pack of ready-made puff pastry to make a **Mushroom en Croûte.** This looks very impressive, particularly for Christmas lunch or as an alternative to meat when putting together a roast. Roll out the pastry into a rectangle approximately 30cm wide by 40cm long and place on a greased baking tray. Spoon the mixture into the middle of the pastry lengthways. Using a sharp knife, cut 2.5–5cm strips either side of the mixture – you will then fold these over the mixture to form a pleated effect. Fold the pastry over the top of the filling and seal well with beaten egg or milk. Bake for 40 minutes until the pastry is golden.

Tip

Make double the amount of mixture to make one nut roast and a Mushroom en Croûte. Freeze both, uncooked, until needed.

Thai Bean Cakes with Chilli Sauce

Originally this was a recipe I read in Rose Elliot's Low-GI Vegetarian Cookbook *and it has become a firm family favourite. We have adapted it to suit our tastes and store cupboard. If we don't have cannellini beans I use chickpeas. I have also made the same recipe with leftover mashed potato (a sort of Thai potato cake) and it has worked well.*

SERVES 4 • COST OF INGREDIENTS: £2 • COST PER SERVING: 50p

- **Suitable for vegetarians**
- **Can be cooked in advance**

1 tin of cannellini beans
½ bunch of spring onions, finely chopped
A handful of coriander leaves, finely chopped
2–3 teaspoons red Thai paste
Zest of 1 lime
Juice of ½ lime
Olive oil

For the sauce
1 red pepper
1 red chilli
1 teaspoon chilli powder
1–2 tablespoons apple juice

1. Drain and rinse the beans in cold water. Shake dry.
2. Place the beans, onions, coriander, Thai paste and zest and juice of lime in a food processor and whizz until combined.
3. Place the mixture on a floured board and form into 4–6 bean cakes.
4. Heat the olive oil in a sauté pan and fry the bean cakes on both sides until golden.
5. While the bean cakes are cooking, whizz together the pepper, chilli, chilli powder and apple juice to make a sauce. Use this as a dipping sauce for the bean cakes.

Vegetable Mornay

SERVES 4 • COST OF INGREDIENTS: £4.67 • COST PER SERVING: 1.17p

- **Suitable for vegetarians**
- **Can be frozen**
- **Can be cooked in advance**
- **Make 2, keep 1**

2–3 carrots
2 leeks
1 head of broccoli
1 cauliflower
25g butter
1 tablespoon plain flour or cornflour
500–750ml milk
2 tablespoons nutritional yeast flakes (optional)
100g mature cheese, grated (75g for the sauce, 25g for the topping)
½ teaspoon mustard
Black pepper to taste

1. Preheat the oven to 180°C/gas mark 4.
2. Chop the carrots into sticks, slice the leeks and cut the broccoli and cauliflower into manageable florets.
3. Place in a steamer and cook until the cauliflower is tender but not soft.
4. Meanwhile, make the sauce. Melt the butter gently in a saucepan on medium heat (not high!). Add the flour or cornflour and stir well with a wooden spoon. Add the milk a little at a time, continuing to stir to avoid lumps.
5. Switch now to a balloon whisk. Continue to stir over a medium heat until the sauce begins to thicken. The balloon whisk will also help to eradicate any lumps that may have materialised. Add more milk as necessary to get the desired thickness. The sauce should be the thickness of custard.
6. If you are using nutritional yeast flakes, add these before the grated cheese as they will reduce the amount of cheese you will need – taste as you go! Add the cheese and mustard and stir well.
7. Season with black pepper.

8. When the vegetables are ready, transfer them to an ovenproof dish. Pour over the sauce and garnish with the remaining grated cheese.
9. Bake in the oven for about 15–20 minutes or grill until the top is golden.

Broccoli and Cheese Bake

SERVES 4 • COST OF INGREDIENTS: £3.31 • COST PER SERVING: 83p

- **Suitable for vegetarians**
- **Can be frozen**
- **Can be cooked in advance**
- **Make 2, keep 1**

1 cauliflower
300g broccoli
25g butter
1 tablespoon plain flour or cornflour
500–750ml milk
2 tablespoons nutritional yeast flakes (optional)
100g mature cheese, grated (75g for the sauce, 25g for the topping)
½ teaspoon mustard
50g wholemeal breadcrumbs
Black pepper to taste

1. Preheat the oven to 180°C/gas mark 4.
2. Cut the cauliflower and broccoli into manageable florets.
3. Place in a steamer and cook until the cauliflower is tender but not soft.
4. Meanwhile, make the sauce. Melt the butter gently in a saucepan on medium heat (not high!). Add the flour or cornflour and stir well with a wooden spoon. Add the milk a little at a time, continuing to stir to avoid lumps.
5. Switch now to a balloon whisk. Continue to stir over a medium heat until the sauce begins to thicken. The balloon whisk will also help to eradicate any lumps that may have materialised. Add more milk as necessary to get the desired thickness. The

sauce should be the thickness of custard.

6. If you are using nutritional yeast flakes, add these before the grated cheese as they will reduce the amount of cheese you will need – taste as you go! Add the grated cheese and mustard and stir well.

7. Season with black pepper.

8. When the vegetables are ready, transfer them to an ovenproof dish. Pour over the sauce. Mix the breadcrumbs with the remaining grated cheese, season with black pepper and sprinkle over the sauce.

9. Heat through in the oven or under the grill for about 15–20 minutes until the top is golden.

Spicy Red Cabbage

The vibrant colour of this dish is perfect to liven up your Christmas lunch. But don't just make this at Christmas, use it to add colour and flavour to your meals at any time of year. It is cheap and easy to prepare.

SERVES 4 • COST OF INGREDIENTS: £3.33 • COST PER SERVING: 84p

- **Suitable for vegetarians**
- **Can be frozen**
- **Can be cooked in advance**
- **Make 2, keep 1**

1 red cabbage
2 onions
2 Bramley apples
4 teaspoons cinnamon powder
1 teaspoon mixed spice
1 teaspoon dried cardamom
25g soft brown sugar
Rind and juice of 1 orange
50ml apple juice
200ml red wine

1. I use my slow cooker to make this, but you can cook it on a low

heat on the hob.

2. Shred the cabbage, chop the onions, core and chop the apples (I leave the peel on, but it is up to you).

3. Place in a pan with all the remaining ingredients and mix thoroughly.

4. Cook on a low heat until the cabbage is soft. This will take approximately 4–6 hours in the slow cooker or 1 hour on a low heat on the hob. Stir occasionally.

5. Serve as a side vegetable dish. If you make a large batch don't waste it; you can bottle it to preserve until needed.

Leek and Stilton Stuffed Cabbage Leaves

Stuffed cabbage leaves make a surprisingly easy dish and a great way to use up some leftovers. This is a vegetarian recipe, but there are other, non-vegetarian variations at the end of the recipe. And, of course, you can always make up your own.

SERVES 4 • COST OF INGREDIENTS: £2.29 • COST PER SERVING: 57p

- **Suitable for vegetarians**
- **Can be cooked in advance**

A spray of olive oil
1 leek, finely chopped
100g chestnut mushrooms, quartered
Black pepper to taste
8–12 large cabbage leaves
50–75g Stilton or blue cheese, crumbled

1. Heat the oil in a sauté pan and fry the leek for 2 minutes. Add the mushrooms and fry for 1 minute. Season with black pepper and leave to one side.

2. Meanwhile, put the cabbage leaves in a pan of boiling water for 2–3 minutes to help soften the leaves. Remove and pat dry with kitchen paper or a clean tea towel, but do not discard the water as you will use it to steam the parcels when they are formed.

3. Place some of the leek and mushroom filling in the centre of each leaf, then sprinkle over a little of the cheese and roll into

a parcel. If you need to, you can use a wooden cocktail stick to help secure the leaves in place.

4. When all the cabbage leaves are parcelled up, place in a steamer. I use a bamboo steamer for this as it seems to give a nicer flavour.

5. Steam for 5–10 minutes before serving.

Variations
Pancetta and Gorgonzola Cheese Parcels;
Mozzarella, Basil and Tomato Parcels;
Bolognese Parcels – great for using up any spare bolognese mince;
Bubble and Squeak Parcels – perfect for using up chopped leftover roast potatoes, vegetables and meat.

Broccoli and Almond (Side dish)

This is a really tasty way to add some superfood broccoli to your diet. I cook my broccoli in a steamer for 4–5 minutes only, in order to retain as much of its flavour and fantastic nutrients as possible.

SERVES 4 • INGREDIENTS COST £1.88 • COST PER SERVING 47P

• **Suitable for vegetarians**

1 head of broccoli, cut into florets
50g toasted flaked almonds
Juice of ½ lemon
25g butter (optional)

1. Steam the broccoli until cooked to your taste.

2. Meanwhile, toast the flaked almonds. Spread them evenly on a baking tray and place them under the grill for a few minutes until they brown. Be careful to watch them as they brown quickly.

3. Mix the lemon juice with the toasted almonds. If you like a buttery taste, you can melt the butter and add this to the lemon juice and almond mix.

4. Pour over the broccoli and serve.

Chinese-style Broccoli

This is a variation on the recipe above and an idea to accompany a Chinese meal or simple rice dish. It's a good idea to roast sesame seeds and other seeds in batches and save them in airtight containers. That way you will always have some to hand when you need them.

SERVES 4 • COST OF INGREDIENTS: £1.81 • COST PER SERVING: 45p

• **Suitable for vegetarians**

1 head of broccoli, cut into florets
2 tablespoons roasted sesame seeds
Olive oil
½ bunch of spring onions, finely chopped
1 tablespoon chopped ginger
1 tablespoon soy sauce
1 tablespoon rice vinegar
1 tablespoon sesame oil

1. Preheat the oven to 200°C/gas mark 6.
2. Steam the broccoli until cooked to your taste.
3. Spread the sesame seeds on a baking tray and bake in the oven for 3–5 minutes.
4. Meanwhile, heat a little olive oil and fry the spring onions and ginger for 2–3 minutes. Leave to one side. Add the roasted sesame seeds when they are ready.
5. Mix the soy sauce, rice vinegar and sesame oil together and add to the onion, ginger and sesame seeds.
6. Place the broccoli in a serving dish and pour over the sesame seed mixture. Toss to ensure an even coating before serving.

Leek and Quorn Pie

*This is quite a substantial pie – really any veg will do. If you aren't vegetarian, you can make a **Chicken and Leek Pie** by adding pieces of cooked chicken.*

SERVES 4
COST OF INGREDIENTS: £4.83 if using Quorn pieces, or £5.43 if using chicken pieces
COST PER SERVING: £1.21 if using Quorn, or £1.36 if using chicken

- **Suitable for vegetarians**
- **Can be frozen**
- **Can be cooked in advance**
- **Make 2, keep 1**

1 large potato, cubed
2–3 carrots, sliced
Olive oil
1 onion, finely chopped
1–2 cloves garlic (optional)
2 leeks, finely chopped
200g Quorn
1 tub of quark
3 tablespoons Greek yoghurt
75g mature Cheddar (optional)
Seasoning to taste
A small handful of fresh tarragon, chopped, or 1 teaspoon dried
½ pack of puff pastry
A handful of sesame seeds for sprinkling

1. Preheat the oven to 200°C/gas mark 6.
2. Chop the potato and carrots and steam for 10 minutes.
3. Meanwhile, heat the oil in a large sauté pan and fry the onion, garlic and leeks for 5 minutes to soften.
4. Add the Quorn and cook for an additional 5 minutes then turn off the heat.
5. Add the quark and the yoghurt (and the cheese if you are using it).
6. When the potato and carrot are cooked, add them to the leek mix. Season and add the herbs.
7. Place the mixture in an ovenproof pie dish. Roll out your pastry larger than required. Wet the edges of the dish with milk or water, and cut thin strips of pastry to place on the edge of the pie dish – dampen again with milk. This will give the top pastry something to hold on to.
8. Cut the top pastry to size and place over the pie. Crimp and seal the edges thoroughly.
9. Brush with milk and sprinkle with sesame seeds. Cut two holes in the middle of the pastry to allow the pie to breathe.
10. Bake in the oven for 30–35 minutes, until the pie crust is golden and flaky.
11. Serve with roast new potatoes and greens.

Chickpea and Vegetable Casserole

SERVES 4–6 • COST OF INGREDIENTS: £2.50 • COST PER SERVING: 63p

- **Suitable for vegetarians**
- **Can be cooked in advance**

Olive oil
1 onion, sliced
1–2 cloves of garlic, crushed
1–2 chillies (optional)
1 pepper, sliced
2 sticks of celery, sliced
2 carrots, sliced
2 courgettes, sliced
1 sweet potato, diced
1 white potato, diced
400g tin chopped tomatoes
1 teaspoon paprika
1 teaspoon ground coriander
1 teaspoon fenugreek (optional)
400g tin chickpeas
200ml water or stock
1 bay leaf
Fresh herbs to taste

1. Heat the oil in a large ovenproof dish and fry the onion and garlic. Stir well and cook until they start to soften.
2. Add the chillies, pepper, celery, potatoes, carrots and courgettes. Cook for another 5 minutes, stirring well to prevent sticking. If necessary, add a few drops of water.
3. Add all the remaining ingredients. Cover with a lid and cook on a low heat for 45 minutes. Check halfway through the cooking time to ensure there is enough fluid in the casserole. Add more water or stock as necessary.
4. Add fresh herbs to taste prior to serving.

Stuffed Peppers with Goats' Cheese

Peppers are, at the time of writing, approximately 50p each, which adds to the price of this dish. You can reduce costs by buying in season or growing your own. This is a really simple dish and perfect for using up leftovers. Alternatively, if you have made Spicy Rice (see 'Rice is Nice', page 158), you could stuff these with the leftover rice. Serve with a delicious salad.

SERVES 4 • COST OF INGREDIENTS: £5.69 • COST PER SERVING: £1.42

- **Suitable for vegetarians**
- **Can be cooked in advance**

4 peppers
A spray of olive oil
400g cooked rice or couscous
A bunch of spring onions, chopped
12 cherry tomatoes, chopped
50g chopped walnuts
Fresh parsley
Seasoning to taste
125g goats' cheese

1. Preheat the oven to 180°C/gas mark 4. Cut the peppers in half and deseed. Spray with olive oil, place in an ovenproof dish and bake in the oven for 15 minutes.
2. Meanwhile, mix the cooked rice or couscous with the spring onions, cherry tomatoes, walnuts and parsley. Season to taste.
3. Remove the peppers from the oven and turn up the oven to 200°C. Stuff the peppers with the rice mixture. Finish with a layer of goats' cheese.
4. Bake in the oven for 10 minutes until the cheese is starting to brown and bubble.

Ratatouille

This is so easy and can be served on its own with some warm crusty bread, or mixed with pasta to create a more filling dish.

SERVES 4 • COST OF INGREDIENTS: £2.70 • COST PER SERVING: 68p

- **Suitable for vegetarians**
- **Can be cooked in advance**

Olive oil
1 aubergine, diced
2 courgettes, sliced
1 red onion, sliced
1–2 cloves garlic, crushed
1–2 red peppers, sliced
400g chopped tomatoes
2 teaspoons tomato purée
100ml red wine
A handful of chopped fresh herbs

1. Heat the olive oil in a large ovenproof dish and fry the aubergine and courgettes for 5 minutes until slightly charred. Remove and place on a plate until later.
2. Add the onion, garlic and peppers and cook for 3–4 minutes.
3. Add the tomatoes, purée and the wine.
4. Finally, add the aubergines and courgettes to the pan. Cover with a lid, reduce the heat to low and cook slowly for 15 minutes until the mixture reduces slightly.
5. Add fresh herbs prior to serving.

Curried Potato and Black-Eyed Beans

SERVES 4 • COST OF INGREDIENTS: £2.20 • COST PER SERVING: 55p

- **Suitable for vegetarians**
- **Can be cooked in advance**

Olive oil
1 teaspoon cumin seeds
1 stick cinnamon
1 teaspoon turmeric powder
1 chilli, chopped
1 red onion
1–2 cloves garlic, crushed
½ red pepper, chopped
750g potatoes, cubed
300ml water
400g tin of chopped tomatoes
300g cooked black-eyed beans, or tinned
2 bay leaves
Juice of 1 lemon
1 tablespoon fresh coriander to garnish

1. Heat a dash of olive oil in a deep-based pan or casserole dish and stir-fry all the spices for 1 minute.
2. Add the onion, garlic and red pepper and cook until soft.
3. Add the potatoes and sweat for a further 5 minutes.
4. Add all the remaining ingredients except the coriander and leave on a low heat, covered, for approximately 1 hour, until tender.
5. Garnish with fresh coriander prior to serving.

Green Bean and Tomato Bredie

A Bredie is a Cape stew. Serve with a fresh salad and rice.

SERVES 4 • COST OF INGREDIENTS: £3 • COST PER SERVING: 75p

- **Suitable for vegetarians**
- **Can be cooked in advance**

Olive oil
2 garlic cloves, chopped
1 teaspoon fresh ginger, grated
1 small chilli, finely chopped
2 onions, chopped
2 carrots, chopped into chunks
400g potatoes, chopped into chunks
400g tin of chopped tomatoes
200ml water
200g green beans cut into 2–3 pieces
3–4 chard leaves, torn into a few pieces
1 tablespoon fresh coriander

1. Heat the olive oil in a pan and fry the garlic, ginger, chilli and onions until the onions soften.

2. Add the carrots and potatoes and sweat for a further 5 minutes, stirring constantly.

3. Add the tomatoes and water, cover and cook on a low heat for 45 minutes.

4. Add the green beans, chard and coriander and continue to cook until the vegetables are tender and the liquid reduced.

Spicy Sweet Potato Balls

SERVES 4 • COST OF INGREDIENTS: £2.30 • COST PER SERVING: 58p

- **Suitable for vegetarians**
- **Can be cooked in advance**

4 sweet potatoes, peeled and cubed
A spray or drizzle of olive oil
1 red onion, chopped
1–2 cloves garlic, crushed
1 chilli, chopped
2 large tomatoes, chopped
1 teaspoon fresh coriander
1 teaspoon turmeric
¼ teaspoon cayenne pepper
A little plain flour
Breadcrumbs for coating

1. Preheat the oven to 180°C/gas mark 4.
2. Steam the sweet potatoes until tender. Mash with a little butter or milk and leave to one side.
3. Heat the oil in a pan and fry the onion, garlic and chilli until tender. Add the tomatoes, coriander and spices and stir for 1 minute.
4. Add to the mash and mix well.
5. With the help of a little flour, form the mash into small balls with your hands. Finally, roll the balls in breadcrumbs to form a crisp coating.
6. Place the balls on a baking tray and heat in the oven for 15–20 minutes.
7. Serve with rice and salad

Black-Eyed Bean Chilli

SERVES 4 • COST OF INGREDIENTS: £2.75 • COST PER SERVING: 69p

- **Suitable for vegetarians**
- **Can be cooked in advance**

Olive oil
1 large onion, chopped
1–2 cloves garlic, crushed
1–2 chillies
1 small red pepper, finely chopped
1 teaspoon chilli powder (or to taste)
¼ teaspoon cayenne pepper (optional)
1 carrot, finely chopped
400g tinned tomatoes, chopped
1 tin of black-eyed beans
1–2 teaspoons oregano
200–300ml water

1. Heat the oil in a pan and fry the onion, garlic, chilli and red pepper until soft.
2. Add the spices and cook for 1 more minute.
3. Add all the remaining ingredients. Cover with a lid and leave to cook on a low heat for 45 minutes.
4. Check occasionally to see if the mixture needs more fluid.
5. Serve with sour cream and rice or tortillas.

Rice is Nice

Not only is rice a nutritional gem, it is also easy to cook and absorbs flavours effortlessly. Brown rice is nutritionally superior to white rice, but don't expect it to be soft and fluffy like white rice – it will have a soft bite to it. People often panic when cooking rice and end up with a soggy mess. The secret is to do very little. As a rough guide for cooking rice (but not risotto), use one part rice to two parts water. Follow the instructions below for perfect rice every time.

Simple Rice

SERVES 4

2 cups basmati rice
4 cups water (always use the same size cup for the rice and the water!)

1. Place the rice and water in a pan and bring to the boil.
2. Simmer for 5–8 minutes and then remove from the heat.
3. Cover the pan with a lid and leave for 10 minutes.
4. When ready to serve, stir up gently with a fork to loosen the rice.

Note: For vibrant yellow rice, add a teaspoon of turmeric.

Simple Risotto

SERVES 4 • COST OF INGREDIENTS: £1.78 • COST PER SERVING: 45p

A splash of olive oil
A knob of butter
1 onion, finely chopped
300g risotto rice
200ml white wine
500–700ml vegetable stock, preferably warm or hot
A handful of fresh, chopped herbs

1. Heat the olive oil and butter in a saucepan and fry the onion until translucent.
2. Stir in the rice, ensuring that it is completely covered in the oil/butter mixture. Don't let this stick! If necessary lower the heat to medium rather than full.
3. Add the wine and stir thoroughly. The wine will evaporate but will flavour the rice.
4. Add the stock, a little at a time. Wait each time until the stock has been absorbed before adding more. Add your chosen herbs.
5. After 10–15 minutes the rice should be tender (not soft as it should still have a little bite to it).
6. Serve immediately.

Variation
Add some lean bacon pieces, covered in a sprinkling of Parmesan to give more flavour. There are endless variations but the main technique remains the same. Once you have mastered the art of cooking risotto, there will be no stopping you!

Mushroom Risotto

SERVES 4 • COST OF INGREDIENTS: £4.25 • COST PER SERVING: £1.06

10g dried porcini mushrooms
A splash of olive oil
A knob of butter
1 onion, finely chopped
400g mixed mushrooms (shiitake, oyster, chestnut, wild, etc.), roughly
  chopped
300g risotto rice
200ml white wine
500–700ml vegetable stock/mushroom water, preferably warm or hot
 A handful of fresh tarragon, chopped
Zest of ½ lemon
2–3 spoonfuls of low fat crème fraiche
A handful of fresh, chopped herbs
A little grated Parmesan to garnish

1. Soak the porcini mushrooms as directed on the pack. This
   normally takes 20 minutes. Retain the fluid to add to your
   stock.
2. Heat the olive oil and butter in a saucepan and fry the chopped
   onion until translucent. Add the fresh and dried mushrooms
   and stir well.
3. Stir in the rice, ensuring that it is completely covered in the
   oil/butter mixture. Don't let this stick! If necessary lower the
   heat to medium rather than full.
4. Add the wine and stir thoroughly. The wine will evaporate but
   will flavour the rice.
5. Add the stock, a little at a time. Wait each time until the stock
   has been absorbed before adding more.
6. After 10–15 minutes the rice should be tender (not soft as it
   should still have a little bite to it). After adding the last of the
   stock, add the tarragon and lemon zest. For a creamy risotto,
   stir in the crème fraiche.
7. Serve immediately, garnished with chopped herbs and
   Parmesan.

Haddock Risotto

SERVES 4 • COST OF INGREDIENTS: £3.67 • COST PER SERVING: 92p

50g butter
1 onion, finely chopped
1 clove garlic, crushed
300g risotto rice
200ml white wine
75g peas
500–700ml fish stock, preferably warm or hot
200g haddock, skinned, boned and chopped
2–3 tablespoons fresh dill (you can use frozen but add this to the hot stock before adding to the rice)

1. Heat the butter in a saucepan and fry the onion and garlic until translucent.
2. Stir in the rice, ensuring that it is completely covered in the butter mixture. Don't let this stick! If necessary lower the heat to medium rather than full.
3. Add the wine and peas and stir thoroughly. The wine will evaporate but will flavour the rice.
4. Add the stock, a little at a time. Wait each time until the stock has been absorbed before adding more.
5. After 10–15 minutes the rice should be tender (not soft as it should still have a little bite to it). When you think the rice is almost cooked, add the chopped haddock and the fresh dill. Stir well. Cover with a lid and remove from the heat for 5 minutes.
6. Serve immediately.

Chicken and Tarragon Risotto

SERVES 4 • COST OF INGREDIENTS: £4.73 • COST PER SERVING: £1.18

A splash of olive oil
A knob of butter
1 onion, finely chopped
1 leek, very finely sliced
1–2 cloves garlic, crushed
300g cooked chicken
300g risotto rice
200ml white wine
500–700ml warm chicken stock
2 tablespoons tarragon, finely chopped

1. Heat the olive oil and butter in a saucepan and fry the onion, leek and garlic until translucent. Add the chicken pieces and stir well.
2. Stir in the rice, ensuring that it is completely covered in the oil/butter mixture. Don't let this stick! If necessary lower the heat to medium rather than full.
3. Add the wine and stir thoroughly. The wine will evaporate but will flavour the rice.
4. Add the stock, a little at a time. Wait each time until the stock has been absorbed before adding more. Add the tarragon.
5. After 10–15 minutes the rice should be tender (not soft as it should still have a little bite to it).
6. Serve immediately.

Beetroot Risotto

This is a vibrant red risotto that looks really dramatic. Top with dark green lettuce leaves such as rocket to help emphasise the fabulous colour.

SERVES 4 • COST OF INGREDIENTS: £2.83 • COST PER SERVING: 71p

A splash of olive oil
A knob of butter
1 onion, finely chopped
2 cloves garlic, crushed
200g cooked beetroot, cut into chunks
300g risotto rice
200ml red wine
700ml vegetable stock, preferably warm or hot
20g Parmesan cheese, grated

1. Heat the olive oil and butter in a saucepan and fry the onion and garlic until translucent. Add the beetroot and stir well.
2. Stir in the rice, ensuring that it is completely covered in the oil/butter mixture. Don't let this stick! If necessary lower the heat to medium rather than full.
3. Add the wine and stir thoroughly. The wine will evaporate but will flavour the rice.
4. Add the stock a little at a time. Wait each time until the stock has been absorbed before adding more.
5. After 10–15 minutes the rice should be tender (not soft as it should still have a little bite to it). Add the grated Parmesan.
6. Serve immediately.

Spicy Rice

This is a really lovely dish that can be served either as a side dish or a main meal.

SERVES 4 • COST OF INGREDIENTS: £2.22 • COST PER SERVING: 56p

Olive oil
1 onion, chopped

2 cloves garlic, crushed
2.5–5cm fresh ginger, grated
1 pepper, chopped
1 red chilli (optional)
1 teaspoon coriander
1 teaspoon cardamom
1 teaspoon ground cumin
1 teaspoon turmeric
½ teaspoon ground nutmeg
250g basmati rice
75g red lentils
750ml water
1 cinnamon stick
1 bay leaf
75g peas (thawed if frozen)
50g sweetcorn
25g sliced almonds
Small handful fresh coriander leaves (optional)

1. Heat the olive oil in a large sauté or casserole pan and fry the onion, garlic, ginger, pepper and chilli for 2 minutes to soften.
2. Add the herbs and spices (apart from the bay leaf and cinnamon stick) and cook for a further 3–4 minutes.
3. Add the rice and lentils and stir well, ensuring all the flavours start to mix with the rice. Top with the water.
4. Add the cinnamon stick and bay leaf and cover. Cook for 10 minutes on medium heat.
5. Turn off the heat. Add the peas, sweetcorn, sliced almonds and coriander leaves. Stir, cover again and leave for 10 minutes.
6. Loosen with a fork before serving.

Note: You can use this to fill the **Stuffed Peppers with Goats' Cheese** on page 147 in 'Give Peas a Chance'.

Thai Rice

You can eat this on its own or serve it as an accompaniment to other dishes, such as Thai Beef Salad. Asda offer a fresh Thai Curry kit, which contains bird eye chillies, lemongrass, shallots, garlic and galangal for only 92p. If you don't already have the ingredients in your store cupboard, this kit is worth buying.

SERVES 4 • COST OF INGREDIENTS: £2.20 • COST PER SERVING: 55p

A drizzle or spray of olive oil
1 onion
2 cloves garlic, crushed
2.5cm piece of ginger, finely sliced
1 chilli (optional)
2.5cm knuckle galangal, finely sliced (optional)
1 small stick of lemon grass
1 teaspoon coriander seeds
1 teaspoon cumin seeds
2 limes
225g basmati rice
750ml water or vegetable stock
A handful of fresh coriander

1. Heat the olive oil in a heavy-based pan and fry the onion, garlic, ginger, chilli, galangal and lemon grass for 2 minutes. Add the coriander and cumin seeds and cook for another minute.
2. Add the zest from the limes (retaining the juice for later). Add the rice and stir for 1–2 minutes before gradually pouring in the water or stock.
3. Cook on medium/high heat for 5 minutes. Reduce heat to low for a further 5 minutes, then pop a lid on the pan and remove from the heat for 10 minutes.
4. Check the rice is cooked; fluff it up with a fork before adding the chopped coriander and lime juice.

Smashing Mash

The humble mashed potato doesn't have to be boring; try some of the variations below for a delicious side vegetable or topping. Boiled mash can be watery and tasteless but steaming vegetables helps retain both their goodness and their flavour. To add fluffiness and a smooth texture to mash, use your food mixer or electric balloon whisk attachment – though mash the potato first or you may buckle your whisk! Alternatively, use a potato ricer, available from cook shops for about £15. These look like giant garlic presses. You literally fill them with your potato and press it through the small holes to form potato rice. Then whip it all together for the smoothest mash ever!

Basic Mash Potato

COST OF INGREDIENTS: 78p

1kg potatoes, cubed
50g butter
50ml milk
Seasoning to taste

1. Steam the potatoes until soft. Place them in a pan or bowl and mash.
2. Add the milk and butter and continue to mash.
3. Season to taste. (For extra lightness use an electric balloon whisk or potato ricer to fluff up the mash.)

Variations
• Mix in a handful of chopped chives and 75g mature Cheddar for a delicious **Cheesy Mash.**
• Add a few spoonfuls of Pesto, to make a wonderful **Herby Mash.**
• Mix in some crème fraiche and herbs for a **Creamy Herb Mash.**

Vegetable Mash

Vegetable mash is a tasty and nutritious accompaniment to a main meal, and a change from the familiar mashed potato. Try some of the following.

Carrot, Potato and Swede Mash: Steam the carrot, swede and potatoes together before mashing with butter and milk. Season with black pepper. This is a lovely mash to place on top of a shepherd's pie, especially when topped with grated cheese!

Sweet Potato Mash: Steam a mixture of sweet potato and white potato together. Mash as above.

Cauliflower Cheesy Mash: Steam the potato and cauliflower until tender. Mash together. Add butter, milk and mature Cheddar. Season to taste before serving.

Garlic Butter Mash: Steam the potatoes as normal. Meanwhile mix 75g butter with 2–3 cloves of garlic and leave to rest. Mash the potato. Add the garlic butter and mix thoroughly.

Leeky Mash: Steam the potatoes and, 5 minutes before they are ready, add some leeks (in another layer of your steamer or, if you have room, in with the potatoes). Mash the potato and leeks together roughly (this will never be a smooth mash). Add milk and butter. You can also add cheese if you like a cheesy flavour. Season to taste before serving.

Watercress Mash: Steam the potatoes as above. When they are cooked, mash them well. Add butter, milk and 50g of finely chopped watercress. Season to taste.

Butternut and Sweet Potato Mash: Steam the potatoes for 10 minutes. Add cubes of butternut squash to the potatoes (either in another layer of your steamer or in with the potatoes if you have room). Cook for a further 10 minutes or until the potatoes are tender. Mash together with milk or butter. Season to taste.

Put a Jacket On

Jacket potatoes are delicious. If you are lucky enough to have an Aga or Rayburn you really should be making use of that lovely steady heat and cooking these as often as possible. Jackets can be cooked in the microwave but, to me, nothing beats the taste of a traditional oven-baked potato. Baking jackets in an electric oven can be expensive, but I have found a solution. I use a halogen oven by JML. It cooks jackets in 45 minutes, so is faster than an electric oven, and cheaper to use.

Baked potatoes can be topped with leftover chilli, bolognese, curry, grated cheese, tuna or even humble baked beans.

Cheesy Jackets

With a bit of imagination jacket toppings can be so much more than a bit of grated cheese or some tuna. Here is a simple suggestion to spice up the popular cheesy jacket.

SERVES 4 • COST OF INGREDIENTS: £1.99 • COST PER SERVING: 50p

4–6 large potatoes
A knob of butter
100g mature Cheddar, grated
1–2 carrots, grated
A dash of Worcestershire sauce
Black pepper to taste

1. Preheat the oven to 200°C/gas mark 6.
2. Select your potatoes. Prick them all over with a sharp knife.
3. Bake the potatoes until they are soft in the middle but the jackets are crunchy. How long this takes will depend on the type of oven you are using.
4. Cut the jackets in half, scoop out the middles and place potato in a large bowl. Return the empty jackets to the oven for 5 minutes to crisp.

5. Meanwhile mix the potato with the butter, cheese, carrots, Worcestershire sauce and black pepper.
6. Restuff the jackets and finish with a sprinkling of grated cheese on top.
7. Bake for another 10 minutes in the oven until the tops are golden. Delicious!

Italian Jackets

SERVES 4 • COST OF INGREDIENTS: £3 • COST PER SERVING: 75p

4–6 large potatoes
A knob of butter
150g Gorgonzola cheese, crumbled
150g pancetta, chopped
1 teaspoon oregano
A dash of milk

1. Preheat the oven to 200°C/gas mark 6.
2. Select your potatoes. Prick them all over with a sharp knife.
3. Bake the potatoes until they are soft in the middle but the jackets are crunchy. How long this takes will depend on the type of oven you are using.
4. Cut the jackets in half, scoop out the middles and place potato in a large bowl. Return the empty jackets to the oven for 5 minutes to crisp.
5. Meanwhile mix the potato with the butter, cheese, pancetta and oregano. Add a dash of milk if the mixture is too dry (it should be the consistency of mashed potato).
6. Restuff the jackets and finish with a sprinkling of grated cheese on top.
7. Bake for another 10 minutes in the oven until the tops are golden. Delicious!

Love–Hate Jackets

This recipe is so named because most people seem to fall into one of two groups: those who love Marmite and those who hate it!

SERVES 4 • COST OF INGREDIENTS: £1.60 • COST PER SERVING: 40p

4–6 large potatoes
A knob of butter
4 teaspoons Marmite or yeast extract
75g mature Cheddar, grated
A dash of milk

1. Preheat the oven to 200°C/gas mark 6.
2. Select your potatoes. Prick them all over with a sharp knife.
3. Bake the potatoes until they are soft in the middle but the jackets are crunchy. How long this takes will depend on the type of oven you are using.
4. Cut the jackets in half, scoop out the middles and place potato in a large bowl. Return the empty jackets to the oven for 5 minutes to crisp.
5. Meanwhile mix the potato with the butter, Marmite and cheese. Add a dash of milk if the mixture is too dry (it should be the consistency of mashed potato).
6. Restuff the jackets and finish with a sprinkling of grated cheese on top.
7. Bake for another 10 minutes in the oven until the tops are golden. Delicious!

Tuna and Mayo Jackets

SERVES 4 • COST OF INGREDIENTS: £2.21 • COST PER SERVING: 55p

4–6 large potatoes
A knob of butter
1–2 large dollops of mayonnaise
1 tin tuna, mashed
50g sweetcorn (optional)
A dash of milk
Grated cheese (optional)

1. Preheat the oven to 180°C/gas mark 4.
2. Select your potatoes. Prick them all over with a sharp knife.
3. Bake the potatoes until they are soft in the middle but the jackets are crunchy. How long this takes will depend on the type of oven you are using.
4. Cut the jackets in half, scoop out the middles and place potato in a large bowl. Return the empty jackets to the oven for 5 minutes to crisp.
5. Meanwhile mix the potato with the butter, mayo, tuna and sweetcorn and mix thoroughly. Add a dash of milk if the mixture is too dry (it should be the consistency of mashed potato).
6. Restuff the jackets and finish with a sprinkling of grated cheese on top.
7. Bake in the oven for another 10 minutes until the tops are golden. Delicious!

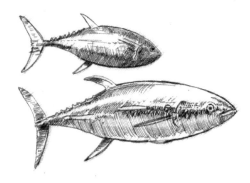

Baked New Potatoes

This must be the simplest recipe of all!

SERVES 4 • COST OF INGREDIENTS: £1.37 • COST PER SERVING: 34p

1kg bag of new potatoes, washed
A dash of olive oil
2–3 cloves garlic, crushed
Herbs (fresh or dried)
Seasoning to taste

1. Preheat the oven to 200°C/gas mark 6.
2. Place the potatoes in a bowl with the olive oil, garlic and herbs. Stir well, ensuring all is the potatoes are coated.
3. Tip all the contents onto a baking tray and bake in the oven for approximately 30 minutes, until golden. Simple!

Bellissimo Pasta

Pasta is quick, easy and very filling. You can buy fresh, but it is quite expensive so, if you prefer the taste of fresh pasta, why not try to make your own. Invest in a pasta maker and experiment! Alternatively, dried pasta is a great standby and perfect for your store cupboard. Wholemeal pasta is a healthier option and wheat-free alternatives are also available. My favourites are rice, spelt or vegetable pasta.

Roasted Cherry Tomato, Pancetta and Ricotta Pasta

You can also make a vegetarian version of this. Simply omit the pancetta from the recipe.

SERVES 4 • COST OF INGREDIENTS: £3.06 • COST PER SERVING: 77p

1 small red onion, quartered
4 cloves garlic, sliced
½ red pepper, sliced
4–5 rashers pancetta or lean bacon
330g cherry tomatoes (one punnet)
4 tablespoons oil
1 teaspoon thyme
1 teaspoon oregano
300g dried pasta
1 bunch fresh basil leaves
125g ricotta (½ tub)
Seasoning to taste

1. Mix the onion, garlic, pepper, pancetta or bacon and cherry tomatoes in a roasting pan (one that can also be used to serve the food in) with the olive oil and dried herbs, ensuring every item is covered in oil. Cook gently on the hob for 10–15 minutes, turning occasionally.

2. Meanwhile, cook the pasta in boiling water according to the instructions on the packet.
3. Drain the pasta and add it to the roasting tin. Mix thoroughly. Add the fresh basil and ricotta and stir well. Season to taste.
4. Serve immediately.

Sweetcorn and Tuna Pasta

SERVES 4 • COST OF INGREDIENTS: £3.09 • COST PER SERVING: 77p

300g dried pasta
10ml olive oil
1 onion, finely chopped
1 tin tuna, drained
1 small tin of sweetcorn or 125g frozen sweetcorn
150ml milk
150g low fat cream cheese (½ a pot)
Seasoning to taste

1. Cook the pasta in boiling water according to the instructions on the pack.
2. Meanwhile, fry the onion in olive oil until soft. Add the tuna and sweetcorn, stir well and turn off the heat. Add the milk and cream cheese as this will start to melt with the heat. Cover the pan with a lid to keep warm.
3. When the pasta is cooked, switch off the heat under the pan. Drain the pasta and return it to the empty saucepan. Add the tuna mixture to the pasta. Return the pan to the hob (it will still be warm from cooking the pasta) and mix well for 1 minute over the heat.
4. Season to taste and sprinkle with some fresh herbs if you have any.
5. Serve immediately.

Bacon and Mushroom Pasta

SERVES 4 • COST OF INGREDIENTS: £3.74 • COST PER SERVING: 94p

300g dried pasta
Olive oil
1 onion, finely chopped
1–2 cloves garlic, crushed
4–5 rashers of lean bacon
100g button mushrooms
100ml white wine
A small handful of mixed fresh herbs such as basil, oregano and thyme
  (alternatively, add 1–2 teaspoons dry or frozen, if out of season)
2–3 tablespoons crème fraiche
Seasoning to taste

1. Cook the pasta in a pan of boiling water according to the instructions on the packet.
2. Meanwhile, heat the olive oil in a large sauté pan and fry the onion and garlic together for a couple of minutes until the onion starts to soften. Add the bacon and cook for a further 5 minutes before adding the mushrooms.
3. Add the white wine and herbs and stir thoroughly.
4. When the pasta is cooked, switch off the heat under the pan. Drain the pasta and return it to the empty saucepan. Add the crème fraiche to the pasta. Return the pan to the hob (it will still be warm from cooking the pasta) and mix well for 1 minute over the heat.
5. Season to taste and serve immediately.

Quick and Easy Garlic Mushroom and Ham Tagliatelle

SERVES 4 • COST OF INGREDIENTS: £4.88 • COST PER SERVING: £1.22

350g tagliatelle
A spray or drizzle of olive oil
2–4 cloves of garlic, crushed
200g button mushrooms, quartered
100g ham, chopped
A dash of white wine (optional)
3–4 tablespoons low fat crème fraiche
A handful of fresh parsley, chopped, plus extra to garnish
A little grated Parmesan to garnish

1. Cook the pasta in boiling water according to the instructions on the packet.
2. Meanwhile, heat the olive oil in a sauté pan and fry the garlic and mushrooms for 2 minutes. Add the ham and cook for 1 more minute.
3. Add the wine, if you are using it, followed by the crème fraiche and parsley. Stir well.
4. When the tagliatelle is cooked, drain and stir in the garlic and mushroom mixture.
5. Garnish with grated Parmesan and parsley.
6. Serve immediately.

Note: Vegetarians can omit the ham in this recipe. If you are not vegetarian, you can add variety by substituting some bacon or pancetta for the ham.

Prawn and Asparagus Pasta

SERVES 4 • COST OF INGREDIENTS: £5.38 • COST PER SERVING: £1.34

300g penne pasta
200g asparagus spears
75g frozen peas
Olive oil
1–2 cloves garlic, crushed
200g prawns
200g low fat crème fraiche
Zest and juice of ½ lemon
Black pepper to taste

1. Cook the pasta in boiling water as directed on the packet. About 4–5 minutes before the end of the cooking time, add the asparagus and peas.
2. Meanwhile heat the olive oil in a pan and fry the garlic. Add the prawns and cook until transparent. Finally, add the crème fraiche and the lemon juice and zest. Season with black pepper.
3. Drain the pasta and vegetables and return them to the empty saucepan. Add the prawn mixture and stir well over a low heat before serving.

Tagliatelle Carbonara

SERVES 4 • COST OF INGREDIENTS: Cost £3.88 • COST PER SERVING: 97p

350–400g tagliatelle
A spray or drizzle of olive oil
1 small red onion, finely chopped
2 cloves garlic, crushed
4 rashers smoky bacon or pancetta, roughly chopped
100ml white wine
2 eggs
30–50g Parmesan, grated
4 tablespoons low fat crème fraiche or quark
1 tablespoon fresh parsley, chopped

1. Cook the tagliatelle in a pan of boiling water according to the instructions on the packet.
2. Meanwhile, heat the olive oil in a pan and fry the onion, garlic and bacon together for 2–3 minutes. Add the white wine.
3. Mix the eggs, Parmesan and crème fraiche or quark together.
4. When the tagliatelle is cooked, drain and return to the saucepan. Add the onion and bacon mix and the parsley and pour on the egg mix. Combine well over a low heat for 1–2 minutes to ensure the eggs cook. Serve immediately.

Note: Vegetarians can replace the bacon with mushrooms, leeks or tofu.

Spinach and Ricotta Lasagne

This is a very quick and easy recipe that will impress your family and friends. When I am in a hurry and don't want to prepare my own pasta sauce, I use Seeds of Change Cherry Tomato and Parmesan, but at £2.20, it is not a cheap option! Instead, try to make your own or you can buy pasta sauces for around £1 a jar.

SERVES 4 • COST OF INGREDIENTS: £3.57 • COST PER SERVING: 89p

- **Cheat alert!**
- **Suitable for vegetarians**
- **Can be frozen**
- **Can be cooked in advance**
- **Make 2, keep 1**

1 onion, finely chopped
1 pot of ricotta
100g mature Cheddar, grated
150g fresh spinach leaves (baby spinach is best)
Grated nutmeg
Black pepper to taste
Lasagne sheets
1 jar of pasta sauce
Grated Parmesan or other cheese for topping

1. Preheat the oven to 200°C/gas mark 6.
2 Place the onion, ricotta and Cheddar in a bowl and mix well. Add the spinach leaves (if you place the spinach in a colander and run it under a hot tap for a few seconds it softens the leaves and makes the mixing easier).
3. Once mixed, add some grated nutmeg and season with black pepper.
4. Place a small layer of ricotta mixture in the bottom of a lasagne dish, followed by a layer of lasagne sheets. Top with a small layer of pasta sauce. Continue with a layer of ricotta, then lasagne, and finally the remaining pasta sauce. Add approximately 30ml of water to the empty jar, rinse the jar and pour the water over the top of the lasagne.
5. Grate some Parmesan or other cheese onto the lasagne and place in the oven to cook for 30–40 minutes.
6. Serve with potato wedges and salad – delicious!

Mushroom and Cottage Cheese Lasagne

SERVES 4 • COST OF INGREDIENTS: £1.93 • COST PER SERVING: 48p

- **Suitable for vegetarians**

10ml olive oil
1 onion, finely chopped
1–2 cloves garlic
250g mushrooms, quartered
100ml white wine (optional)
1 teaspoon thyme (or fresh thyme if you have it)
1 tub cottage cheese
Black pepper to taste
Lasagne sheets
Grated Parmesan or other cheese for topping

1. Preheat the oven to 200°C/gas mark 6.
2. Heat the olive oil in a large sauté pan and fry the onion and garlic until the onion becomes translucent.
3. Add the mushrooms and wine if using and cook for another 5 minutes.
4. Remove from the heat and stir in the herbs and cottage cheese. Season to taste. Leave to one side.
5. Place a layer of mushroom mix in a lasagne dish, followed by a layer of lasagne sheets, and alternate the two, finishing with a layer of lasagne.
6. Add a grating of Parmesan or other cheese and place in the oven to cook for 30–40 minutes.

Tuna and Sweetcorn Lasagne
Another very quick and easy recipe!

SERVES 4 • COST OF INGREDIENTS: £4.24 • COST PER SERVING: £1.06

- **Cheat alert!**
- **Can be frozen**
- **Can be cooked in advance**
- **Make 2, keep 1**

400g tuna (roughly 2 tins), mashed
3–4 spring onions, chopped
200g sweetcorn (tinned or frozen)
Seasoning to taste
Lasagne sheets
500ml passata
Grated Parmesan or other cheese for topping

1. Preheat the oven to 200°C/gas mark 6.
2. Mix the tuna, spring onions and sweetcorn together in a bowl. Season to taste.
3. Add a layer of tuna mash to the bottom of a lasagne dish, cover with a layer of lasagne sheets and top with a layer of passata. Continue this process once more, ending with a layer of passata.
4. Grate Parmesan or other cheese over the final layer of passata and place in the oven to bake for 40 minutes.

Asparagus and Cherry Tomato Tagliatelle

SERVES 4 • COST OF INGREDIENTS: £4.20 • COST PER SERVING: £1.05

- **Suitable for vegetarians**

175g asparagus tips
Dried or fresh tagliatelle for 4 servings (fresh is much more expensive unless you make your own)
3–4 tablespoons crème fraiche
300g cherry tomatoes, halved
50g Parmesan cheese, grated

Fresh basil, chopped

1. Steam the asparagus tips for 8–10 minutes until tender. Don't overcook – the asparagus needs to be tender but still have a bit of a bite.
2. Meanwhile, cook the tagliatelle in a pan of boiling water. Both should be ready about the same time (if using fresh tagliatelle, allow for the time difference in cooking to ensure the asparagus and tagliatelle are cooked at the same time).
3. When the asparagus and tagliatelle are cooked, drain and place in a pan together. Add the crème fraiche, cherry tomatoes, Parmesan and basil and stir well.
4. Serve immediately.

Broccoli and Red Pepper Linguine

This is a delicious way to get some broccoli into your family's meals.

SERVES 4 • COST OF INGREDIENTS: £2.69 • COST PER SERVING: 67p

• **Suitable for vegetarians**

250–300g linguine or spaghetti
1 head of broccoli
Olive oil
1 small red onion, chopped
3 cloves garlic, crushed
1 red pepper, chopped
A handful of fresh oregano
50g Parmesan, finely grated

1. Cook the pasta in a pan of boiling water according to the instructions on the packet. About 5 minutes before the end of the cooking time, put the broccoli in a steamer and place over the pasta pan to cook.
2. Meanwhile, heat the olive oil in a pan and fry the onion, garlic and red pepper for 5 minutes to soften.
3. When the pasta is cooked, drain and place in a large serving dish. Add the broccoli, red pepper mixture, oregano and Parmesan and stir well before serving.

Ooh, Saucy!

Basic White Sauce

25g butter
1 tablespoon plain flour or cornflour
500–750ml milk
Black pepper to taste

1. Melt the butter gently in a saucepan on medium heat (not high!). Add the flour or cornflour and stir well with a wooden spoon. Add the milk, a little at a time, continuing to stir to avoid lumps.

2. Switch now to a balloon whisk. Continue to stir over a medium heat until the sauce begins to thicken. The balloon whisk will also help eradicate any lumps that may have materialised. Add more milk as necessary to get the desired thickness. The sauce should be the thickness of custard.

3. Season with black pepper.

Cheese Sauce

This is also known as Mornay.

25g butter
1 tablespoon of plain flour or cornflour
500–750ml milk
75g mature cheese, grated
2 tablespoons nutritional yeast flakes (optional)
½ teaspoon mustard
Black pepper to taste

1. Melt the butter gently in a saucepan on medium heat (not high!). Add the flour or cornflour and stir well with a wooden spoon. Add the milk, a little at a time, continuing to stir to avoid lumps.

2. Switch now to a balloon whisk. Continue to stir over a medium heat until the sauce begins to thicken. The balloon whisk will also help eradicate any lumps that may have materialised. Add more milk as necessary to get the desired thickness. The sauce should be the thickness of custard.

3. If you are using nutritional yeast flakes, add these before you add the cheese as they will reduce the amount of cheese you may need – taste as you go! Add the cheese and mustard and stir well.

4. Season with black pepper.

Parsley Sauce

25g butter
1 tablespoon of plain flour or cornflour
500–750ml milk
A handful of fresh parsley, finely chopped
Black pepper to taste

1. Melt the butter gently in a saucepan on medium heat (not high!). Add the flour or cornflour and stir well with a wooden spoon. Add the milk, a little at a time, continuing to stir to avoid lumps.

2. Switch now to a balloon whisk. Continue to stir over a medium heat until the sauce begins to thicken. The balloon whisk will also help eradicate any lumps that may have materialised. Add more milk as necessary to get the desired thickness. The sauce should be the thickness of custard.

3. Add the parsley and season with black pepper.

Bread Sauce

This is best when made with old or slightly stale bread. You can crumble the bread with your fingers to produce small pieces or, if you prefer a smoother sauce, whizz it into breadcrumbs (any unused breadcrumbs can be frozen until needed for other dishes).

1 onion, finely chopped
4 whole cloves
5–8 peppercorns
1–2 bay leaves
500ml milk
Seasoning to taste
50g–75g breadcrumbs (see above)
100ml single cream (optional)
A sprinkling of nutmeg

1. Place the onion, cloves, peppercorns, bay leaves and milk in a pan.
2. Slowly bring the milk to the boil and simmer gently for 5 minutes. Remove from the heat and leave to one side to infuse (this is great to leave while your roast is cooking).
3. About 5 minutes before you are ready to serve, reheat the milk gently. Remove the cloves, peppercorns and bay leaves. Season to taste before adding your crumbled bread, a little at a time until you get the desired consistency.
4. Remove from the heat, stir in the cream if you prefer a creamier consistency, sprinkle with nutmeg and serve.

Tomato and Herb Sauce

If I am making something with a tomato sauce base, I double up the recipe and then store half in the fridge. This can then be used as a pizza topping, pasta sauce or as an addition to any other savoury dish. Here is a basic recipe for you to add to.

Olive oil
2–3 cloves garlic, finely chopped
2 red onions, finely chopped
1kg tomatoes (I prefer fresh, ripe tomatoes, but you can use 2–3 tins of tomatoes)
½ red pepper, chopped
1–2 splashes of balsamic vinegar
1–2 splashes of red wine
A handful of fresh herbs, such as basil, thyme, oregano, or fresh frozen herb cubes
Seasoning to taste

1. Heat the olive oil in a pan and fry the garlic and onions until translucent.
2. Chop the tomatoes. (I never peel my tomatoes as I think it an unnecessary faff; however, if you prefer to peel them, take a sharp knife and lightly score the skins of the tomatoes. Place the tomatoes in a bowl of boiling water until the skins start to curl slightly. Remove from the water and peel off the skins before chopping.)
3. Add the tomatoes and red pepper to the onions. Cook for 1–2 minutes before adding the balsamic vinegar and red wine. Simmer gently for 10 minutes.
1. Add the herbs. Season to taste.

Pesto

I love pesto, and at almost £2 for a small jar, it is great to make your own, especially if you have some fresh herbs that need using up. This recipe uses the traditional basil leaves, but you can try coriander for a variation in flavour.

2–3 handfuls of basil
1–2 cloves garlic, crushed
25g pine nuts
25g Parmesan cheese
Olive oil
Seasoning to taste

1. I use a small food processor and mix all the ingredients together thoroughly. Add olive oil until you are happy with the consistency.
2. Leave to rest for 20–30 minutes to help enhance the flavours.
3. Serve with pasta, mashed potato, salads, dips, or even as a topping or marinade.

Gravy

I know most people tend to grab the gravy granules but home-made gravy really is simple – and delicious. Nothing beats the flavour of home-made onion gravy served with bangers and mash,. Here are some recipes to help motivate you.

Onion Gravy

A dash of oil (you can use the fat from a roast)
A small knob of butter
4 red onions
1 cloves garlic, crushed
5 tablespoons red wine vinegar (or balsamic will do)
1 tablespoon flour
1 teaspoon Marmite or yeast extract (optional)
350ml stock (Marigold vegetable stock is good)

1. Combine the oil and butter as this prevents the butter from burning, and fry the onions and garlic in a pan on a low heat until very soft – this usually takes about 15–20 minutes, so remember to allow this time when cooking your roast or bangers and mash.
2. Add the red wine vinegar and cook until this reduces to half the liquid.
3. When the onions and garlic are soft, stir in the flour and Marmite. Add the stock a bit at a time and stir well. Cook gently, allowing the gravy to thicken. You can add more water or stock if it is too thick.

Red Wine Gravy

1 tablespoon plain flour or cornflour
300ml hot meat stock (if roasting a joint, use meat juices for this)
2 teaspoons redcurrant jelly
300ml red wine
Seasoning to taste

1. Place the flour in a saucepan, add a little stock and stir well. Add the redcurrant jelly and continue to add more stock as the gravy thickens.
2. Add the wine and season to taste. Continue to cook until the gravy thickens to the desired consistency (this takes about 8–10 minutes).

Stocks

I will probably make good chefs cry but I don't often use stocks; I find water and a good selection of herbs and spices does the trick. However, there are certain dishes where stock really does add good flavour. It's better not to buy stock cubes – they contain far too much salt and tend to give all the food an overpowering salty taste. Instead, you can make your own stock using any leftover and past their best vegetables. Bottle it in the fridge or freeze it until required.

Vegetable Stock

There really is no recipe for stock – anything goes. I normally raid my vegetable drawer and pull out anything that is really no longer suitable for fresh vegetable dishes. I also include some of the bits of veg we would normally throw away, which I have saved up over a few days, as it still has lots of flavour. Don't use anything from the brassica family as it will make your stock smell – so no cauliflower, cabbage, broccoli etc.

1. Place your chosen ingredients in a stock pan and cover with water. Add any chosen herbs and seasoning.
2. Allow to simmer, and then reduce the heat to low and leave to cook on a very low heat for 1–2 hours.
3. Strain and retain the liquid. Bottle in the fridge for up to 4 days or freeze for up to 3 months.

Note: Use the same principle to make **Fish Stock** or **Meat Stock**. When making a meat or fish stock, you can use the bones of the carcasses and even the heads of the fish, so there is no waste. Add wine and vegetables to suit the stock you are making. If you are making a meat stock, stick to one animal or bird source. Remember to strain thoroughly before bottling. Label and date stock, especially if you are storing it in the freezer.

Pie and Mash Shop Liquor

My husband was raised in south-east London so is a big fan of the traditional Manzes Pie and Mash Shops. The pie liquor looks a bit dubious but tastes divine. Here is a variation to the traditional recipe.

25g butter
25g flour or cornflour
200ml water
100ml white wine
A large bunch of fresh parsley, finely chopped
Seasoning to taste

1. Melt the butter in a pan on a medium heat. Add the flour or

cornflour and stir continuously with a wooden spoon.

2. Gradually add the water, stirring well. When approximately half the water has been added, switch to a hand whisk. Keep stirring to remove any lumps.

3. Add the remaining water and wine and continue to stir.

4. Add the chopped parsley and season to taste.

5. Continue to heat the liquor until it starts to thicken. You don't want this too thick, it should be the consistency of gravy.

Butters

Butters can be used on fish, but also to add flavour to a jacket potato, bread, or even a soup. They can be made in advance and stored in an airtight container in the fridge (or in an old margarine container), or they can be frozen until needed. I have frozen them in silicone ice-cube trays as they are simple to remove and in handy-sized portions. Remember to label the butters clearly.

150g butter
1 tablespoon fresh herbs or 1–2 teaspoons dried

1. Mix the butter and herbs together thoroughly. Store in an airtight container until needed. If you want to use this immediately, wait at least 30 minutes to allow the butter to absorb the flavours of the herbs.

Garlic Butter

150g butter
2–3 garlic cloves, crushed
1 tablespoon fresh herbs or 1–2 teaspoons dried

1. Mix the butter, garlic and herbs together thoroughly.

2. Store in an airtight container until needed. If you want to use this immediately, wait at least 30 minutes to allow the butter to absorb the flavours.

Ginger and Lime Butter

150g butter
2.5cm knuckle of ginger, grated
Zest and juice of 1 lime
A touch of cayenne pepper (optional)

1. Mix the butter, ginger, lime and cayenne pepper together thoroughly.
2. Store in an airtight container until needed. If you want to use this immediately, wait at least 30 minutes to allow the butter to absorb the flavours.

Chilli Butter

150g butter
1–2 chillies, finely chopped
A dash of Tabasco sauce

1. Mix the butter, chillies and Tabasco together thoroughly.
2. Store in an airtight container until needed. If you want to use this immediately, wait at least 30 minutes to allow the butter to absorb the flavours.

Dips

Dips have become increasingly popular but can be expensive to buy ready made. Why not try to make your own. They are quick and easy and they can save you money.

Hummus

Both my sons are mad about hummus. Many years ago we went to a fabulous restaurant in Bromley with my husband's family. Orri asked for a hummus starter and was gobsmacked when out came a huge platter of chopped vegetables and fruit, alongside a large bowl of hummus. He ate it all up and declared it was the best meal he had ever had (which did not do much for my ego, I can tell you!). Tamlin, my younger son, has hummus every day (that and his other favourite, rice and beans!). He has hummus sandwiches for his school packed lunch, or we fill tiny containers with hummus and he takes some chopped veg and fruit. It is cheap, simple to make and packed with nutrients.

400g chickpeas (you can use canned)
2–3 tablespoons olive oil or flax oil (great to get some omega into your diet)
Juice of ½ lemon
2–4 cloves garlic, depending on personal taste
1 tablespoon tahini paste (made from sesame seeds)

1. Place all the ingredients into a blender and whizz until smooth. Add more lemon juice or olive oil until you get the desired consistency.
2. If you taste this and think it is not garlicky enough, don't be tempted to add more until you have let it rest for at least 20 minutes. Then taste again and add more if you think it needs it.
3. Store in an airtight container in the fridge. The hummus should last 3–4 days.

Pesto Hummus

400g chickpeas (you can use canned)
2–3 tablespoons olive oil or flax oil (great to get some omega into your diet)
Juice of ½ lemon
2–4 cloves garlic, depending on personal taste
1 tablespoon tahini paste (made from sesame seeds)
1 tablespoon pesto

1. Place all the ingredients into a blender and whizz until smooth. Add more lemon juice or olive oil until you get the desired consistency.
2. If you taste this and think it is not garlicky enough, don't be tempted to add more until you have let it rest for at least 20 minutes. Then taste again and add more if you think it needs it.
3. Store in an airtight container in the fridge. The hummus should last 3–4 days.

Red Pepper Hummus

400g chickpeas (you can use canned)
2–3 tablespoons olive oil or flax oil (great to get some omega into your diet)
Juice of ½ lemon
1 sweet red pepper
2–4 cloves garlic, depending on personal taste
1 tablespoon tahini paste (made from sesame seeds)

1. Place all the ingredients into a blender and whizz until smooth. Add more lemon juice or olive oil until you get the desired consistency.
2. If you taste this and think it is not garlicky enough, don't be tempted to add more until you have let it rest for at least 20 minutes. Then taste again and add more if you think it needs it.
3. Store in an airtight container in the fridge. The hummus should last 3–4 days.

Red Pepper and Chilli Hummus

400g chickpeas (you can use canned)
2–3 tablespoons olive oil or flax oil (great to get some omega into your diet)
Juice of ½ lemon
1 sweet red pepper
1 chilli, finely chopped
A dash of Tabasco sauce (optional – only if you like it very hot!)
2–4 cloves garlic, depending on personal taste
1 tablespoon tahini paste (made from sesame seeds)

1. Place all the ingredients into a blender and whizz until smooth. Add more lemon juice or olive oil until you get the desired consistency.
2. If you taste this and think it is not garlicky enough, don't be tempted to add more until you have let it rest for at least 20 minutes. Then taste again and add more if you think it needs it.
3. Store in an airtight container in the fridge. The hummus should last 3–4 days.

Lemon and Coriander Hummus

400g chickpeas (you can use canned)
2–3 tablespoons olive oil or flax oil (great to get some omega into your diet)
Juice and zest of ½ lemon
2–4 cloves garlic, depending on personal taste
1 tablespoon tahini paste (made from sesame seeds)
A handful of fresh coriander leaves

1. Place all the ingredients into a blender and whizz until smooth. Add more lemon juice or olive oil until you get the desired consistency.
2. If you taste this and think it is not garlicky enough, don't be tempted to add more until you have let it rest for at least 20 minutes. Then taste again and add more if you think it needs it.
3. Store in an airtight container in the fridge. The hummus should last 3–4 days.

Salsa

Salsa is another gem to help use up any unwanted items lurking in your fridge. If you don't know what to do with the handful of tomatoes, end of a cucumber or those two spring onions that have slipped behind the salad drawer, this is for you. I was watching Jamie Oliver on TV one day and he was using up some fresh tomatoes. He made a salsa, but used the same recipe to mix with spaghetti for an instant dish with a bit of a kick. I now do this at home and it works brilliantly.

2–3 tomatoes, chopped
5–7.5cm of cucumber, diced
1–2 chillies, finely chopped
½ of a red pepper, finely chopped
2–3 spring onions, finely chopped, including green stalks
1–2 cloves garlic, crushed
A dash of balsamic vinegar
A dash of olive oil
A dash of lemon or lime juice
Seasoning to taste

1. Mix all the ingredients together in a bowl. Add more balsamic vinegar, olive oil or lemon/lime juice to taste.
2. Leave to settle for at least 15 minutes, allowing the flavours to infuse.

Note: You can add more chillies, or even a splash of Tabasco sauce, according to your taste. Some people add chopped apple or other vegetables they may have in the fridge. I always use fresh tomatoes as I prefer the flavour and it is also a great way to use up any ripe tomatoes, but others find tinned are perfectly acceptable.

Slow-Baked Tomatoes

Strictly speaking this is not a sauce, dip or salsa, but I have placed it in the sauce chapter as I use it so often in a variety of meals. You can use this as a quick and easy pasta sauce, a topping for a pizza, an accompaniment to a meat, fish or vegetable dish or in a salad. The sweetness of the tomatoes alongside the hit of basil and garlic is truly heaven. I bake this in large batches, especially when I have ripe tomatoes that need using up, or if I see cherry tomatoes on special offer. You can then store it in jars (covered in olive oil) or in an airtight container in the fridge for one week maximum.

A batch of ripe tomatoes, halved
4 cloves garlic, crushed (more if preferred)
A sprinkle of balsamic vinegar
A drizzle of olive oil
A handful of fresh herbs

1. Preheat the oven to 50–100°C (very low).
2. Place the tomatoes in a baking tray. Sprinkle on the garlic and balsamic vinegar. Finish with a drizzle of olive oil.
3. Place in the oven for 2–3 hours.
4. When cooked, add a handful of fresh herbs. I prefer oregano or fresh basil.
5. Use or store as required.

Sour Cream and Chive

This is a great favourite, particularly with those who love dipping crisps or corn chips.

150g cream cheese
100ml sour cream
A handful of chives, chopped
A dash of lemon juice
Seasoning to taste

1. Place the cream cheese in a bowl and mix to soften. Add the sour cream and chives, with a little lemon juice if you prefer a creamier consistency.
2. Season to taste

Tzatziki Dip

1–2 cloves garlic, crushed (optional)
2 tablespoons olive oil or flax oil (great to get some omega into your diet)
500g thick low fat yoghurt (I use Total Greek Yoghurt)
2 teaspoons dried mint
5–7.5cm piece of cucumber, chopped into small cubes
1 tablespoon lemon juice

1. Place all the ingredients in a bowl and mix thoroughly.
2. If you prefer a lump-free dip, mash the cucumber with a fork before adding to the yoghurt mixture.

Pomegranate Molasses

This is great as a marinade. You can buy it in bottles from specialist shops – it is popular in Lebanese and Moroccan stores – or from specialist delis. But it's so easy to make, why not have a go and bottle it ready for use? If you store it in a sterilised jar it will keep for up to six months.

750ml pomegranate juice
100g sugar
250ml lemon juice

1. Place all the ingredients in a pan and simmer gently until the liquid has reduced by at least half.
2. Use immediately or bottle until required.

Fruit Sauce

I made this sauce one Christmas as a bit of an experiment to go with some pink pears. My mum loved it so it has become a bit of a family favourite.

2 teaspoons cornflour
250ml orange juice
Zest of 1 orange
1 teaspoon cinnamon
A little grated nutmeg
½ teaspoon vanilla essence

1. Mix the cornflour with 50ml of the juice. Stir well.
2. Gently heat the remaining juice and add all the other ingredients. Add the cornflour mix gradually. Stir continuously.
3. Cook on a low heat until the sauce is thick and smooth.
4. Serve with pies, fruit or crumble.

Buttermilk Alternative

Buttermilk is becoming increasingly popular, especially for making cakes or muffins. If you don't have buttermilk, you can make your own by warming some milk, adding a little lemon juice and leaving it at room temperature overnight. You can make this with any sort of milk, including skimmed, and even soya milk.

Sumptuous Salads

Salads shouldn't be prepared simply to provide a garnish to your dish; they can make delicious main meals in their own right. Experiment with different flavours, textures and colours. Create two or three salad dishes for one delicious main meal – the perfect way to bring some sunshine into your food, winter or summer.

Couscous and Mint Salad

SERVES 4 • COST OF INGREDIENTS: £1.34 • COST PER SERVING: 34p

200g couscous
A large bunch of fresh mint
Juice of ½ lemon
2 large ripe tomatoes, finely chopped
¼ length of cucumber, finely chopped
½ bunch of spring onions, finely chopped
Seasoning to taste

1. Following the instructions on the packet for exact quantity, add freshly boiled water to the couscous. Leave to absorb for 5–10 minutes.
2. Meanwhile, chop the remaining ingredients into small pieces ready to mix into the couscous.
3. Mix all the ingredients together in a bowl. Season to taste before serving.

Delicious Bitza Salad

Excuse the name but this really does use up any spare ingredients in your fridge to make bits of this and bits of that salad.

SERVES 4 • COST OF INGREDIENTS: £2.30 • COST PER SERVING: 58p

A selection of leaf lettuce
½ bunch spring onions, sliced
½ pepper, thinly sliced
4–5 mangetout or sugar snap peas, roughly chopped
4 eggs, boiled and halved
A handful of fresh chives and mint
50ml olive oil or omega-rich oil
Juice of ½ lemon
Seasoning to taste

1. Place the lettuce leaves in the base of a large serving bowl. Add the spring onions, pepper and mangetout/sugar snap peas.
2. Place the boiled egg halves over the lettuce leaves. Sprinkle with freshly chopped herbs.
3. To make a dressing, mix the oil, lemon juice and seasoning together. Drizzle over the salad just before serving.

Note: You can add just about any spare item from your fridge: cold meat, chopped tomatoes, tinned tuna or chunks of feta cheese. Experiment and make something out of nothing!

Rocket, Parmesan and Pomegranate Salad

I love the vibrant colour of pomegranate and, when it's combined with one of my favourite salads, I am truly in heaven.

SERVES 4 • COST OF INGREDIENTS: £3.50 • COST PER SERVING: 88p

100g rocket, washed
75g Parmesan cheese, shaved
I pomegranate
2 tablespoons balsamic vinegar
1 tablespoon olive oil or flax oil (great to get some omega into your diet)

1. Place the rocket and the Parmesan shavings in a bowl.
2. Cut the pomegranate in half and squeeze out the juice and seeds. An easy way to extract the seeds is to tap the bottom of the pomegranate. You may need to use a fork to help extract them, but try to avoid getting any pith in the salad. Add the juice and seeds to the salad leaves in the bowl.
3. Drizzle on the mixture of olive oil and balsamic vinegar. Serve and enjoy!

Tuna and Rocket Salad

SERVES 4 • COST OF INGREDIENTS: £5.22 • COST PER SERVING: £1.31

80g rocket leaves
1 red onion, sliced
½ red pepper, diced
12 cherry tomatoes
350g tinned tuna, drained and in chunks

For the dressing
3 tablespoons olive oil
2 tablespoon white wine vinegar
½ teaspoon Dijon mustard
Black pepper to taste

1. Place all the salad ingredients in a bowl and mix thoroughly.

2. To make the dressing, place all the dressing ingredients in a screw-top jar and shake well before drizzling over the salad. Serve immediately.

Tomato and Mozzarella Salad

This is one of my favourites, especially when I use fresh, juicy tomatoes just off the vine. It takes minutes to prepare. You can use olive oil for the dressing or, if you want to increase your Omega 3 intake, opt for healthy oils such as flax or Good Oil – rich in Omega 3, 6 and 9.

SERVES 4 • COST OF INGREDIENTS: £2.60 • COST PER SERVING: 65p

1 clove garlic, crushed
2 tablespoons fresh parsley, chopped
75ml olive or omega-rich oil
2 teaspoons balsamic vinegar
Black pepper to taste
450g mozzarella cheese (roughly 2 packs)
5 ripe tomatoes, sliced
1 red onion, finely chopped

1. Place the garlic and parsley in a bowl and add the oil. Mix thoroughly.
2. Add the balsamic vinegar,season to taste and leave to settle.
3. Drain the mozzarella and slice. Generously slice the tomatoes. Layer the mozzarella and tomatoes on a large serving dish. Cover with a sprinkling of red onion and season with black pepper.
4. Drizzle the oil dressing over the tomato and mozzarella salad and leave to rest for 10 minutes before serving.

Brown Rice, Lentil and Chicken Salad

SERVES 4 • COST OF INGREDIENTS: £6 • COST PER SERVING: £1.50

200g Puy lentils
600ml water
200g long-grain brown rice
1 onion, chopped
1 red pepper, chopped
6 spring onions, sliced
300g cooked chicken pieces
250g mushrooms, sliced
1 teaspoon thyme
2 tablespoons red wine vinegar
1 tablespoon balsamic vinegar
75ml olive oil
Seasoning to taste
75g chopped walnuts

1. Place the lentils, water and rice in a large saucepan and cook until the rice is tender. Drain of any excess fluid.
2. Meanwhile, in a large sauté pan, fry the onion in a little olive oil. Add the pepper and the spring onions and cook until soft.
3. Add the chicken, mushrooms and thyme. Cook until the chicken is reheated thoroughly.
4. In a small bowl, mix the wine vinegar, balsamic vinegar and olive oil together. Season to taste. If you like dressing with a bit of a kick you could add some chilli oil or Dijon mustard.
5. Combine the drained rice and lentils with the chicken mixture in one large serving dish. Mix in the chopped walnuts and pour over the dressing. Serve while still warm.

Green Bean and Cashew Stir-fry

I have included this with the salads as to me it is just like a hot salad – deliciously crunchy with a light tangy dressing.

SERVES 4 • COST OF INGREDIENTS: £4.50 • COST PER SERVING: £1.13

2 tablespoons dry sherry
1 tablespoon soy sauce
1 tablespoon red wine vinegar
6–8 spring onions, very finely chopped
1 stick of celery, very finely chopped
2 teaspoons sesame oil
2 cloves garlic, crushed
2 teaspoons grated ginger
1–2 fresh chillies, chopped
150g French beans, trimmed
150g mangetout
75g cashew nuts
1 teaspoon fresh coriander

1. Mix the sherry, soy sauce and red wine vinegar together and leave to stand.
2. Chop the spring onions and celery into small pieces. Heat the sesame oil in a wok or large sauté pan.
3. Add the spring onions, celery, garlic, ginger and chilli. Cook for 2 minutes.
4. Add the beans, mangetout and cashew nuts and cook for a further 2–3 minutes.
5. Pour over the sauce and toss the ingredients for 1 minute until covered. Add the coriander leaves and serve immediately.

Greek-style Salad

SERVES 4 • COST OF INGREDIENTS: £3.50 • COST PER SERVING: 88p

½ cucumber, in chunks
1 small red onion, sliced
75g olives
4 ripe tomatoes (ideally fresh home-grown)
A large handful of mixed lettuce leaves
A handful of fresh coriander, chopped
100g feta cheese, crumbled

For the dressing
75ml olive or flax oil (great to get some omega into your diet)
1 tablespoon red wine vinegar
1 teaspoon dried oregano
Black pepper to taste

1. Make the dressing by mixing the ingredients together thoroughly. Season to taste with black pepper.
2. Place all the remaining ingredients in a large bowl. Pour over the dressing when ready to serve.

Goats' Cheese, Brown Lentil and Rocket Salad

This is one of my absolute favourite salads. The flavours really complement each other and it is surprisingly filling.

SERVES 4 • COST OF INGREDIENTS: £4.69 • COST PER SERVING: £1.17

175g Puy lentils
100g rocket
1 small punnet of cherry tomatoes
1 red onion, sliced
125g goats' cheese, crumbled

For the dressing
2 tablespoon olive oil
2 tablespoon balsamic vinegar
Black pepper to taste

1. Cook the lentils in boiling water for 15 minutes until soft. Drain and leave to one side.
2. Meanwhile make the dressing. Mix the olive oil and balsamic vinegar together and season.
3. Place the rocket, tomatoes, onion, lentils and goats' cheese in a serving bowl. Stir well before pouring over the dressing.

Simple Puy Lentil Salad

I love Puy lentils and often cook this to add to a basic salad, ensuring that my family has some wonderful nutrients as well as a great taste.

SERVES 4 • COST OF INGREDIENTS: £1 • COST PER SERVING: 25p

250g Puy lentils
A drizzle or spray of olive oil
1 red onion, finely chopped
Zest and juice of ½ lemon
2–3 teaspoons dried mint

1. Cook the lentils in boiling water until they are tender but not soggy – this takes approximately 20 minutes.
2. Meanwhile, heat the oil in a frying pan and fry the onion until soft. Leave to one side.
3. Drain the lentils and return them to the saucepan. Add the onion, lemon zest and juice and the dried mint. Stir thoroughly.
4. You can serve this hot or cold.

Feta and Chickpea Salad

I enjoy making lots of different salads so people can dip in and out and choose what they prefer. This is a really easy dish and is perfect to accompany a variety of salad dishes. You can use freshly cooked or tinned chickpeas. It is ideal if you have cooked a batch of chickpeas for hummus or a casserole and have some left over.

SERVES 4 • COST OF INGREDIENTS: £4.20 • COST PER SERVING: £1.05

400g chickpeas (cooked or tinned)
100g fresh garden peas (you can use good-quality frozen)
6 spring onions, finely chopped, including the green stalks
Juice and zest of 1 lemon
200ml olive or flax oil (great to get some omega into your diet)
A handful of fresh mint, finely chopped
A handful of fresh parsley, finely chopped
2–3 teaspoons fresh chives, finely chopped
Seasoning to taste
250g feta cheese, crumbled

1. Place the cooked chickpeas, peas and spring onions in a bowl. Mix the lemon juice and zest, oil, herbs and seasoning together before pouring onto the chickpeas.
2. Leave to soak until ready to serve. Add the crumbled feta cheese just before serving.

Potato Salad

Potato salad is delicious, especially for picnics on summer days. It's great for using up leftover potatoes and any spare bits and pieces in the fridge. This is a basic recipe, but you can add cucumber, celery, boiled eggs, fresh peas or even bits of chicken or bacon. If you like it spicy, add some chopped chillies or even a dash of Tabasco sauce.

SERVES 4 • COST OF INGREDIENTS: £1.50 • COST PER SERVING: 38p

400g cooked potatoes, cubed, or if using new potatoes, halved
1 onion, finely chopped
1–2 tablespoons fresh mint, finely chopped
A handful of fresh chives, finely chopped
Juice of ½ lemon
2–3 tablespoons mayonnaise, ideally low fat
Seasoning to taste

1. Place the potatoes in a large bowl. Add all the remaining ingredients and stir well.
2. Season to taste.

Carrot and Ginger Coleslaw

This is very simple and made even easier by using your food processor to grate the carrot. It can be made in seconds and is ideal for barbecues, picnics or to add some colour to your salads.

SERVES 4 • COST OF INGREDIENTS: £1.80 • COST PER SERVING: 45p

3–4 carrots, grated
100g sultanas
50g chopped walnuts
2.5–5cm knuckle of fresh ginger
Juice and zest of ½ lemon
250g low fat natural yoghurt
Seasoning to taste

1. Place the carrots in a bowl. Add the sultanas and chopped walnuts and stir well.
2. Finely grate the ginger and add to the carrot mix. Add the lemon zest and juice and finally stir in the yoghurt.
3. Stir the mixture thoroughly and season to taste before serving.

Fruity Coleslaw

SERVES 4 • COST OF INGREDIENTS: £2.20 • COST PER SERVING: 55p

½ white cabbage, finely shredded
1 carrot, grated
1 apple, cored and chopped
2 sticks of celery, chopped
2–3 teaspoons lemon juice
50g sultanas
50g chopped walnuts
4 tablespoons Greek yoghurt or low fat mayonnaise
Black pepper to taste

1. Place the cabbage, carrot, apple and celery together in a bowl. Mix in the lemon juice.
2. Add the sultanas and walnuts. Stir well.
3. Add the yoghurt or mayonnaise, stir and season well before serving.

Green Snap Salad

I love the taste of mangetout and sugar snap peas and use them in my everyday salads to add taste and crunch. Experiment and enjoy.

SERVES 4 • COST OF INGREDIENTS: £3.90 • COST PER SERVING: 98p

200g mangetout
200g sugar snap peas
50g walnuts, chopped
75ml olive or omega-rich Good Oil
30ml white wine vinegar
Juice of ½ lemon
1–2 cloves garlic, crushed
2 teaspoons fresh tarragon, roughly chopped

1. Place the mangetout, sugar snap peas and walnuts in a bowl.
2. Combine the oil, white wine vinegar, lemon juice, garlic and tarragon together. Pour over the pea mixture and stir well.

Thai Beef Salad

This is a very simple dish. You can use up any leftover beef from a joint or use beef pieces. If you are feeling extravagant, you could use beef steak, grilled and then sliced into small strips.

SERVES 4 • COST OF INGREDIENTS: £3 • COST PER SERVING: 75p

1–2 chillies, depending on taste
1 stick of lemon grass, finely chopped
1–2 cloves garlic, crushed
2.5cm knuckle of ginger, finely chopped
Zest and juice of 2 limes
1–2 tablespoons Thai fish sauce
75g cooked beef, cut into strips
½ cucumber, cut into sticks
1 red onion, finely sliced
½ bunch of spring onions, thickly sliced at an angle
A handful of fresh coriander
A handful of fresh mint

1. Place the chillies, lemon grass, garlic, ginger, zest and juice of the limes and the fish sauce in a bowl and mix thoroughly.
2. Meanwhile, place the sliced beef, cucumber sticks and onions in a serving dish and mix thoroughly.
3. Pour over the chilli mixture and leave to infuse for 10 minutes. Just before serving garnish with fresh coriander and mint.

Avocado, Grapefruit and Feta Salad

SERVES 4 • COST OF INGREDIENTS: £2.80 • COST PER SERVING: 70p

- **Suitable for vegetarians**
- **Can be cooked in advance**

1 cos lettuce
½ cucumber, diced
½ bunch of spring onions, chopped
1 pink grapefruit, peeled and chopped
1 avocado, diced
100g feta cheese, crumbled
Fresh herbs to garnish

1. Place the lettuce leaves in the bottom of a serving bowl. Add the cucumber, spring onions, grapefruit and avocado and finish with the feta cheese.
2. Garnish with fresh herbs from the garden, such as chives, mint or parsley.

Traffic Light Salad with Citrus Dressing

SERVES 4 • COST OF INGREDIENTS: £2.60 • COST PER SERVING: 65p

300g green leaves of your choice: watercress, baby spinach, lettuce,
   endive etc.
2 carrots, finely grated
½ cucumber, diced
8 cherry tomatoes, halved
1 small red onion, thinly sliced
Juice of 1 orange
Juice of 1 lime
30g fresh basil, chopped
30g fresh dill, chopped
30g fresh cilantro, chopped
Seasoning to taste

1. Place the salad leaves in a serving bowl. Add the carrots,
cucumber, tomatoes and onion.
2. Mix the orange and lime juice together. Add the chopped onion
and herbs and season before pouring over the salad leaves just
prior to serving.

Roll out the Pastry

Pastry dishes are so British, aren't they? Think of apple pies or the cockney pie and mash shops. This book encompasses three main elements: healthy eating, eating on a budget, and family food. Some of these concepts can appear to contradict the others – is pastry healthy? Certainly, pastry – particularly puff pastry – is quite high in fat so, if you are watching your weight, limit the amount you eat. However, a home-made pasty for lunch is a healthier and cheaper option than a fast food takeaway and should sustain you for longer. It's really a question of balance: a home-made pie or pasty every now and again is a real treat and won't do you any harm, particularly if you use wholemeal or granary flour, which both make wonderful savoury pastry and are a healthier option.

I use several pastry variations: plain, wholemeal, granary, sweet and puff pastry. I tend to buy puff pastry ready made, but I always buy supermarket own brands, which are normally located in the freezer and are about a third of the price of the refrigerated ready-to-roll varieties.

Most of the pies and pastries in this chapter can be placed, uncooked, in the freezer, so it makes sense to double up the recipe and make one for the oven and one for the freezer. Remember to label and date the food before placing in the freezer.

Savoury Pastry

This is the basic method for shortcrust pastry. You can make it by hand or in a food processor. The amounts given will make enough pastry to serve 4–6 people. If you want a flaky pastry, freeze the butter, and then grate it into the flour. You can also substitute wholemeal, granary or malted flour, for a healthier option.

200g plain flour
100g cold butter
A little cold water

Hand method

Place the flour in a large bowl and add small pieces of the chilled butter. Using your fingertips, rub the butter into the flour until the whole mix resembles breadcrumbs. Add 5–6 tablespoons of cold water (a little at a time) and mix until it forms a dough. Wrap the dough in cling film and place in the fridge to cool until needed.

Food processor method

Place the flour and butter in a processor and whizz for a few seconds. Add 5–6 tablespoons of water, gradually, while the machine is on, until the mixture forms into a ball of dough. Wrap the dough in cling film and place in the fridge to cool until needed.

Cornish Pasties

As I am from the West Country, I could not miss the opportunity of including pasties!

The recipes below are easy to make. I have given you four recipes to choose from but you can create your own fillings if you like. You can also make more wholesome pasties by using wholemeal or multigrain flour. The recipes below make 4–6 pasties, but why not make mini pasties – ideal for kids or for quick snacks. Simply reduce the size of the pastry circle!

Traditional Cornish Pasties

MAKES 4 PASTIES • COST OF INGREDIENTS: £4.22

- **Can be frozen**
- **Can be cooked in advance**
- **Use up your leftovers**
- **Make 2, keep 1**

Shortcrust pastry (see above)
1 onion
1 carrot
1 potato
100g swede
350g lean rump steak
1 teaspoon paprika
1 teaspoon mixed herbs (optional)
Seasoning to taste

1. Preheat the oven to 210°C/gas mark 7.
2. Make the pastry as instructed above.
3. Chop the vegetables and steak into small dice-sized pieces.
4. Place in a bowl and mix thoroughly. Add the paprika and herbs and season well.
5. Roll out the pastry on a floured surface until even. Using a small round plate approximately 20cm in diameter as a template, cut 4 circles.
6. Place some of the steak and vegetable mix in the centre of each circle – do not overfill. Use beaten egg or water to brush the edges of the pastry before bringing the edges together and crimping until sealed.
7. Place the pasties on a lined baking tray. Brush with beaten egg and bake in the oven for 15 minutes until the pastry starts to turn golden. Reduce the heat to 150°C/gas mark 2 and cook for a further 30 minutes.

Corned Beef and Potato Pasties

MAKES 4–6 PASTIES • COST OF INGREDIENTS: £3.22

- **Can be frozen**
- **Can be cooked in advance**
- **Make 2, keep 1**

Shortcrust pastry (see page 209)
3–4 potatoes, cooked and mashed (you can use leftover mash for this)
350g or 1 tin of corned beef
1 onion, diced
1–2 teaspoons Worcestershire sauce
1 egg, beaten
Seasoning to taste

1. Preheat the oven to 200°C/gas mark 6.
2. Make the pastry as instructed on page 209.
3. Cook and mash the potatoes.
4. Place the corned beef, mashed potato and diced onion in a bowl and mix thoroughly. Add the Worcestershire sauce and beaten egg and season well.
5. Roll out the pastry on a floured surface until even. Using a small round plate approximately 20cm in diameter as a template, cut 4–6 circles.
6. Place some of the corned beef mix in the centre of each circle – do not overfill. Use beaten egg or water to brush the edges of the pastry before bringing the edges together and crimping until sealed.
7. Place the pasties on a lined baking tray. Brush with beaten egg and bake in the oven for 20–25 minutes, until the pastry is golden.

Cheese and Potato Pasties

MAKES 4–6 PASTIES • COST OF INGREDIENTS: £3.09

- **Suitable for vegetarians**
- **Can be frozen**
- **Can be cooked in advance**
- **Use up your leftovers**
- **Make 2, keep 1**

Shortcrust pastry (see page 209)
3–4 potatoes, cooked and mashed (or use leftover mash)
1 onion, diced
1 carrot, grated
125g mature Cheddar, grated
1 egg, beaten
1 teaspoon mixed herbs (optional)
Seasoning to taste

1. Preheat the oven to 200°C/gas mark 6.
2. Make the pastry as instructed on page 209.
3. Cook and mash the potatoes.
4. Place the potatoes, diced onion, grated carrot and cheese in a bowl and mix thoroughly. Add the beaten egg and herbs and season well.
5. Roll the pastry out on a floured surface until even. Using a small round plate approximately 20cm in diameter as a template, cut 4 to 6 circles.
6. Place some of the cheese and potato mixture in the centre of each circle – do not overfill. Use beaten egg or water to brush the edges of the pastry before bringing the edges together and crimping until sealed.
7. Place the pasties on a lined baking tray. Brush with beaten egg and bake in the oven for 20–25 minutes until the pastry is golden.

Cheese and Vegetable Pasties

MAKES 4–6 PASTIES • COST OF INGREDIENTS: £2.50

- **Suitable for vegetarians**
- **Can be frozen**
- **Can be cooked in advance**
- **Use up your leftovers**
- **Make 2, keep 1**

Shortcrust pastry (see page 209)
1 onion
1 carrot
1 potato
100g swede
125g mature Cheddar, grated
1 egg, beaten
1 teaspoon paprika
1 teaspoon mixed herbs (optional)
Seasoning to taste

1. Preheat the oven to 210°C/gas mark 7.

2 Make the pastry as instructed on page 209.

3. Chop the vegetables into small dice-sized pieces.

4. Place the vegetables in a bowl, add the cheese and egg and mix thoroughly. Add the paprika and herbs and season well.

5. Roll the pastry on a floured surface until even. Using a small round plate approximately 20cm in diameter as a template, cut 4 circles.

6. Place some of the vegetable mix in the centre of each circle – do not overfill. Use beaten egg or water to brush the edges of the pastry before bringing the edges together and crimping until sealed.

7. Place the pasties on a lined baking tray. Brush with beaten egg and bake in the oven for 15 minutes until the pastry starts to turn golden. Turn the oven down to 150°C/gas mark 2 and cook for another 30 minutes.

Sausage Rolls

You can make traditional sausage rolls with sausage meat or vegetarian sausage mix, as shown in the recipe below; or, for a change, try some of the spicier variations.

Traditional Sausage Rolls

- **Can be frozen**
- **Can be cooked in advance**
- **Make 2, keep 1**

Pastry (either puff pastry, page 222, or shortcrust, page 209)
Sausage meat
Beaten egg to glaze
A sprinkle of sesame seeds (optional)

1. Preheat the oven to 200°C/gas mark 6.
2. Roll your sausage meat into a thumb-thick length.
3. Roll out your pastry to the desired size and thickness (it should be just over twice as wide as your roll of sausage meat, and 1cm longer at each end).
4. Place the sausage mix 1–2cm from the long edge of the pastry.
5. Coat the edges of the pastry with beaten egg before folding it over the sausage meat. Press down firmly on the edge before cutting the sausage rolls to the desired length.
6. Place the sausage rolls on a baking tray. Brush with beaten egg and sprinkle with sesame seeds before baking in the oven for 20–25 minutes, until golden brown.

Variations

For a great variation to the standard sausage roll, mix some herbs with the sausage meat to create delicious **Herby Sausage Rolls.** If you like things hot, mix your sausage meat with some fresh chillies and a dollop of Tabasco sauce to create tempting **Hot, Hot, Hot Sausage Rolls.** Vegetarians can opt for any of the above by mixing with vegetarian sausage mix, or why not use one of the vegetarian burger mix ideas in 'Fast Food That's Good For You' to create your own veggie variation?

Spinach and Ricotta Sausage Rolls

COST OF INGREDIENTS: £3.56

- **Suitable for vegetarians**
- **Can be frozen**
- **Can be cooked in advance**
- **Make 2, keep 1**

Pastry (either puff pastry, page 222, or shortcrust, page 209)
300g fresh baby leaf spinach
1 tub of ricotta
75g mature Cheddar, grated
A sprinkle of grated nutmeg
Beaten egg to glaze
A sprinkle of sesame seeds (optional)

1. Preheat the oven to 200°C/gas mark 6.
2. Place the spinach in a colander and wash under hot water for a few seconds to help soften the leaves.
3. Mix the spinach and ricotta together with the cheese and a sprinkle of grated nutmeg.
4. Roll out your pastry to the desired size and thickness.
5. Place the spinach and ricotta mix 1–2cm from the edge of the pastry.
6. Coat the edges of the pastry with beaten egg before folding the pastry over the ricotta mix. Press down firmly on the edge before cutting the sausage rolls to the desired length.
7. Place the sausage rolls on a baking tray. Brush with beaten egg and sprinkle with sesame seeds before baking in the oven for 20–25 minutes until golden brown.

Revival of the Quiche

Quiche was very popular in the 1970s and still usually appears in most buffets. It was supposed to provide a balanced meal containing essential milk, egg and bacon. Today we are less reliant on the traditional quiche, but it is the inspiration for these great recipes for pies and tarts.

Among the recipes below you'll find some vegetarian and vegan suggestions. If you are a meat eater, don't discount these – they are very tasty and often cheaper than versions that contain meat. However, the beauty of these recipes is you can add whatever ingredients you wish. For example, Cheese and Spring Onion Quiche is great with some Parma ham or pancetta added. Once you are confident, experiment with your own creations.

Bacon and Egg Quiche

COST OF INGREDIENTS: £2.70

- **Can be frozen**
- **Can be cooked in advance**
- **Make 2, keep 1**

Shortcrust pastry (see page 209)
500g low fat cottage cheese
4 eggs, beaten
3 rashers of lean bacon, chopped
1 small onion, finely chopped
Seasoning to taste
1 tomato, sliced

1. Preheat the oven to 200°C/gas mark 6.
2. Make the pastry as instructed on page 209.
3. Roll out the pastry on a floured surface to the correct size and thickness to line a 23cm greased flan tin. Place a sheet of baking parchment over the pastry and cover with baking beans.
4. Bake in the oven for 10 minutes. Remove the baking beans and parchment and cook for a further 5 minutes. Remove the pastry case from the oven and turn the oven down to 180°C/gas mark 4.

5. Meanwhile, mix the cottage cheese and eggs together thoroughly. Add the bacon pieces and chopped onion. Season well before pouring into the pastry case.
6. Garnish with slices of tomato and bake in the oven for 30–35 minutes until golden and firm in the centre.

Quiche Lorraine

COST OF INGREDIENTS: £4.52

- **Can be frozen**
- **Can be cooked in advance**
- **Make 2, keep 1**

Shortcrust pastry (see page 209)
200ml milk
3 eggs
½ teaspoon mustard powder
A pinch of cayenne pepper
150g Gruyère cheese, grated
1 small onion, finely chopped
75g cooked ham or lean bacon, diced
Seasoning to taste

1. Preheat the oven to 200°C/gas mark 6.
2. Make the pastry as instructed on page 209.
3. Roll out the pastry on a floured surface to the correct size and thickness to line a 23cm greased flan tin. Place a sheet of baking parchment over the pastry and cover with baking beans.
4. Bake in the oven for 10 minutes. Remove the baking beans and parchment and cook for a further 5 minutes. Remove the pastry case from the oven and turn the oven down to 180°C/gas mark 4.
5. Meanwhile, mix the milk and eggs together thoroughly before adding the mustard powder and a tiny dash of cayenne pepper. Add the cheese, onion and bacon or ham. Season well before pouring into the pastry case.
6. Bake in the oven for 30–35 minutes until golden and the centre is firm.

Goats' Cheese, Pesto and Cherry Tomato Tart

COST OF INGREDIENTS: £3.39

• **Suitable for vegetarians**

Shortcrust pastry (see page 209)
200g low fat crème fraiche
3 eggs, beaten
3–4 teaspoons pesto
Seasoning to taste
125g goats' cheese, crumbled
150g cherry tomatoes, halved

1. Preheat the oven to 200°C/gas mark 6.
2. Make the pastry as instructed on page 209.
3. Roll out the pastry on a floured surface to the correct size and thickness to line a 23cm greased flan tin. Place a sheet of baking parchment over the pastry and cover with baking beans.
4. Bake in the oven for 10 minutes. Remove the baking beans and parchment and cook for a further 5 minutes. Remove the pastry case from the oven and turn the oven down to 180°C/gas mark 4.
5. Meanwhile, mix the crème fraiche, beaten eggs, pesto and seasoning together thoroughly and leave to one side.
6. Place the goats' cheese and cherry tomatoes in the bottom of the pastry case. Pour over the crème fraiche mix.
7. Bake in the oven for 30–40 minutes until golden.

Cheese and Spring Onion Quiche

COST OF INGREDIENTS: £3.14

- **Suitable for vegetarians**
- **Can be frozen**
- **Can be cooked in advance**
- **Make 2, keep 1**

Shortcrust pastry (see page 209)
200g low fat crème fraiche
100g low fat single cream
4 eggs, beaten
100g mature Cheddar, grated
1 bunch spring onions, including green stalks, chopped
Seasoning to taste

1. Preheat the oven to 200°C/gas mark 6.

2. Make the pastry as instructed on page 209.

3. Roll out the pastry on a floured surface to the correct size and thickness to line a 23cm greased flan tin. Place a sheet of baking parchment over the pastry and cover with baking beans.

4. Bake in the oven for 10 minutes. Remove the baking beans and parchment and cook for a further 5 minutes. Remove the pastry case from the oven and turn the oven down to 180°C/gas mark 6.

5. Meanwhile, mix the crème fraiche, cream and eggs together thoroughly. Add the grated cheese and spring onions, including the green stalks. Season well before pouring into the pastry case.

6. Bake in the oven for 30–35 minutes until golden.

Tofu Quiche

This quiche is one of my favourites and it is a big hit with meat eaters as well as vegetarians – most don't realise they are eating tofu! It can be adapted for vegans (see below for ingredient substitutions if needed). It is also very simple to make and there's no risk of a soggy, eggy middle that some quiche recipes can suffer from!

COST OF INGREDIENTS: £3.10

- **Suitable for vegetarians**
- **Can be frozen**
- **Can be cooked in advance**
- **Make 2, keep 1**

Shortcrust pastry (see page 209)
1 onion, finely chopped
1 box tofu, mashed
125g mature Cheddar, grated (you can use vegan Cheddar if you want a vegan quiche)
1 tablespoon Marigold Nutritional Yeast Flakes (optional but gives a cheesier taste and is full of B vitamins)
Seasoning to taste

1. Preheat the oven to 200°C/gas mark 6.
2. Make the pastry as instructed on page 209.
3. Roll out the pastry on a floured surface to the correct size and thickness to line a 23cm greased flan tin. Place a sheet of baking parchment over the pastry and cover with baking beans.
4. Bake in the oven for 10 minutes. Remove the baking beans and parchment and cook for a further 5 minutes. Remove the pastry case from the oven and turn the oven down to 180°C/gas mark 6.
5. Meanwhile mash the tofu thoroughly. Add grated cheese, onion and nutritional yeast flakes if using. If the mixture is too dry, add a dash of milk and mix well. Season well before pouring into the pastry case. Cover with a sprinkling of grated cheese before placing in the oven.
6. Bake in the oven for 30 minutes until golden.

Goats' Cheese and Red Onion Tarts

You can use savoury shortcrust pastry (as shown in the basic recipe at the start of this chapter), or you could buy a sheet of puff pastry and roll it out (this is more expensive so buy unbranded frozen, not ready-to-roll refrigerated).

COST OF INGREDIENTS: £1.80

- **Suitable for vegetarians**
- **Can be cooked in advance**

Shortcrust pastry (see page 209)
A drizzle or spray of olive oil
1 large red onion, sliced
A splash of balsamic vinegar
A splash of red wine or sherry
2–3 teaspoons sugar
125g goats' cheese, crumbled
Black pepper

1. Preheat the oven to 180°C/gas mark 4.
2. Heat a little oil in a pan and fry the onion until soft.
3. Add the balsamic vinegar, wine or sherry, and sugar and cook on a low heat until the mixture starts to caramelise. Don't let it burn!
4. If you are using savoury pastry, you can fill individual tart cases, or one 23cm flan case. If using puff pastry, simply roll out to the desired thickness and place the filling in the middle of the pastry, leaving at least 1cm around the outside of the pastry. This will naturally form a crust when baking.
5. Fill the pastry cases with the red onion layer, followed by the cheese and a garnish of black pepper.
6. Bake in the oven for 15–20 minutes until golden.

Puff Pastry

I am a big fan of puff pastry, but don't overdo it; it's not too good for the waistline. I have made my own but I find ready-made is so much easier – a girl is allowed to cheat occasionally! However, I always buy the supermarket own brand which is normally located in the freezer and is about a third of the price of the refrigerated ready-to-roll varieties. It is a great standby and produces near-perfect results every time.

Mozzarella and Cherry Tomato Tarts

These take minutes to prepare and look much more impressive than they really are. You can either make one large tart, or individual ones. Here I have given the recipe for 6 individual tarts.

COST OF INGREDIENTS: £2.80

- **Cheat alert!**
- **Suitable for vegetarians**
- **Can be cooked in advance**

1 pack of ready-made puff pastry
1 pack of mozzarella
A handful of basil leaves
8–10 cherry tomatoes
Seasoning to taste

1. Preheat the oven to 200°C/gas mark 6.
2. Roll out the pastry 2–3mm thick.
3. Cut into 6 squares. Carefully score around the edge of each square, 1cm from the edge of the pastry – do not cut the pastry, just make a slight indent.

4. Place pieces of mozzarella and a few leaves of basil inside the scored line. Add a few cherry tomatoes, halved or whole, depending on your preference. Season to taste and bake in the oven for about 15 minutes until the pastry is golden.

5. Before serving, add a garnish of basil leaves.

Variations

Pizza Puffs – make the pastry as above then spread a layer of pasta sauce or tomato purée over the pastry square (staying within the 1cm edge). Add pizza topping ingredients such as onion and peppers and finish with cheese. Bake in the oven for 15 minutes and serve hot.

Red Onion and Goats' Cheese Tarts – make the pastry as above, remembering to mark it 1cm from the edge. Add a filling of red onion marmalade, or make your own red onion mixture: fry some chopped red onions until soft, add a splash of red wine, balsamic vinegar and a teaspoon of sugar and cook until reduced. Cover the red onion filling with goats' cheese and season with black pepper. Bake in the oven for 15 minutes and serve hot.

Tuna and Sweetcorn Puff Tarts – make the pastry as above, remembering to mark it 1cm from the edge. Fill with red onion marmalade or mixture as above. Bake in the oven for 15 minutes until golden. While the tarts are baking, mix some tuna, mayonnaise and sweetcorn together. When the tarts come out of the oven, fill the cases with tuna mix and serve.

Roasted Vegetables and Feta Tart – roll out the pastry for 1 large tart and roll the edges inwards to form a crust/edge. Place roasted vegetables and squares of feta cheese in the centre of the tarts. Garnish with herbs before baking in the oven for 20–25 minutes.

Sausage and Herb en Croûte

My mum used to make this when we were children – although it did not have the posh 'en croûte' name then! En croûte basically means wrapped in pastry and baked – simple. This recipe is made with puff pastry.

COST OF INGREDIENTS: £3.21

- **Cheat alert!**
- **Can be frozen**
- **Can be cooked in advance**
- **Make 2, keep 1**

1 pack of ready-made puff pastry
500g quality lean sausage meat
1 onion, chopped
2–3 teaspoons mixed herbs
1 egg, beaten
A sprinkle of sesame seeds (optional)

1. Preheat the oven to 200°C/gas mark 6.
2. Roll out the pastry 2–3mm thick.
3. Mix the sausage meat, onion and herbs together in a bowl and form into a thick sausage shape.
4. Roll out the pastry into a rectangle three times the width of your roll of sausage meat, and 5cm longer at each end
5. Place the sausage meat roll in the centre of the pastry, allowing at least 5–7.5cm of pastry either side of the meat.
6. Brush the egg over the exposed pastry – you will use this pastry to fold over the sausage meat (see below).
7. Using a sharp knife, cut the pastry into 5cm-wide strips, either side of the sausage meat, stopping about 2.5–3cm away from the sausage meat.
8. Fold the top and bottom ends of the pastry over the sausage meat, leaving the pastry strips free.
9. Moisten the ends of the pastry strips and fold these strips over the sausage meat, alternating from one side of the sausage meat to the other, to form a pleated pattern.
10. Ensure the pastry is secure and the whole of the sausage meat is covered.

11. Brush with any remaining egg or milk and sprinkle with herbs or sesame seeds if you like. Bake in the oven for 30–40 minutes until golden.

12. Serve hot or cold.

Cheating Cheesy Straws

I am a big fan of the TV chefs the Hairy Bikers, and this idea came from their BBC show. It is a great idea and creates light straws with little effort.

COST OF INGREDIENTS: £1.95

- **Cheat alert!**
- **Suitable for vegetarians**
- **Can be frozen**
- **Can be cooked in advance**
- **Make 2, keep 1**

1 pack of ready-made puff pastry
100g mature Cheddar, grated
A handful of dried onions
A sprinkle of freshly chopped chives (optional)

1. Preheat the oven to 200°C/gas mark 6.

2. Roll out the pastry 2–3mm thick, as if you were making a pie.

3. Sprinkle with some of the cheese, onions and chives and carefully fold in half.

4. Sprinkle with more cheese, onions and chives and fold again. If possible, do this once more.

5. Carefully roll out the pastry again to the same thickness as before. If the filling falls out, just replace it.

6. Once rolled, cut the pastry into thin strips. You can give these a little twist before placing them on a lined baking tray.

7. Bake in the oven for 15 minutes until golden. Leave on the tray for 5 minutes before transferring the straws to your cooling rack.

Variations

Bacon and Cheese Straws – add bacon or pancetta for added flavour.

Marmite Straws – spread the pastry with yeast extract before each fold.

Stilton Straws – use Stilton instead of Cheddar for extra cheesy zing.

Chilli Straws – add a sprinkle of paprika and chilli powder to each layer. For added kick, sprinkle with a few finely chopped chillies.

Garlic Butter Straws – mix some butter, crushed garlic and mixed herbs together. Spread thinly over each layer before folding.

Chocolate Straws – chocolate lovers can spread the pastry with chocolate spread, or sprinkles of dark chocolate chips, before each fold.

Cinnamon Straws – add a generous sprinkling of cinnamon and mixed fruit (sultanas or raisins) before each fold.

Filo Pastry

Filo pastry always looks so dramatic and impressive when the reality is very different. It is really child's play to create delicious snacks and pies. When Christmas approaches, I normally spend an afternoon listening to my favourite radio station while creating some savoury and sweet pastry snacks. I don't bake them; I simply freeze them once created. When the time comes, or friends call unexpectedly, I can look like the unfazed domestic goddess (in my dreams!) and bake tasty snacks without breaking into a sweat.
Filo pastry consists of very thin layers of pastry. Placing a little melted butter between each sheet creates a light and crunchy pastry.

Stilton, Leek and Mushroom Filo Parcels

COST OF INGREDIENTS: £2.40

- **Suitable for vegetarians**
- **Can be frozen**
- **Can be cooked in advance**
- **Make 2, keep 1**

Ready-made filo pastry sheets, defrosted
50g butter
1–2 leeks
6–8 chestnut mushrooms, halved
50–75g Stilton or blue cheese
Black pepper

1. Preheat the oven to 200°C/gas mark 6.
2. Melt the butter gently in a pan. Fry the leeks and mushrooms for 5 minutes.
3. Drain and retain the melted butter.
4. Place your filo sheets on a floured work surface. Cut into 15cm squares; you will need roughly 5 x 15cm squares per parcel.
5. Lay the first square on a floured surface. Brush with the melted butter. Add the next layer slightly at an angle to the first, so that

you create an 8-point star shape. Continue layering and brushing with butter like this until all 5 sheets are in place. You will end up with a rough star shape.

6. Place a little of the mushroom/leek mixture in the middle, season with black pepper and add a couple of small chunks of cheese.

7. Gather all the edges of the pastry together to form a sack. Press the edges together at the base of the sack (to look as if you have tied the sack), leaving some filo pastry edges to flare out at the top. You may need to dab with some melted butter to help secure.

8. Place these on a tray lined with baking parchment and freeze them. When they are frozen, transfer them into bags or a container. Freezing the parcels before placing them in a container or bag prevents them from sticking together and helps them keep their shape.

9. When you are ready, simply remove the parcels from the freezer and bake in the oven for 20 minutes until golden.

Spinach and Ricotta Filo Parcels

COST OF INGREDIENTS: £3.03

- **Suitable for vegetarians**
- **Can be frozen**
- **Can be cooked in advance**
- **Make 2, keep 1**

Ready-made filo pastry sheets, defrosted
50g butter
200g baby leaf spinach
1 tub of ricotta cheese
½ onion, finely chopped
Black pepper
Nutmeg

1. Preheat the oven to 200°C/gas mark 6.

2. Melt the butter gently in a pan.

3. Meanwhile place the spinach in a colander under hot running water for 2–3 seconds to help soften the leaves.

4. Mix the ricotta, spinach and onion together. Season with black pepper and nutmeg.

5. Place your filo sheets on a floured work surface. Cut into 15cm squares; you will need roughly 5 x 15cm squares per parcel.

6. Lay the first square on a floured surface. Brush with the melted butter. Add the next layer slightly at an angle to the first, so that you create an 8-point star shape. Continue layering and brushing with butter like this until all 5 sheets are in place. You will end up with a rough star shape.

7. Place a little of the ricotta mixture in the middle.

8. Gather all the edges of the pastry together to form a sack. Press the edges together at the base of the sack (to look as if you have tied the sack), leaving some filo pastry edges to flare out at the top. You may need to dab with some melted butter to help secure.

9. Place these on a tray lined with baking parchment and freeze them. When they are frozen, transfer them into bags or a container. Freezing the parcels before placing them in a container or bag prevents them from sticking together and helps them keep their shape.

10. When you are ready, simply remove from the freezer and bake in the oven for 20 minutes until golden.

Salmon and Spinach Filo Parcels

COST OF INGREDIENTS: £5.37

- **Can be frozen**
- **Can be cooked in advance**
- **Make 2, keep 1**

Filo pastry sheets
50g butter
150g baby leaf spinach
300g salmon fillets (you can use tinned salmon)
1 small tub of ricotta or cream cheese
2–3 spring onions, finely chopped
Black pepper

1. Melt the butter gently in a pan.

2. Meanwhile place the spinach in a colander and run under a hot tap for 2–3 seconds to help soften the leaves.

3. Mix the spinach, salmon, ricotta or soft cheese and spring onions together. Season with black pepper.

4. Place your filo sheets on a floured work surface. Cut into 15cm squares; you will need roughly 5 x 15cm squares per parcel.

5. Lay the first square on a floured surface. Brush with the melted butter. Add the next layer slightly at an angle to the first, so that you create an 8-point star shape. Continue layering and brushing with butter like this until all 5 sheets are in place. You will end up with a rough star shape.

6. Place a little of the salmon mixture in the middle. Gather all the edges of the pastry together to form a sack. Press the edges together at the base of the sack (to look as if you have tied the sack), leaving some filo pastry edges to flare out at the top. You may need to dab with some melted butter to help secure.

7. Place these on a tray lined with baking parchment and freeze them. When they are frozen, transfer them into bags or a container. Freezing the parcels before placing them in a container or bag prevents them from sticking together and helps them keep their shape.

8. When you are ready, simply remove from the freezer and bake in the oven for 20 minutes until golden.

Sweet Pastry

Pastry offers endless possibilities for making gorgeous desserts and sweet dishes. The favourite – and probably the quickest and easiest – is a sweet pie. Here are some of my family favourites. Double up the amounts for the recipes and make two. You can freeze one, uncooked, ready for the uninvited guest or for a pudding on a day when you don't feel like cooking. Remember to label and date the food before placing in the freezer.

Apple, Sultana and Cinnamon Pie

COST OF INGREDIENTS: £2.70

- **Suitable for vegetarians**
- **Can be frozen**
- **Can be cooked in advance**
- **Make 2, keep 1**

For the pastry
250g plain flour
125g butter
25g caster sugar or icing sugar
2 teaspoons cinnamon powder
Zest and juice of 1 orange

For the filling
1kg cooking apples, peeled and sliced
50g sultanas
A sprinkle of cinnamon powder
25–50g sugar
1 egg for glazing

1. Preheat the oven to 190°C/gas mark 5.
2. It is easier to make the pastry with a food processor. Add the flour, butter, caster or icing sugar, cinnamon, zest of the orange and whizz for a couple of seconds. Add the orange juice slowly until the dough forms. Place the dough in the fridge to cool for 5 minutes.

3. Roll out ½ of the pastry on a floured board to the desired size and thickness to line your pie dish. To scoop up the pastry without breaking it, flip one end over the rolling pin and roll it back. To line the pastry dish, simply unroll it over the dish.

4. Press the pastry down firmly around the bottom of the dish and the sides. To trim, hold the dish and use a knife to remove excess dough. To avoid a soggy bottom to your pie, place a sheet of baking parchment over the pastry and cover with baking beans. Cook the base for 10 minutes, then take the pastry out of the oven and remove the baking beans and parchment. Alternatively, sprinkle some ground semolina over the pastry base.

5. Layer the apple slices in the pie dish with the sultanas and sprinkle with cinnamon to taste. Sprinkle over the sugar.

6. Roll out the remaining pastry to the desired size and thickness to make a top crust for your pie. Brush some egg over the edges of the pastry base to help secure the lid. Place the pastry over the pie base and crimp/secure the edges.

7. Brush with egg and sprinkle with sugar before baking in the oven for 30–40 minutes until golden.

8. Serve with a dollop of crème fraiche or low fat yoghurt – delicious!

Note: You can top with puff pastry to make a lighter pie topping or make a lattice pattern over the filling with strips of pastry instead of a full crust to your pie.

Apple and Blackberry Pie

This is a wonderful way of using up freshly picked blackberries.

COST OF INGREDIENTS: £2.30 if using home-picked blackberries

- **Suitable for vegetarians**
- **Can be frozen**
- **Can be cooked in advance**
- **Make 2, keep 1**

For the pastry
250g plain flour
25g caster sugar or icing sugar
125g butter
1 egg, beaten

For the filling
1kg cooking apples, peeled and sliced
200g blackberries
25–50g sugar

1. Preheat the oven to 190°C/gas mark 5.

2. It is easier to make the pastry with a food processor. Add the flour, caster or icing sugar and butter and whizz for a couple of seconds. Add the egg slowly until the dough forms. You may only use half the egg, so leave whatever is left to one side to use to coat the pie. Place the dough in the fridge to cool for 5 minutes.

3. I prefer apples in a pie to have a slight bite to them so, to avoid a soggy mush, I tend to put the apples and blackberries straight into the pie (as below). However, if you prefer, you can place the fruit in a pan with a very small amount of water and cook for 10 minutes on a medium heat until soft.

4. Roll out ½ of the pastry on a floured board to the desired size and thickness to line your pie dish. To scoop up the pastry without breaking it, flip one end over the rolling pin and roll it back. To line the pastry dish, simply unroll it over the dish.

5. Press the pastry down firmly around the bottom of the dish and the sides. To trim, hold the dish and use a knife to remove excess dough. To avoid a soggy bottom to your pie, place a sheet of baking parchment over the pastry and cover with baking beans. Cook the base for 10 minutes, then take the pastry out of the oven and remove the baking beans and parchment. Alternatively, sprinkle some ground semolina over the pastry base.

6. Place the apples and blackberries in the pie dish. Sprinkle over the sugar. Roll out the remaining pastry to the desired size and thickness to make a top crust for your pie. Brush some egg over the edges of the pastry base to help secure the lid. Place the pastry over the pie base and crimp/secure the edges.

7. Brush with remaining egg and sprinkle with sugar before baking in the oven for 30–40 minutes until golden.

8. Serve with a dollop of crème fraiche or low fat yoghurt – delicious!

Simple Cheating Eccles Cakes

These were my dad's favourite when I was growing up. I never really liked them when I was a child – along with garibaldi biscuits, we thought they were packed with dead flies! I have matured since then and I really love these. They don't last long in our home, so here is a very fast and easy recipe to suit the craving.

COST OF INGREDIENTS: £1.20

- **Cheat alert!**
- **Suitable for vegetarians**
- **Can be frozen**
- **Can be cooked in advance**
- **Make 2, keep 1**

½ pack of ready-made puff pastry
½ small jar of mincemeat
25g butter, melted
A sprinkling of brown sugar

1. Preheat the oven to 190°C/gas mark 5.
2. Roll out the puff pastry to about 4–5mm thick. Cut into squares, approximately 15–20cm square.
3. Place 2–3 teaspoons of mincemeat in the centre of each pastry square.
4. Using a pastry brush, brush melted butter around the edges of the square. I normally fold diagonally, bringing each corner to the centre to form an envelope/parcel. Alternatively, you can simply fold over and secure either to form a rectangle or a triangle.
5. On a floured surface, turn cakes over so the seam is on the bottom. Apply a bit of pressure with your rolling pin or fingers and gently roll the cakes flat, taking care not to split the pastry.
6. Using a sharp knife, score 2–3 slits in the top of the cakes. Brush with butter and a sprinkle of brown sugar.
7. Bake in the oven for 15 minutes until golden.

Jam Turnovers

If I am making some Eccles cakes, my younger son usually demands to help and inevitably wants to make Jam Turnovers. The recipe is similar to the above so I would suggest, to save time and money, that you make them both together.

COST OF INGREDIENTS: 75p

- **Cheat alert!**
- **Suitable for vegetarians**
- **Can be frozen**
- **Can be cooked in advance**
- **Make 2, keep 1**

½ pack of ready-made puff pastry
Jam of your choice
Beaten egg or milk

1. Preheat the oven to 190°C/gas mark 5.
2. Roll out the puff pastry to about 4–5mm thick. Cut into squares, approximately 15–20cm square.
3. Place 2–3 teaspoons of jam in the centre of each pastry square.
4. Using a pastry brush, brush the milk or egg around the edges of the square. I normally fold diagonally to form a triangle. Secure the edges by crimping.
5. Bake in the oven for 15 minutes until golden.

Apple Turnovers

These are great if you have any spare puff pastry or stewed apple to use up. Stewed apple is easiest, but you can simply slice some cooking apples into the centre of the pastry, add some sugar and off you go.

COST OF INGREDIENTS: £1.30

- **Cheat alert!**
- **Suitable for vegetarians**
- **Can be frozen**
- **Can be cooked in advance**
- **Make 2, keep 1**

½ pack of ready-made puff pastry
Stewed apple, or 2 cooking apples, finely sliced
Brown sugar to sprinkle
Cinnamon to sprinkle
Beaten egg or milk

1. Preheat the oven to 190°C/ gas mark 5.
2. Roll out the puff pastry to about 4–5mm thick. Cut into squares, approximately 15–20in square.
3. Place 2–3 teaspoons of stewed apple or apple slices in the centre of each pastry square. If using apple slices, add a sprinkle of sugar and cinnamon to taste.
4. Using a pastry brush, brush a little milk or egg around the edges of the square. I normally fold diagonally to form a triangle. Secure the edges by crimping.
5. Brush with milk or egg and sprinkle with brown sugar.
6. Bake in the oven for 15 minutes until golden.

French Prune Tart

My Great-Aunt Sylvia provided this recipe (thank you!). It is quite decadent and the pastry is lovely – though it does have more fat than traditional pastry. If you are concerned about your fat intake, swap this for a lighter pastry. This is baked in a 25–30cm flan dish and serves up to 8 people.

COST OF INGREDIENTS: £4

- **Suitable for vegetarians**
- **Can be cooked in advance**

For the pastry
225g plain flour
75g semolina
50g caster sugar
150g unsalted butter
2 eggs, beaten

For the filling
250g Californian pitted prunes
120g dried, ready-to-eat apricots
50g unsalted butter, melted
75g light brown sugar
3 tablespoons Amaretto liqueur

1. Preheat the oven to 180°C/gas mark 4.
2. To help plump up the fruit, place in a bowl and cover with warm water while you prepare the pastry.
3. Place the flour in a bowl with the semolina and sugar. Rub in the butter to form breadcrumbs. Add the eggs and mix to form a dough.
4. Place in the fridge to cool until ready to use.
5. To make the filling, pour the melted butter into the base of your flan dish. Sprinkle over the brown sugar.
6. Drain your fruit and arrange in the dish. Spoon over the liqueur.
7. Roll out your pastry large enough to cover the flan dish. Carefully press down around the edges of the fruit to secure.
8. Bake in the oven for 20 minutes; reduce the heat to 150°C/gas mark 2 and cook for another 20 minutes.
9. Allow to stand for 10 minutes before turning out onto a serving plate.
10. Serve with yoghurt or low fat crème fraiche.

Just Desserts

I absolutely adore puddings, particularly zesty desserts that leave your taste buds tingling. Here are some favourites that are easy to make, and not too naughty!

Summer Pudding

For ease of pricing, I have priced this pudding using mixed frozen summer fruits. During the berry season, you should be able to reduce this price.

SERVES 4 • COST OF INGREDIENTS: £2.20 • COST PER SERVING: 55p

- **Suitable for vegetarians**
- **Can be cooked in advance**

500g of mixed berries (strawberries, raspberries, blueberries, cherries, blackberries – you can use frozen mixed fruit)
50g golden caster sugar
6 slices bread

1. Heat the fruit and sugar very gently in a saucepan for 2–3 minutes until the sugar is dissolved. Make sure the fruit does not lose it shape. Remove from the heat.
2. Drain off some of the fruit juice and leave to one side.
3. Meanwhile line a 1.2 litre pudding basin with the bread slices, ensuring that there are no gaps and the edges overlap.
4. Place the fruit mixture into the basin. Cover with a layer of bread to help seal the top.
5. Place a saucer over the basin – ideally, one that fits inside the basin rim – and press down gently. Place a weight onto the saucer to keep the shape of the pudding and chill overnight.
6. When you are ready, turn the pudding onto a serving plate and drizzle with the remaining fruit juice.
7. Serve with crème fraiche.

No Messing Rice Pudding

Most people cook rice pudding in the oven, but I find making it in a saucepan so much easier. I have also prepared it in a slow cooker – though don't do this in a crockery slow cooker as you may find the flavour of garlic from your savoury dishes will taint your pudding – yuck!

I make this with soya milk as I prefer not to have too much dairy, but you can use any milk you like. Full fat adds creaminess, or stir in some double cream prior to serving. If you want to use soya milk, try stirring in some Alpro soya alternative to cream – surprisingly, it gives the same result as cream.

SERVES 4 • COST OF INGREDIENTS: 98p • COST PER SERVING: 25p

- **Suitable for vegetarians**
- **Can be cooked in advance**

75g pudding rice or Arborio risotto rice
1 litre of milk (see above)
2–3 teaspoons cinnamon
1–2 teaspoons pure vanilla extract
25g sugar

1. Place all the ingredients into a heavy-based pan – make sure this pan is at least a third larger in volume than the contents.
2. Cook the rice on a low heat until soft, stirring occasionally to avoid the rice sticking to the base of your pan. The rice will thicken and you may have to add more liquid. This should take 20–30 minutes on a hob, or longer if you are using a slow cooker.
3. Prior to serving, you can stir in some cream (see above) if you like. Spoon the pudding into bowls and sprinkle with nutmeg.

Note: My family love a **Raspberry Rice Pudding Brûlée.** I place some raspberries in the base of an ovenproof dish (or mini ramekin dishes), add rice pudding and finish with a sprinkle of brown sugar. I then use my cook's blow torch to caramelise the top (you can get a similar effect by placing under the grill but it does take longer). This also works with other leftover fruit. Another favourite is **Rhubarb and Ginger Rice Pudding Brûlée.**

Using the same technique as above, place rhubarb chunks in the base of the ramekins or ovenproof dish. Add a sprinkle of fresh grated ginger to the rhubarb – be careful as it can give quite a kick! Cover with rice pudding and sprinkle with brown sugar before caramelising as above. Lovely!

Simple Baked Apples

This is a delicious and very simple autumnal pudding that always leaves people satisfied. You can stuff the apples with whatever you fancy, but I tend to cheat and add a generous dollop of mincemeat, or if there is none in the store cupboard, I will fill them with a mixture of dried fruit and a sprinkle of brown sugar.

SERVES 4 • COST OF INGREDIENTS: £1.80 • COST PER SERVING: 45p

• **Suitable for vegetarians**

4 Bramley apples, cored but not peeled
Mincemeat, or mixed dried fruit
Brown sugar

1. Preheat the oven to 180°C/gas mark 4.
2. Wash and core your apples, leaving the skins intact.
3. Place the apples on a baking tray or ovenproof dish.
4. Fill the empty cores with mincemeat or dried fruit. Finish with a sprinkling of brown sugar.
5. Bake in the oven for 30–40 minutes until soft.
6. Serve with low fat crème fraiche or natural yoghurt.

Note: In early September, try to make use of the plump ripe blackberries in the hedgerows, and fill the apple cores with these delicious bulging berries to make **Baked Blackberry Apples**. Place these in an ovenproof dish as you will get plenty of sticky juice oozing out from the apples.

Baked Peach and Almond Delights

Just like baked apples, this is a very simple dish but tastes wonderful. You can add a touch of luxury by drizzling a dash of Cointreau, or whichever is your favourite liqueur, over the peaches just before adding the yoghurt mixture. Remember, as with most fruit and vegetables, it is cheaper, and better environmentally, to buy them when they are in season.

SERVES 4 • COST OF INGREDIENTS: £4.30 • COST PER SERVING: £1.08

• Suitable for vegetarians

4 ripe peaches, halved and stoned

4 teaspoons honey

18–24 raspberries (you can use frozen or, if you have no raspberries, raspberry jam – but omit the honey!)

75g flaked almonds

For the topping

100ml natural yoghurt

100ml quark

1 teaspoon honey

Zest of 1 orange

1 teaspoon vanilla essence

1. Preheat the oven to 180°C/gas mark 4.

2. Place the peaches in an ovenproof tray, flesh facing upwards.

3. In the centre of each peach half, where the stone was, add ½ teaspoon of honey and top with 2–3 raspberries.

4. Sprinkle the flaked almonds over the top of the peaches, retaining a few for later.

5. Bake in the oven for 15 minutes.

6. Meanwhile, mix the yoghurt, quark, honey, orange zest and vanilla essence together.

7. When the peaches are ready, place them in serving bowls with a dollop of the yoghurt mixture. Sprinkle with the remaining almonds before serving.

Easy-Peasy Chocolate Mousse

I first saw a variation of this recipe on Nigella Lawson's TV show. Since then, we have adapted the recipe to suit our own taste. I can't claim that this is a healthy sweet, other than the fact that it uses organic chocolate, but who can resist a chocolate hit? I use Green & Black's Maya Gold chocolate as I like the spicy flavour and the quality of the chocolate. I have also used G&B Dark Chocolate with Ginger, which was really special. This is a seriously good mousse, but quite rich, so don't be tempted to give large portions.

SERVES 4 • COST OF INGREDIENTS: £2.99 • COST PER SERVING: 75p

- **Suitable for vegetarians**
- **Can be cooked in advance**

75g mini marshmallows
50g unsalted butter
100g bar of Green & Black's Maya Gold chocolate
50ml orange juice
200ml whipped or extra thick double cream
1 teaspoon vanilla extract

1. Place marshmallows, butter, chocolate and orange juice in a pan and cook gently on a low heat until melted. You will need to watch over this and stir well to avoid it sticking.

2. While the mixture is cooling slightly, choose your serving dishes. I normally use small shot glasses; this is very rich so you don't need big servings.

3. Place the cream in a bowl and carefully fold in the chocolate mixture. This may look a bit curdled but carry on as it will form into a nice rich mousse.

4. Spoon into your shot glasses and leave at room temperature to set. If you place the mousse in the fridge it will go quite hard.

Simple Gooseberry Fool

Gooseberry fools are lovely, but they can be high in fat, especially when made with full fat cream. I use Total Greek Yoghurt as it is low fat and holds it thickness. I suppose really this is gooseberry yoghurt. For those who would like a creamy fool, you can substitute cream for half the yoghurt. Buy your gooseberries in season or grow your own.

SERVES 4 • COST OF INGREDIENTS: £3 • COST PER SERVING: 75p

- **Suitable for vegetarians**
- **Can be cooked in advance**

400g gooseberries
50g sugar
250g Total Greek Yoghurt

1. Place the gooseberries in a pan with the sugar and gently cook until the gooseberries pop when pushed with a spoon.
2. Leave the gooseberries to cool and then fold in the yoghurt. Place in serving dishes to set.

Note: You can make **Rhubarb Fools** by following the same process. If you have a very sweet tooth you may want to add more sugar.

Chocolate Fondue

Fondues are a quick and easy dessert to make for dinner parties and guarantee good conversation. They are also a great way to get some fresh fruit into your children. OK, we are coating the fruit in chocolate, but if you use dark organic chocolate you will avoid unnecessary sugar hits and hopefully educate your children in the delights of great dark chocolate instead of the inferior sugary, milky confectionery.

200g dark chocolate, opt for at least 70% cocoa
A selection of fresh fruit, chopped

1. If you have a fondue set, this is easy – simply melt the chocolate in your bain-marie (otherwise known as a double boiler where you place water in the bottom pan and the chocolate in the top pan. The heat of the boiling water melts the chocolate.)

2. Transfer the chocolate to your fondue set. If you don't have a fondue set, keep the chocolate over the bain-marie as it will stay warm for approximately 10 minutes.

3. While the chocolate is melting, place your fruit on a platter ready for dipping.

4. Simply dip your chosen fruit into the chocolate and enjoy!

Note: Why not offer some small sweet dips alongside the chocolate? Try fruit yoghurt; crème fraiche mixed with crushed strawberries; cream cheese mixed with lemon zest, juice and a spoonful of cream; or try a sweet dressing made from fruit juice, sweetened with honey.

Blackberry and Apple Crumble

There is nothing nicer than the taste of blackberries and apples to tell you autumn is on its way. Go out late August/early September and pick these gorgeous fat blackberries ready to use fresh or to freeze. Mix them with tart cooking apples such as Bramleys and you'll find a little goes a long way.

I'm very fond of crumbles, but my recipe does not involve flour, butter or sugar. Instead I use muesli or a combination of key store cupboard ingredients such as oats, dried fruit, granola and nuts. The nutty texture you get from muesli is much nicer than a stodgy, heavy flour and butter combination! You can buy value supermarket own-brand muesli for as little as 58p per kg.

SERVES 4–6 • COST OF INGREDIENTS: £2 • COST PER SERVING: 33–50p

- **Suitable for vegetarians**
- **Can be frozen**
- **Can be cooked in advance**
- **Make 2, keep 1**

4 cooking apples, ideally Bramley
1 or 2 handfuls of blackberries (fresh or frozen)
25g brown sugar
200g muesli (or a combination of your choice, as above)

1. Preheat the oven to 180°C/gas mark 4.
2. Place the apples in a saucepan or ovenproof dish with 1–2 tablespoons of water. Cook on medium heat for 5–8 minutes until the apples start to soften, but ideally most remain firm.
3. Mix in the blackberries and sugar. Stir well.
4. Pour into an ovenproof dish, sprinkle on the muesli mix. Bake in the oven for 15 minutes.

Variations
There are endless combinations for a good fruit crumble. Go with the seasons and try to use up any spare fruit in your fruit bowl. Here are some ideas:

Spiced Apple Crumble – after stewing your apple, stir in some nutmeg, cinnamon and mixed spice with a handful of dried fruit.

Apple and Blackcurrant Crumble – just like blackberries, black-currants add a wonderful flavour and vibrant colour to your crumble. Place the blackcurrants in the saucepan with the apple to stew together before pouring the fruit into the ovenproof dish and covering it in crumble topping.

Apple and Blueberry Crumble – blueberries are marketed as superfoods, but really all berries are good for you. Mix fresh or frozen blueberries into the stewed apple before placing in an ovenproof dish and covering in your crumble mix.

Summer Fruit Crumble – this is a great 'cheat' crumble. All you need is a pack of frozen summer fruits and a some own-brand muesli or combo ingredients. Place the summer fruits in the bottom of an ovenproof dish (no need to precook if you don't want to!). Add two tablespoons of water and a sprinkle of sugar if you have a sweet tooth. Cover with your crumble mix and place in the oven for 15–20 minutes.

Rhubarb Crumble – I love rhubarb. You can make a simple rhubarb crumble by cooking some fresh or frozen rhubarb in a pan with a little water. Or try mixing in some fresh strawberries to create a delicious **Strawberries and Rhubarb Crumble,** or some fresh or frozen raspberries to make a mouthwatering **Raspberry and Rhubarb Crumble.** Another great combo is **Rhubarb and Orange Crumble.** Add some orange segments alongside the rhubarb for a great citrus/rhubarb hit. If you like a bit of spice, try **Rhubarb and Ginger Crumble.**

Gooseberry and Elderflower Crumble – this is one of my favourites. Place prepared gooseberries in a saucepan with 2 tablespoons of elderflower cordial and 25g of sugar. Cook gently until the gooseberries just start to burst under pressure. Place in an ovenproof dish and cover with your crumble topping.

Pink Pears

This is a really simple dish and perfect to use up any stray pears in your fruit bowl.

SERVES 4 • COST OF INGREDIENTS: £3.75 • COST PER SERVING: 94p

- **Suitable for vegetarians**
- **Can be cooked in advance**

4 pears, skinned
400ml apple juice
300ml red grape juice or red or mulled wine
200g raspberries
Juice and zest of 1 orange
1 teaspoon vanilla essence
50g sugar (optional, but needed if you have a sweet tooth)
1 cinnamon stick

1. Peel the pears, retaining their stalks if you can. Lightly steam the whole skinned pears for 5 minutes.
2. Meanwhile gently heat the apple and grape juice. Sieve the raspberries to remove the seeds and add the fruit to the grape juice. Add the juice and zest of the orange, vanilla essence, sugar and the cinnamon stick.
3. Place the pears in the liquid and leave to heat gently for 30 minutes. Turn the pears occasionally to ensure they are fully covered in juice.
4. Place the pears in a dish and pour over the sauce. Serve with a dollop of low fat crème fraiche.

Note: This can be made in advance, allowing the flavours more time to be absorbed by the pears. Reheat gently prior to serving.

Baked Bananas with Dark Chocolate Sauce

Wow, what a combination: bananas and dark chocolate covered in a dollop of crème fraiche ... yum-yum. I use cacao or Green & Black's 85% Dark as I like a very bitter dark chocolate to complement the sweetness of the bananas, but you can buy dark chocolate for as little as 27p per 100g.

SERVES 4 • COST OF INGREDIENTS: £1.55 • COST PER SERVING: 39p

4 bananas
100g bar of dark chocolate
A spoonful of crème fraiche per serving

1. Preheat the oven to 180°C/gas mark 4.
2. Place the bananas in an ovenproof tray in their skins and bake for 10 minutes, or until the skin goes completely black.
3. Meanwhile, melt the chocolate.
4. When you are ready to serve, pour the chocolate over the bananas and finish with a generous dollop of crème fraiche.

Apple and Fruit Bread Pudding

This is a really easy dish to make, and avoids the need for the eggy custard the traditional puddings have. It is a bit of a cheat dish but very tasty – especially soothing on a cold winter's evening! As with all my puddings, serve with a dollop of low fat yoghurt or crème fraiche.

SERVES 4 • COST OF INGREDIENTS: £1.50 • COST PER SERVING: 38p

75g dried mixed fruit
1–2 teaspoons cinnamon
2–3 cooking apples, diced
150ml apple juice
125g stale/leftover bread, cut into small chunks
150ml milk
1–2 tablespoons brown sugar

1. Preheat the oven to 180°C/gas mark 4.
2. Put the dried fruit, cinnamon, apples and apple juice into a pan,

bring to the boil for 5 minutes then remove from the heat.
3. Stir in the bread and milk.
4. Pour into a greased ovenproof dish. Sprinkle over the brown sugar and bake in the oven for 25–30 minutes.

Lemon and Ginger Cheesecake

This is one of my son's favourite desserts. If you don't like the ginger base, you can swap the ginger biscuits for digestives. I have also made a similar cheesecake using muesli as a base, which has worked surprisingly well. I then topped it with raspberries.

SERVES 4 • COST OF INGREDIENTS: £1.80 • COST PER SERVING: 45p

150g (½ pack) of ginger biscuits, crushed
50g butter, melted
1 tub of low fat cream cheese
Zest and juice of 2 small lemons
150g Greek yoghurt
150g crème fraiche
50g plain chocolate

1. Place the crushed biscuits in a saucepan with the melted butter. Stir well until the biscuit crumbs are thoroughly coated.
2. Pour the crumbs into a greased cheesecake tin (ideally one where the bottom pushes out). Push down the biscuit crumbs to form a solid base.
3. Chill in the fridge while you continue with the filling.
4. In a large bowl beat the cream cheese with a wooden spoon to help soften it. Add the zest of both lemons and the juice of 1 lemon. Add the yoghurt and crème fraiche. Stir well.
5. Taste to see if it is lemony enough. If not, add some more lemon juice. When you are happy with the mixture, pour it over the biscuit crumbs.
6. Spread the mixture evenly over the biscuit base.
7. Replace in the fridge to set.
8. Melt the chocolate. I make an icing bag out of parchment, but if you don't want precise swirls, you can use a spoon and dribble the chocolate over the cheesecake to form a pattern.
9. Return the cheesecake to the fridge until you are ready to serve.

Apple and Granola Bird's Nest Layer

When I was a child my mum used to make this really simple dish. This is a variation of her recipe. Serve it in glasses or syllabub dishes for a dramatic look. In the summer months, you can swap the apple for some delicious crushed berries. Amounts vary depending on the size of the glasses – so simply layer!

SERVES 4 • COST OF INGREDIENTS: £2 • COST PER SERVING: 50p

• **Can be prepared in advance**

2–3 cooking apples, stewed and slightly sweetened
Granola
Crème fraiche (or cream if you prefer)
Dark chocolate to decorate

1. After you have cooked your apples, allow them to cool.
2. In your chosen serving glasses, place a layer of apple, followed by granola, followed by the crème fraiche.
3. Repeat this process, finishing with the crème fraiche.
4. Decorate with swirls of dark chocolate

Let them Eat Cake

When I was little, Sunday mornings used to be all about baking for the week ahead. This passion has stayed with me and I am at my happiest when baking cakes. My dream would be to open a tea room by the sea.

Most of my recipes use self-raising flour. I find this makes a much nicer cake, and I use brown, golden sugar. I always sieve the flour as it does make a lighter cake. Buttermilk is becoming more readily available now, or you can use milk, add a few splashes of lemon juice and leave for 5 minutes before using, as this does have a similar effect. Another ingredient that's becoming increasingly popular in cakes is natural yoghurt. Surprisingly it can help create light and fluffy cakes and even scones.

You don't need any fancy equipment to make great cakes. You can make very light cakes by hand; however, you will save time if you have a good food mixer. I have several mixers but the one I use most is my 1970s Kenwood. Kenwoods cost over £200 new, but I paid £10 at a local boot sale for mine, so keep your eyes peeled for bargains!

I would advise spending a little extra on good cake tins. For example, if you want nice sponges, go for deep sponge tins with removable bottoms. Always opt for non-stick, but don't rely on this to work. It's a good idea to grease even non-stick tins with butter and sprinkle with a little flour before adding the cake mixture. There is nothing more frustrating than tipping out a gorgeous cake with half the bottom still stuck to the tin. You can buy cake tin liners though I have never used them myself.

Some of the recipes below are for eggless cakes. My husband doesn't eat eggs so I have mastered the art of cooking wonderful eggless cakes for the whole family. These are suitable for vegans if you substitute a vegan alternative for any butter.

Chocolate Melts

We used to make these as children. I think it was a ploy of my mum's to try to get some fruit and fibre into us without us realising. A good plan as they are seriously yummy!

SERVES 4–6 • COST OF INGREDIENTS: £1.22 • COST PER SERVING: 30p

- **Suitable for vegetarians**
- **Can be cooked in advance**

225g plain/dark chocolate
100g Bran Flakes or Fruit & Fibre cereal
50g raisins
50g mixed nuts
6–8 apricots, chopped

1. Melt the chocolate in a bain-marie or a basin placed over a pan of hot water.
2. Add the remaining ingredients and stir well.
3. Spoon dollops of the mixture onto a sheet of greaseproof paper and leave to set.

Lemon Curd Cupcakes

This is one of my mum's favourite recipes. The cupcakes are ideal for packed lunches, but beware, they might not last that long – they are yummy eaten warm!

SERVES 8–12 • COST OF INGREDIENTS: £2.27 • COST PER SERVING: 28p each

- **Suitable for vegetarians**
- **Can be frozen**
- **Can be cooked in advance**
- **Make 2, keep 1**

175g butter
150g sugar
3 large eggs, beaten
175g self-raising flour
1 teaspoon baking powder
125g sultanas
2 tablespoons lemon curd
Zest and juice of 1 lemon for topping
100g sugar for topping

1. Preheat the oven to 180°C/gas mark 4.
2. Cream the butter and sugar together until pale and fluffy.
3. Add the eggs a little at a time and continue to beat well.
4. Sift the flour and baking powder and fold into the mixture gently.
5. When thoroughly mixed, roughly fold in the sultanas and lemon curd. Don't over fold as you want the lemon curd to be more like a ripple effect.
6. Place in cupcake or muffin cases in a muffin/cupcake tray. This mixture should make 8–12 cakes depending on their size. Bake for 15 minutes.
7. Juice and zest 1 lemon. Mix the zest and juice together.
8. Pour a little over each hot cake and finish with a sprinkle of sugar.

Healthy Fruit Cake

I discovered this recipe in my great-aunt's recipe scrapbook. I don't know where she acquired it but it is a fatless, sugarless, eggless fruit cake and very simple to make.

COST OF INGREDIENTS: £2.25

- **Suitable for vegetarians**
- **Can be cooked in advance**

200g dates
300ml tea or water
175g self-raising flour
1 teaspoon baking powder
2 teaspoons mixed spice
400g dried mixed fruit
Grated rind of 1 orange
1 tablespoon orange juice

1. Preheat the oven to 180°C/gas mark 4 (slightly lower for fan-assisted ovens).
2. Put the dates and tea into a saucepan and gently heat until the dates are soft. Remove the pan from the heat and mash to break up the dates.
3. In a large mixing bowl sift the flour, baking powder and mixed spice. Add the dried fruit, orange rind and orange juice and mix thoroughly. Add the date mixture and stir well.
4. Spoon the mixture into a greased or lined 1kg (2lb) loaf or cake tin. Level the top. If your oven is quite fierce, you may want to place a sheet of greaseproof or brown paper over the top of the cake halfway through cooking to avoid a burnt top.
5. Bake for 1 hour, then reduce the heat to 160°C/gas mark 3 and cook for a further 15–30 minutes (until a skewer or knife inserted into the cake comes out clean).

Fatless Sponge

My mum makes a mean fatless sponge, especially when she uses her home-made raspberry jam to fill it – yum! I have pinched her recipe to share with you, so go on, and enjoy a guilt-free pleasure!

COST OF INGREDIENTS: £1.16

- **Suitable for vegetarians**
- **Can be cooked in advance**

3 eggs, separated
225g sugar (ideally golden caster sugar)
75ml warm water
150g self-raising flour
Raspberry jam filling

1. Preheat the oven to 180°C/gas mark 4.
2. Grease 2 deep sponge tins with butter and sprinkle over a little flour, ensuring the butter is fully coated. This forms a perfect non-stick base.
3. Mix the egg yolks and sugar together, adding the warm water a little at a time. This normally takes about 10 minutes to ensure a light and fluffy texture.
4. Sift the flour and gently add a little at a time into the egg/sugar mix – *don't whisk*!
5. Whisk the egg whites until firm, and then very gently fold into the cake mixture.
6. Spoon the mixture into the 2 greased sponge tins. Bake for 15–20 minutes until firm.
7. Allow to cool on a cooling rack before filling with raspberry jam. Sprinkle a little sugar over the top to complete – delicious!

Fatless Chocolate and Raspberry Sponge

COST OF INGREDIENTS: £2.81

Suitable for vegetarians
Can be cooked in advance
4 eggs, separated
225g sugar (ideally golden caster sugar)
75ml warm water
150g self-raising flour
75g good-quality cocoa
200g low fat fromage frais
100g raspberries

1. Preheat the oven to 180°C/gas mark 4.
2. Grease 2 deep sponge tins with butter and sprinkle over a little flour, ensuring the butter is fully coated. This forms a perfect non-stick base.
3. Mix the egg yolks and sugar together, adding the warm water a little at a time. If using a mixer, this takes a good 5 minutes, or by hand at least 10 minutes to ensure a light and fluffy texture.
4. Sift the flour and cocoa and gently add a little at a time into the egg/sugar mix – *don't whisk*!
5. Whisk the egg whites until firm, and then very gently fold into the cake mixture.
6. Spoon the mixture into the 2 greased sponge tins. Bake for 15–20 minutes until firm.
7. Allow to cool on a cooling rack.
8. Once cool, combine the fromage frais with the raspberries and sandwich between the sponge bases. Sprinkle with icing sugar to garnish.

Decadent Marble Cake

I used to think my mum was a magician when she conjured up marble cake in a variety of vibrant colours. Now I try to avoid using food colours, but still like the look of a marble cake. One day I was making a batch of different flavoured muffins and I got a bit bored waiting to reuse my two small muffin trays. The result was a marble cake made out of the muffin mixes. Here is the recipe below. Feel free to ignore the marble cake and instead opt for two different flavours of muffins ... enjoy!

SERVES 16 • COST OF INGREDIENTS: £4.04 • COST PER SERVING: 25p

- **Suitable for vegetarians**
- **Can be frozen**
- **Can be cooked in advance**
- **Make 2, keep 1**

100g butter
250g self-raising flour
250g sugar
4 eggs, beaten
400ml milk
50g white chocolate chips
100g raspberries (frozen or fresh)
50g cocoa
1 teaspoon vanilla essence
50g plain chocolate chips

1. Preheat the oven to 190 °C/gas mark 5.
2. Melt the butter in a saucepan.
   In the meantime, place the sifted flour and sugar in a bowl.
   Mix the eggs, melted butter and milk together.
3. Pour over the dry ingredients and mix until thoroughly combined.
4. Separate the mixture into two bowls.
5. To the first bowl, add the white chocolate chips and gently fold in the raspberries.
6. To the second bowl, add the cocoa, vanilla essence and plain chocolate chips.
7. In a greased or lined cake tin, place a spoonful of each mixture randomly to create a mottled marble effect when cooking. You can use a sharp knife and gently combine the mixtures if you wish, or just let nature take its course. Bake for 20–25 minutes.

Yummy Chocolate Cake

This is a real favourite in our house as we are all chocolate addicts. I recently treated myself to some cacao (Willie Harcourt-Cooze produces the most amazing 100% pure cacao bars, available from Waitrose, or visit www.williescacao.com) and it is well worth the money! You don't need much to make a real difference to your recipes. This is a standard chocolate sponge recipe but instead of using 25g of cocoa, I use 50g–75g, depending on the quality. I also add some grated cacao. The result is a rich dark chocolate sponge.

COST OF INGREDIENTS: £2.41

- **Suitable for vegetarians**
- **Can be frozen**
- **Can be cooked in advance**
- **Make 2, keep 1**

For the cake
175g butter
150g sugar
3 eggs, beaten
1 teaspoon vanilla essence
175g self-raising flour
50–100g cocoa powder (depending on desired intensity of chocolate taste)
15g grated cacao chocolate (optional)

For the butter icing
30g butter
50–75g icing sugar
1 teaspoon vanilla essence
75g plain chocolate

1. Preheat the oven to 180°C/gas mark 4.
2. Mix the butter and sugar together to form a light, fluffy cream.
3. Gradually add the beaten eggs and the vanilla essence.
4. Add the sifted flour and cocoa, ensuring it is thoroughly mixed. If using the grated chocolate, add this now.
5. Spoon the mixture into two deep lined or greased sponge tins.

6. Bake for 20–25 minutes until firm and the edges are starting to pull away from the sides.

7. Tip out onto a cooling rack and allow to cool.

8. To prepare the butter icing, beat the butter with the icing sugar, a little at a time. Add the vanilla essence and more icing sugar until you are happy with the taste and consistency. If too dry add a tiny drop of water, if too wet, add some more icing sugar.

9. Spread over the base of one of the cooled sponges and sandwich the two together.

10. Meanwhile, melt the plain chocolate in a bain-marie or a bowl placed over a pan of hot water. Pour the melted chocolate over the top of the sponge and spread to form an even but generous topping. Allow to cool before serving.

Moist Carrot Cake

*I love carrot cake and tend to fluctuate between this recipe and my boil-in-a-pan **Fruity Eggless Carrot Cake** (see page 273). You can decorate this cake with frosted icing, or low fat cream cheese mixed with icing sugar and lemon juice, but I tend to leave it bare and add a dollop of yoghurt or crème fraiche if I feel like it. This way the cake keeps longer in an airtight tin.*

COST OF INGREDIENTS: £3.14

- **Suitable for vegetarians**
- **Can be frozen**
- **Can be cooked in advance**
- **Make 2, keep 1**

For the cake
4 eggs, beaten
250g golden caster sugar
2 teaspoons vanilla extract
200ml very mild/light olive oil
300g self-raising flour
1 teaspoon bicarbonate of soda
2 teaspoons cinnamon
½ teaspoon grated nutmeg
400g grated carrots
50g chopped walnuts or pecan nuts

For the icing
1 x 200g tub of low fat cream
    cheese, softened
400g icing sugar
2–3 teaspoons lemon juice
2 drops vanilla extract
Chopped nuts to decorate

1. Preheat the oven to 180°C/gas mark 4.
2. Beat the eggs and sugar together until fluffy. Add the vanilla extract and oil and continue to whisk.
3. Sift the flour, bicarbonate of soda, cinnamon and nutmeg together and gradually add to the egg mix.
4. Stir in the carrots and nuts. Mix thoroughly.
5. Spoon the mixture into a greased or lined baking tin (I use a 25cm cake tin) and bake in the oven for 1 hour. Test if cooked by inserting a clean knife or skewer into the centre of the cake. If it comes away clean, the cake is cooked.
6. Place on a cooling rack to cool.
7. If you are icing the cake, mix the cream cheese, icing sugar,

lemon juice and vanilla extract together. When the cake has cooled, spread the icing over the top and decorate with some chopped nuts.

Blueberry Scones

COST OF INGREDIENTS: £1.87

- **Suitable for vegetarians**
- **Can be cooked in advance**

225g self-raising flour
½ teaspoon baking powder
25g sugar
50g butter
100g blueberries
150ml natural yoghurt
1 teaspoon vanilla essence
Milk to glaze
A sprinkling of brown sugar

1. Preheat the oven to 200°C/gas mark 6.
2. Sift the flour, baking powder and sugar into a bowl. Rub the butter into the flour until it resembles breadcrumbs.
3. Add the blueberries, yoghurt and vanilla essence and mix to form a dough.
4. On a floured surface roll out the dough into a thick sausage. Cut 2.5–5cm pieces and place these flat onto a greased or lined baking tray.
5. Brush with milk and sprinkle over some brown sugar before placing in the oven for 12–15 minutes.

Variations
Omit the blueberries to make **Plain Scones**. Add 75g of dried mixed fruit to make **Fruit Scones,** or choose your own fabulous flavours.

Apple and Walnut Loaf

Apple cakes of any description are a great favourite of mine. The flavour of apple combined with cinnamon is delicious. Thankfully, my husband agrees, so does not mind me cooking apple cakes on a regular basis – shame about my waistline though!

COST OF INGREDIENTS: £2.20

- **Suitable for vegetarians**
- **Can be cooked in advance**

100g butter
150g golden sugar
2 eggs, beaten
200g self-raising flour, sifted
2 teaspoons cinnamon powder
2 cooking apples, chopped
50g chopped walnuts

1. Preheat the oven to 180°C/gas mark 4.

2. Mix the butter and sugar together until light and fluffy.

3. Add the eggs a little at a time and continue to mix well.

4. Add the sifted flour and cinnamon powder and combine until thoroughly mixed.

5. Add the chopped apples and walnuts. When combined thoroughly, spoon the mixture into a lined or greased 1kg loaf tin.

6. Bake in the oven for 50–60 minutes, until a skewer or knife inserted into the centre of the cake comes out clean.

7. Cool on a cooling rack before storing in an airtight container.

Blackcurrant and Apple Bran Loaf

In the early eighties my mum was keen to get as much fibre into our diets as possible. She sent away for a booklet of recipes from Kellogg's All-Bran and this became a bit of a bible for her. Years later we are still making some of these recipes. This is one of our favourites which we have adapted over the years.

COST OF INGREDIENTS: £2.65

- **Suitable for vegetarians**
- **Can be cooked in advance**

75g sugar
100g butter
2 eggs, beaten
150g low fat yoghurt
75g All-Bran
150g self-raising flour, sifted
100g nuts, finely chopped
1 large cooking apple, chopped
125g blackcurrants, fresh or frozen

1. Preheat the oven to 180°C/gas mark 4.
2. Beat the sugar and butter together until light and fluffy. Gradually add the eggs and yoghurt and continue to whisk.
3. Add the All-Bran and gradually fold in the sifted flour. Stir well.
4. Finally add the nuts, apple and blackcurrants. When thoroughly mixed, place in a 1kg greased or lined loaf tin.
5. Bake for 40 minutes. Leave in the tin for 10 minutes before turning out onto a cooling rack.
6. This is delicious hot as a pudding served with yoghurt or low fat crème fraiche, or leave to cool and slice.

Out-of-Nothing Fruit Loaf

Don't let the simple ingredients of this loaf put you off. This is a really yummy fruit loaf, made with All-Bran, fruit, flour, milk and sugar – go on, give it a try! It is a fabulous cake to make when you have run out of other traditional cake ingredients. Even better, it's fatless and packed full of fibre – so it's actually good for you!

COST OF INGREDIENTS: £1.55

- **Suitable for vegetarians**
- **Can be cooked in advance**

100g All-Bran
275g dried mixed fruit
75g sugar
300ml milk
100g self-raising flour
1–2 teaspoons cinnamon
1 teaspoon ground coriander

1. Place the All-Bran, fruit, sugar and milk in a bowl and leave to stand for 30 minutes.
2. Preheat the oven to 180°C/gas mark 4.
3. Sift in the flour and spices. Stir well and transfer the mixture to a 500g lined or greased loaf tin.
4. Bake in the oven for 30–40 minutes, until firm to the touch. To ensure the middle is cooked, insert a clean knife into the centre of the cake – if it comes out clean, the cake is cooked.

Simple Muesli Bars

These are great fillers, and healthy too, so they're perfect for packed lunches. You would pay £1.50 each for these in a coffee shop, so why not make your own? This recipe is very simple and a bit of a cheat!

COST OF INGREDIENTS: Cost £1.70

- **Suitable for vegetarians**
- **Can be cooked in advance**

125g butter
125g brown sugar
2 tablespoons honey or (if you have a very sweet tooth) golden syrup
300g value muesli
50g dried mixed fruit

1. Preheat the oven to 180 °C/gas mark 4.
2. Melt the butter and sugar in a large saucepan over a gentle heat. Add the honey or golden syrup when the butter has dissolved.
3. Add the muesli and fruit and stir well.
4. Pour into a lined baking tin, and press down with the back of a spoon to form a solid base.
5. Bake for 15–20 minutes until golden.
6. Cut into slices when cool.

Note: For extra decadence (if you aren't worried about your waistline), melt some plain chocolate and cover the slices.

Chocolate Brownies

COST OF INGREDIENTS: £3.66

- **Suitable for vegetarians**
- **Can be cooked in advance**

200g butter
300g sugar
1 teaspoon vanilla extract
4 eggs, beaten
225g plain flour, sifted
150g cocoa
½ teaspoon baking powder
100g plain chocolate chips
25g chopped dates

1. Preheat the oven to 180 °C/gas mark 4.
2. Mix the butter and sugar together until light and fluffy.
3. Add the vanilla extract and eggs (a little at a time).
4. Gently fold in the sifted flour, cocoa and baking powder until thoroughly combined.
5. Add the chocolate chips and dates and stir again.
6. Place in a greased or lined baking tray and cook for 20 minutes. These brownies are better if slightly undercooked, so the middle is still gorgeously sticky.
7. Allow to cool before cutting into slices or squares.

Bran and Raisin Cakes

These are fantastic for breakfast. You can use either All-Bran or bran flakes from health food shops for this recipe. For a change, substitute Bramley apple chunks for the raisins – delicious!

COST OF INGREDIENTS: £1.32

- **Suitable for vegetarians**
- **Can be frozen**
- **Can be cooked in advance**
- **Make 2, keep 1**

50g butter
100g self-raising flour, sifted
1–2 teaspoons cinnamon
40g bran (see above)
100g brown sugar
75g raisins
1 egg, beaten
250ml milk or buttermilk
Juice of ½ lemon

1. Preheat the oven to 190 °C/gas mark 5.
2. Melt the butter in a saucepan.
3. In the meantime, place the sifted flour and all the remaining dry ingredients in a bowl. Add the raisins and stir well.
4. Mix the egg, melted butter, milk and lemon juice together.
5. Pour over the dry ingredients and mix until thoroughly combined
6. Place the mixture in paper cake cases or directly into a greased cupcake tray. Bake for 15–20 minutes.

Raspberry and White Chocolate Muffins

I made these for my dad one day as a special treat when he was going through his chemotherapy treatment. He ate three with one cup of tea so I think we can safely say he liked them!

COST OF INGREDIENTS: £3.74

- **Suitable for vegetarians**
- **Can be frozen**
- **Can be cooked in advance**
- **Make 2, keep 1**

50g butter
125g self-raising flour, sifted
125g sugar
2 eggs, beaten
200ml milk
100g white chocolate chips
175g raspberries (frozen or fresh)

1. Preheat the oven to 190 °C/gas mark 5.
2. Melt the butter in a saucepan.
3. In the meantime, place the sifted flour and sugar in a bowl.
4. Mix the eggs, melted butter and milk together.
5. Pour over the dry ingredients and mix until thoroughly combined.
6. Add the white chocolate chips and gently fold in the raspberries.
7. Spoon the mixture into paper cake cases or direct into a greased cupcake tray. Bake for 15–20 minutes.

Lemon and Banana Muffins

These are really tasty and low in fat. I find banana cakes quite sweet so I reduce the sugar content, but you can adjust this to suit your personal taste.

COST OF INGREDIENTS: £1.20

- **Suitable for vegetarians**
- **Can be frozen**
- **Can be cooked in advance**
- **Make 2, keep 1**

1 egg
4 tablespoons golden caster sugar
200g mashed banana
60g low fat natural yoghurt
1 teaspoon vanilla essence
Zest and juice of ½ lemon
125g self-raising flour, sifted
½ teaspoon nutmeg

1. Preheat the oven to 180°C/gas mark 4.
2. Mix the egg and sugar together. Add the mashed banana, yoghurt, vanilla essence, lemon juice and zest. Mix thoroughly
3. Add the sifted flour and nutmeg.
4. Spoon into muffin cases and bake in the oven for 20–25 minutes.
5. Leave to cool on a cooling rack. If you like, you can ice the muffins with lemon icing (mix icing sugar with some lemon juice).

Banana and Walnut Loaf

This is the perfect recipe to use up any browning bananas. It is quite low in fat, but very sweet.

COST OF INGREDIENTS: £2.10

- **Suitable for vegetarians**
- **Can be frozen**
- **Can be cooked in advance**
- **Make 2, keep 1**

50–75g sugar
200g self-raising flour
1 teaspoon cinnamon powder
1 teaspoon allspice
50g chopped walnuts
3–4 tablespoons wheatgerm
3 ripe bananas, mashed
2 eggs, beaten
4 tablespoons stewed apple

1. Preheat the oven to 180°C/gas mark 4.
2. Place the dry ingredients in a bowl and combine well.
3. In a separate bowl, mix the mashed banana, eggs and stewed apple. Combine with the dry ingredients until thoroughly mixed.
4. Place in a 500g greased loaf tin and bake for 50–60 minutes or until a skewer or knife inserted into the centre of the loaf comes out clean.
5. Place on a cooling rack to cool.

Eggless Cakes

The secret to making an eggless cake is to recognise the correct consistency needed for a cake mix: too wet and you will end up with a stodgy cake that burns on the outside and is still doughy in the middle; too dry and the cake will be heavy. It should be like a thick double cream. Don't be afraid to adjust as you go if you are concerned. Add more sieved flour if it is too wet; if too dry, add a touch of water, milk or even juice.

Eggless Chocolate Brownies

These are a huge favourite in our house and they are so simple to make. I use a Pyrex glass measuring jug which gives me flour and sugar weights as well as liquid measures.

COST OF INGREDIENTS: £1.71

- **Suitable for vegetarians**
- **Can be frozen**
- **Can be cooked in advance**
- **Make 2, keep 1**

225g self-raising flour
200g brown sugar
100–150g plain cocoa powder
350ml water (or orange juice if you like chocolate orange flavour)
200ml light olive oil
1 teaspoon vanilla extract
50g plain chocolate chips
50g mixed nuts (optional)
15g grated cacao chocolate (optional – this gives extra dark chocolate zing)

1. Preheat the oven to 180°C/gas mark 4.
2. In a large bowl, stir together the dry ingredients.

3. Add the water, vegetable oil and vanilla extract. Whisk until thoroughly mixed.
4. Add the chocolate chips (and the nuts and cacao if you are using them). Pour the mixture into a lined or greased baking tray.
5. Bake for 25–30 minutes until firm to the touch. Leave in the tray for 10 minutes before cutting into squares.

Variations
I have also added chopped nuts, white chocolate chips and even dates to this mix and all variations come out well. Serve warm with a rich chocolate sauce for a naughty but very nice dessert!

Eggless Apple Cake

COST OF INGREDIENTS: £3.19

- **Suitable for vegetarians**
- **Can be cooked in advance**

125g butter
150g golden sugar
3 cooking apples, stewed
100g raisins
100g sultanas
1 cooking apple, sliced
220g self-raising flour, sifted
75g mixed chopped nuts
2–3 teaspoons ground cinnamon

1. Preheat the oven to 180°C/gas mark 4.
2. Cream the butter and sugar together thoroughly until it has a light creamy texture.
3. Add the cold stewed apple, cream again, and add the dried fruit and sliced apple.
4. Add the flour, nuts and cinnamon and stir thoroughly.
5. Spoon into a buttered and floured or lined cake tin and sprinkle a few nuts on top. Bake for 1 hour or until a knife inserted into the centre of the cake comes out clean.

Fruity Eggless Carrot Cake

COST OF INGREDIENTS: £2.11

- **Suitable for vegetarians**
- **Can be cooked in advance**

3 carrots, grated
200g brown sugar
400ml water
100g dates, chopped
100g currants or raisins
110g butter
2 teaspoons cinnamon powder
1 teaspoon ground cardamom
220g self-raising flour
75g chopped nuts

1. Preheat the oven to 180°C/gas mark 4.
2. Boil the carrots, sugar, water, dates and currants for about 2 minutes in a large saucepan.
3. Add the butter and spices and allow to cool.
4. Sift in the flour. Add the nuts and mix well.
5. Spoon into a buttered and floured or lined cake tin. Bake for 50 minutes or until a knife inserted into the centre of the cake comes out clean.

Eggless Chocolate Date Cake

COST OF INGREDIENTS: £2.04

- **Suitable for vegetarians**
- **Can be cooked in advance**

110g butter
150g golden sugar
1 tablespoon golden syrup
300ml milk and water mixed
220g self-raising flour, sifted
75g cocoa
75g chopped dates
50g plain chocolate chips (optional)

1. Preheat the oven to 180°C/gas mark 4.
2. Cream the butter, sugar and golden syrup together until light and creamy.
3. Add the milk and water mixture a little at a time while gradually mixing in the sifted dry ingredients.
4. Add the dates and chocolate chips, if you are using them. Mix well.
5. Spoon into a buttered and floured or lined cake tin and sprinkle a few nuts on top. Bake for 20–30 minutes or until a knife inserted into the centre of the cake comes out clean.

Eggless Fruit Cake

COST OF INGREDIENTS: £3.79

- **Suitable for vegetarians**
- **Can be cooked in advance**

250g butter
500ml tea (without milk!)
200g sugar
750g mixed fruit
1 small apple, grated
2 teaspoons ground cinnamon
2 teaspoons ground ginger
1 teaspoon nutmeg
1 teaspoon allspice
2 tablespoons golden syrup
Juice of ½ lemon and finely grated peel
200g self-raising flour
1 teaspoon vanilla and/or almond essence

1. Preheat the oven to 180°C/gas mark 4.
2. Place the butter, tea, sugar, fruit and spices in a pan and simmer for 10 minutes. Leave to cool.
3. When cold, add all the other ingredients and mix thoroughly.
4. Spoon into a buttered and floured or lined cake tin. Bake for 1 hour then turn down the oven to 160°C/gas mark 3 and bake for another 45 minutes–1 hour until the cake is cooked. If you are concerned about the top burning, place a sheet of parchment paper over the cake.

Eggless Apple and Oat Muffins

COST OF INGREDIENTS: £1.98

- **Suitable for vegetarians**
- **Can be frozen**
- **Can be cooked in advance**
- **Make 2, keep 1**

110g butter
150g sugar
2 apples, stewed
50–75g dried fruit (raisins are best)
75g oats
50g mixed chopped nuts
125ml milk
110g self-raising flour, sifted
1 teaspoon ground cardamom
2 teaspoons cinnamon

1. Preheat the oven to 180°C/gas mark 4.
2. Cream the butter and sugar together until light and fluffy.
3. Add the stewed apple, raisins, oats and nuts. Add the milk, flour and spices, mixing well.
4. Spoon the mixture into muffin cases and bake for approx 20–30 minutes.

Eggless Raisin and Walnut Tea Loaf

Ingredients Cost £1.52

- **Suitable for vegetarians**
- **Can be frozen**
- **Can be cooked in advance**
- **Make 2, keep 1**

100g raisins
200ml boiling water
200g sugar
50g butter
100g chopped walnuts
1 teaspoon vanilla extract
200g self-raising flour
1 teaspoon ground ginger

1. Preheat the oven to 180°C/gas mark 4.
2. Combine the raisins, boiling water, sugar, butter and walnuts in a bowl.
3. Allow to cool.
4. Add the vanilla extract. Sift the flour and ginger and mix into the raisin mix. Combine well.
5. Place in a greased 500g loaf tin and bake in the oven for 30–40 minutes until firm and golden.

Smooth and Juicy

Smoothies and juices are a great way of getting your minimum five a day, but also a great stopgap when you are feeling peckish, have a sugar craving or just need a pick-me-up.

Smoothies

Smoothies are normally made in a liquidiser, smoothie maker or electric hand blender (I use my electric hand blender or my liquidiser). Smoothies are only good for soft fruits. Place whole berries into the liquidiser. Fruit with an inedible skin, such as kiwi, mango etc., should be peeled before adding to the liquidiser. Apples and pears can be added but they are best juiced.

Juice

Most fruit and vegetables can be juiced. I use my Green Life masticating juicer (available from www.nutrigold.co.uk), which chews the fruit and vegetables and leaves very little waste. Unlike centrifugal juicers, masticating juicers don't suck air into the juice or spin the fruit around, bruising it and destroying nutrients. They are much more expensive than centrifugal (approximately £300), but if you are serious about juicing, buying one is a good long-term investment. Centrifugal juicers are less powerful so you may have to chop your ingredients into small pieces to feed into the machine. Most juicers will separate the juice from the fibre and skin so there is no need to peel the ingredients. Use a citrus juicer to extract the juice from citrus fruits. This avoids adding pith and unwanted fibre into your drink, especially if you are making a smoothie.

Vegetable juices can help you reach your minimum five a day. Carrot juice mixed with apple or other fruits is delicious and most children are unaware they are drinking a vegetable. If you are making green juices, be aware that some greens, such as watercress, are very strong, so only add a tiny amount until you are happy with the taste.

Quantities

When juicing and making smoothies, don't get too hung up on quantities. By trial and error you will find the proportions that suit you. I have listed some simple recipes below to get you started. All the recipes make enough for 1 large or 2 small glasses.

Smooth Operator

This juice is made using a blender. It's so sweet, smooth and creamy, you feel as if you are having something wicked rather than a nutrient-packed smoothie. Sit back and enjoy!

Juice of 2 oranges
Flesh of ½ mango
1 banana, peeled
50g blueberries
2 tablespoons bio yoghurt

1. Place all the ingredients into the blender.
2. Whizz until smooth.

M and M

Mango and melon make a lovely juice when blended together. I use watermelon for its extra juice, but any melon will do. If you want a more liquid juice, you can add a base juice of either apple, pear or orange to suit your palate. Remember, mangos are far better to juice when they are ripe and the juice pours through your fingers as you cut into the flesh. Lovely.

Equal amounts of mango and melon flesh

1. Place the mango and melon in a blender.
2. Whizz until smooth.

Indian Summer

This juice uses a traditional recipe for a popular pick-me-up (apple and carrot) together with orange and turmeric to form a delicious, highly beneficial and nutritious juice. Turmeric contains curcumin, and is increasingly used by naturopathic practitioners as an anti-inflammatory, digestive aid and a wound healer. Turmeric gives the juice an earthy taste which is masked very well by the sweetness of the orange and apple juice.

2 carrots
2 apples
Juice of 2 oranges
1 teaspoon turmeric

1. Juice the carrots and apples.
2. Extract the juice from the oranges (I use my citrus press for this).
3. Mix all the juices together thoroughly with the turmeric powder.

Club Tropicana

The yoghurt, coconut milk and banana are high in carbohydrates, so this is almost a meal in itself. Fancy escaping to a tropical paradise? Sip this juice and away you go!

Flesh of ½ mango
Flesh of ½ pineapple
50ml coconut milk
1 banana, peeled
1 tablespoon yoghurt
Nutmeg

1. Put all the ingredients, apart from the nutmeg, in a blender and whizz until smooth.
2. To finish, sprinkle some nutmeg over the juice – delicious!

John Lemon

You may want to play around with this juice to suit your palate, as it is very zesty and will leave your mouth tingling. It's really refreshing, and fantastic as a replacement for the traditional fresh orange juice in the morning. Awaken your senses!

1 orange
1 grapefruit
½ lemon
½ lime

1. Using a citrus press, extract the juice from all the fruits.
2. Blend together well.

The Kiss

This is a deliciously wicked juice, which leaves you lips smacking together with the sheer pleasure of it all. Pucker up and get ready for the ultimate seduction!

1 peach
1 nectarine
2 oranges
1 passion fruit

1. Using a citrus press, squeeze the oranges to extract the juice.
2. Add this juice, along with the other fruits, to the blender and whizz until smooth.

Crimson King

What a great combination! Watermelon makes a fantastic juice, and is so refreshing.

2 oranges
50g raspberries
¼ watermelon

1. Juice all the fruits together, and mix thoroughly before drinking.

The Green Smile

This juice is really sweet and fruity, and the fresh mint adds a special touch.

1 apple
1 kiwi
1 pear
A handful of fresh mint

1. Juice all the ingredients together. Place the mint leaves alongside any fruit pieces to help it go through the juicer efficiently.
2. As a finishing touch, decorate with a couple of mint leaves.

Sweet Sunset

This is a very simple juice, but that does nothing to detract from its fantastic taste.

1–2 oranges
Flesh of ½ pineapple

1. Using a citrus press, squeeze the oranges to extract the juice.
2. If the pineapple is nice and juicy you can place all the ingredients in a blender and whizz. If the pineapple is not so ripe, place everything in your juicer. Mix well before serving.

Strawberries and Dream

This is a wonderful smoothie, perfect for a summer's day, and very simple to make. I have added oranges as an optional extra as some people like a more fluid juice. This makes one glass.

5–8 strawberries
1 dessertspoon bio yoghurt
Juice of 1 orange (optional)

1. Simply put all the ingredients into a blender and whizz until smooth. Absolutely scrumptious!

Sweet and Sour Delight

The sweetness of the papaya and raspberries contrasts with the sharpness of the grapefruit and lime to make this a very special juice.

Juice of ½ grapefruit
Juice of ½ lime
½ papaya
50g raspberries

1. Using a citrus press, extract the juice from the grapefruit and lime.
2. If you don't mind having raspberry pips in your juice, you can save time by whizzing the fruit in your blender. If you want a finer, smoother juice, put it through the juicer.

Medicine Mango

This is pure, sweet luxury in a juice – and packed full of fabulous nutrients. It will satisfy the most ardent sweet cravings.

1–2 apricots
Flesh of ½ mango
Flesh of ½ pineapple
1 passion fruit

1. Place all the ingredients in a blender and whizz until smooth.

Blue Moon

This is a lovely creamy smoothie, packed with goodness. It makes a great start to the day.

50g blueberries
1–2 tablespoons natural yoghurt
2–3 teaspoons oats
Juice of 1 orange

1. Place all the ingredients in a blender and whizz until smooth.

Purple Rain

This juice really is fit for a prince and the colour delights children. Powerful antioxidants in the blueberries, combined with the sweetness of the kiwi, make this a big favourite with both parents and children. If you make this in a blender, peel the kiwi, apple and pear first. There is no need to peel if you make it in a juicer.

50g blueberries
1 kiwi
1 apple
1 pear

1. Place all the ingredients in a blender and whizz until smooth.

Bridge Over the River Kiwi

The only battle you will have with this juice is fighting over the glass. It is deliciously sweet and very nutrient rich. Sit back and enjoy!

A handful of seedless grapes
1 orange
¼ pineapple
1 kiwi, peeled
1 passion fruit

1. Place all the ingredients in a blender and whizz until smooth.

The Big Apple

Kids love this juice – and it's so simple to make!

2 apples
Flesh of ½ mango
1–2 oranges

1. Simply juice all the ingredients together and stir well.

The Peach Boys

Sweet and tropical, this is a delicious and decadent smoothie – perfect for those seeking a touch of paradise.

1 peach
1 apricot
1 nectarine
1 orange (optional)

1. Place all the ingredients in a blender and whizz until smooth.

Papaya Don't Peach

I'm sure Madonna would love this smoothie – sweet and sumptuous with the kick of lime.

Flesh of 1 ripe papaya
1 peach
25g raspberries
Juice of ½ lime

1. Place all the ingredients in a blender and whizz until smooth.

Frank Flu Zapper

This is a wonderful juice for those winter months. The ginger adds warmth and zing – it really does pack quite a punch.

1–2 carrots
1–2 apples
Fresh ginger root to taste
Juice of 2 oranges

1. Juice the carrots, apples and ginger root (not too much!).
2. In a citrus press squeeze the oranges and then blend the two juices together. Alternatively, you can use freshly squeezed orange juice. Stir well.

Menu Planning

In this section I will hopefully start to make your lives easier by providing you with some weekly menu suggestions and shopping lists. The secret of good menu planning is to think ahead, be aware of what you have in your store cupboard and make the most of the resources at your disposal.

You may notice that some days include more cooking than others. This is to utilise my 'make two, keep one' philosophy. It is a waste of expensive energy to heat up a half-empty oven, so make the most of it while it's on and cook several dishes at the same time, both main meals and cakes, pastries and puddings. Many of the recipes can be frozen, enabling you to fill your oven with meals that can be kept for another day. This is a much more efficient use of energy – both your own and the kind you have to pay for! Make sure you list all the items you have in your freezer and plan them into your weekly menus.

Store cupboard essentials, such as flour, butter, milk, olive oil, herbs and spices, are not included in the menus, so take this into consideration when planning your meals and make sure you have stocked up on these basics.

On Sundays I have planned for a traditional roast dinner. Feel free to choose a different meat but, if you do, consider what you will do with leftovers. Play the supermarkets off against each other – almost every week you will find an offer on a particular meat joint, so keep an eye out for the best deals.

Week 1

Sunday: Roast chicken, roast potatoes (page 21), 2 seasonal vegetables, home-made gravy (pages 182–183) (double up)

Get a chicken that is slightly bigger than your needs. Strip this of flesh (thighs, legs, breast; turn the bird over to pull off the meat). Put the leftover meat to one side ready for tomorrow's chicken pie, plus sandwiches.

Fill the oven – choose some cakes, pastries or savouries to make the most of the free heat! And if you are making pastries, why not prepare two and freeze one uncooked?

Monday: Leftover Chicken Pie (page 86) and Mash (page 161) (double up)

Prepare double the mash and keep it in the fridge for tomorrow's fish pie.

You are using your oven so add a pudding, such as Baked Apples (page 240).

Use up your spare puff pastry by making Eccles Cakes (page 234), jam puffs or savoury dishes.

Tuesday: Creamy Fish Pie (page 124) with yesterday's mash

You already have the mash prepared from yesterday's meal, so now all you have to do is prepare the fish pie.

I use my Halogen oven as it is a simple dish that does not need a full oven's heat. You can also use a combination microwave or top oven to save on electricity.

Wednesday: Chickpea and Vegetable Casserole (page 146)

This can be made in a slow cooker or casserole dish on a hob – so no need to turn on the oven. If you are out at work all day, prepare this in the slow cooker before you leave, ready for your return in the evening.

Make extra and heat up leftovers for next day's lunch. Or take to work in a flask for a wholesome packed lunch.

Thursday: Spaghetti Bolognese (page 107) (double up)

Double up the recipe and freeze half to make another bolognese or a lasagne for next week.

Friday: Fish and Chunky Chips (page 75), Peas

Simple and a great way to end the week.

Saturday: Bacon and Egg Quiche (page 216), new potatoes, salad (pages 194–207)

Make extra pastry and fill the oven with other pastry dishes.

Shopping List

Large chicken for roasting	£6.97
800g mince	£1.94
1kg fish fillets	£3.88
(or 500g white fish pieces and 4–6 fillets)	
1 pack of bacon	£1.48
4 eggs	88p (for 6)*
500g low fat cottage cheese	£1.49
(650g Be Good to Yourself)*	
200g mature Cheddar	£3.75 (for 500g)*
4kg potatoes	£3.96 (for 5kg)*
2kg new potatoes	£1.56
Seasonal vegetables	£2.60
(enough for 3 meals)	
Seasonal salad (enough for 1 meal)	£2.57
6–8 onions	75p (for 1.5kg)*
150g Mushrooms	89p (for 400g)*
Celery (you will use 4–6 sticks)	78p (bunch)
1 bulb of garlic	39p (for 2 bulbs)*
2 peppers	£1.48 (for 3)*
2 courgettes	39p
1 bag of carrots	89p
(can use some of these for second vegetables)	
1 sweet potato	£1.58 (for 1kg bag)*
1 large tomato	79p (for 450g)*
2 tins of tomatoes	70p
1 tin of chickpeas	48p
Condensed chicken soup	40p
1 block of puff pastry	91p
1 bottle of beer	75p
Frozen peas	£1*
Total	**£43.26**

*Denotes items that are far greater in weight than needed as it is more economical to buy in these quantities. Make a note of these as you can store them for the following week to reduce next week's bill. In the case of the sweet potato, why not make a tasty sweet potato soup?

Week 2

Sunday: Roast beef, Yorkshire puddings, 2 seasonal vegetables, roast potatoes (page 21), home-made gravy (pages 182–183) (double up)
Your roast beef will also provide you with spare beef for sandwiches and tomorrow's dinner.

Monday: Beef and Mushrooms in Red Wine (page 96) (using leftover beef), steamed new potatoes, seasonal vegetables
This can be prepared in the slow cooker or in a casserole dish on the hob. Steam your vegetables to avoid having to use your oven.
If you can, prepare this dish in the morning before you leave for work, or even the night before.

Tuesday: Salmon Fish Cakes (page 126) with Green Snap Salad (page 204) and Steamed New Potatoes
Another quick and easy meal that avoids the use of the oven.
Remove last week's leftover bolognese/lasagne base from the freezer ready for tomorrow's dinner.

Wednesday: Lasagne (page 108) with Salad (pages 194–207) and Potato Wedges (page 85)
Using last week's spaghetti bolognese base, prepare the lasagne.
You will need to cook the lasagne and the potato wedges in the oven so make use of the heat and cook something extra!

Thursday: Mediterranean Fish Pot (page 130)
Cook this in a slow cooker or a casserole dish on the hob to avoid using the oven.

Friday: Meatballs (page 113-115) and Tomato Sauce (page 181) on a bed of spaghetti (double up)
Prepare your meatballs (double up and freeze some for another meal).
   Your tomato sauce can be prepared fresh or, if you are in a hurry, cheat and purchase a pasta sauce – though make sure it's on offer!

Saturday: Pizza (page 78), Salad (pages 194–207), Chunky Chips (page 76)
Pizza bases are simple to prepare. Make several and freeze them between layers of foil or greaseproof paper ready for another meal.

Shopping List

Beef roasting joint	£11.79
500g fish fillets/pieces	£1.94
400g salmon	£4.00
400g mince	97p
2.5kg potatoes	£1.98 *
(you should have potatoes left from last week)	
2kg new potatoes	£1.56
Seasonal vegetables (enough for 3 meals)	£2.60
Seasonal salad (enough for 2 meals)	£3.97
Celery (you will use 3–4 sticks)	£0.00*
(you should have these left from last week)	
1 bulb of garlic	£0.00*
(you should have these left from last week)	
150g mushrooms	89p (for 400g)
3 onions	£0.00
(you should have these left from last week)	
1 bag of carrots	89p
2 Leeks	89p
1 tin of tomatoes	35p
200g mature Cheddar	£3.75 (for 500g)
2 eggs	£0.00
(you should have 2 left from last week)	
Spaghetti	39p
Jar of pasta sauce	89p
Total	**£36.87**

*This figure is including the non-perishable extras you purchased in the previous week.

Week 3

Sunday: Roast chicken, roast potatoes (page 21), 2 seasonal vegetables and home-made gravy (pages 182–183) (double up)
As with Week 1's menu, get a chicken that is slightly bigger than your needs, and when it is cold strip the bird of all the meat, ready for the chicken casserole for tomorrow's dinner, plus sandwiches.

Monday : Hearty Chicken Casserole (page 83)
This can be made in a slow cooker or casserole dish on a hob – so no need to turn on the oven. If you work all day, prepare this in the slow cooker before you leave and it will be ready when you return.

Tuesday: Smoked Haddock with Leek and Parsley Sauce (page 131), new potatoes and green salad
This can be prepared on a hob so no need to use your oven.

Wednesday: Red Pepper and Tomato Soup with Pesto Swirl (page 42), crusty bread and fresh hummus (page 186)
This can be made in a slow cooker or casserole dish on a hob – so no need to turn on the oven.

Make extra and heat it up for tomorrow's lunch (you can take some to work in a flask for a wholesome packed lunch).

Thursday: Cottage Pie (page 111) and 2 seasonal vegetables (double up)
Double up the recipe and store half in the freezer ready to make another meal.

You don't have to use your oven for this meal. Prepare the mince mix and the mashed potato and pop it under the grill.

Friday: Lemon and Herb Pan-Fried Cod (page 127), new potatoes and Green Snap Salad (page 204)
This can be cooked on a hob so no need to use your oven.

Saturday: Chicken Burgers (page 70), Chunky Chips (page 76) and salad (pages 194–207) (double up)
Burgers are so simple, so double up and make extra to freeze for another week. Layer them with greaseproof paper to prevent them sticking together.

Remember to use your oil spray when preparing the chunky chips.

Shopping List

Large chicken for roasting	£6.97
4 haddock fillets	£2.78
500g fish fillets/pieces	£1.94
800g minced beef	£1.94
400g chicken mince	£1.79
Seasonal vegetables (enough for 3 meals)	£2.60
2.5kg potatoes	£1.98
6–8 onions	75p (for 1.5kg)*
2kg new potatoes	£1.56
Seasonal salad (enough for 3 meals)	£5
5 peppers	£3.96 (for 6)*
Tomatoes	96p (for 6)
2 bulbs of garlic	39p
Celery (you will use 4–6 sticks)	78p (bunch)
1 lemon	23p
5–6 leeks	£2.50
1 bag of carrots	89p
1 tin of tomatoes	35p
Jar of pesto	£1.19
200g mature Cheddar	£3.75 (for 500g)
30g pine nuts	£1.89 (for 100g)
4–6 burger baps	65p
Total	**£44.85**

Week 4

Sunday: Leg of lamb, roast potatoes (page 21), 2 seasonal vegetables, home-made gravy (pages 182–183) (double up)
Put the leftover meat to one side ready for baking a Lamb Hotpot for tomorrow's dinner, plus sandwiches.

Monday: Lamb Hotpot (page 92) and Potato Mash (page 161)
This can be cooked in a slow cooker or casserole dish on a hob – so no need to turn on the oven.

Tuesday: Haddock Risotto (page 156)
This can be cooked on a hob so no need to use your oven.

Wednesday: Sausage and Tomato Casserole (page 105) and Mini Roast Potatoes (page 22)
The casserole can be cooked in a slow cooker or casserole dish on a hob – so no need to turn on the oven unless you want to cook the mini roasts (otherwise swap these for mashed or steamed potatoes).

Thursday: Tuna and Sweetcorn Pasta (page 176)
This can be prepared on a hob so no need to use your oven.

Friday: Breaded Fish Fillets (page 129), Chunky Chips (page 76) and Peas
Remember, you are using your oven, so fill it up. Think of cakes, desserts or pastries.

Saturday: Chicken Chow Mein (page 80)
This can be prepared on a hob so no need to use your oven.

Shopping List

Leg of lamb	£9.99
2 haddock fillets	£2.80
8 pork sausages	£3
500g fish fillets/pieces	£1.94
Chicken breast pieces	£2.39 (300g)
2.5kg potatoes	£1.98
Seasonal vegetables	£2.60
4 leeks	£2
1 bulb of garlic	39p (for 2 bulbs)
4 onions	£0.00
(you should have some left from last week)	
Chilli	53p
2 peppers	£1.48 (for 3)*
Broccoli head	83p
Spring onions	68p (bunch)
Spring cabbage	68p
Mushrooms	87p (for 250g)
1 bag of carrots	89p
200g mature Cheddar	£3.75 (for 500g)
Parmesan cheese	£2
Risotto rice	95p (500g)
1 tin of tomatoes	35p
Tomato purée	25p
Noodles	70p
2 tins of tuna	£1.16
1 tin of sweetcorn	34p
400g cream cheese	90p
(for 2 packs of 200g)	
Dried pasta	43p (for 500g)
1 lemon	23p
Total	**£44.11**

Veggie Menu Planners
Week 1

Sunday: Mushroom and Cashew Nut Roast (page 135), roast potatoes (page 21) and 2 seasonal vegetables (double up)
Double up the recipe for the Nut Roast and freeze one, or make Mushroom en Croûte (page 000) and freeze it.
If you have any puff pastry left you could make some Eccles Cakes (page 000).

Monday: Country Vegetable Broth (page 50) with Stuffed Pitta Bread
Stuff your pitta breads with grated carrot, sliced peppers, cheese, hummus or a selection of your own choice.
This soup can be made in the morning before you go to work – prepare in your slow cooker or hob-proof casserole dish.
Why not make a delicious No Messing Rice Pudding (page 239) for dessert?

Tuesday: Veggie Spaghetti Bolognese (page 107, substitute vegetarian mince) (double up)
Double up the recipe and store half in the freezer ready to make another bolognese or a lasagne.

Wednesday: Spicy Chickpea, Spinach and Potato Curry (page 120) with Lentil Dahl (page 121) and Rice (double up)
It's curry night again; you can double up the recipes and freeze one for another day – so simple and takes very little extra work.

Thursday: Spinach and Ricotta Lasagne (page 174), salad (pages 194–207) and Potato Wedges (page 85) (double up)
This is a really easy dish that tastes great. You can prepare this in the morning before leaving for work.
Double up the recipe and bake one, freeze one for another meal in Week 3.

Friday: Chickpea and Vegetable Casserole (page 146)
This can be cooked in a slow cooker or casserole dish on a hob – so no need to turn on the oven.
Why not make a little more? You can heat up leftovers for a quick and tasty lunch, or take some to work in a flask for a wholesome packed lunch.

Saturday: Spicy Tofu Burgers (page 73), Chunky Chips (page 76) and Salad (pages 194-207) (double up)
Burgers are so simple, so double up and make extra to freeze for Week

3. Layer them with greaseproof paper to prevent them sticking together. Remember to use your oil spray when preparing the chunky chips.

Shopping List

2 packs of veggie mince	£3.56
10 onions	£1.14
Cashew nuts	£3.69
600g mushrooms (2 x 400g basics)	£1.78
1 bulb of garlic	39p (for 2 bulbs)
1 parsnip	24p
2.5kg potatoes	£1.98
1 sweet potato	£1.58 (for 1kg bag)*
Chilli	56p
Celery (you will use 4–6 sticks)	78p (bunch)
2 x 300g spinach	£2.32
Seasonal vegetables (enough for 3 meals)	£2.60
Seasonal salad (enough for 2 meals)	£3.97
1 bag of carrots	89p
3–4 peppers	£1.48 (for 3)*
4 courgettes	78p
2 x ricotta	£1.50
2 x tofu	£3.18
Green split peas	49p (for 500g)
Red lentils	£1.02 (for 500g)
1 tin of tomatoes	35p
4 tins of chickpeas	£1.92
Tomato purée	25p
2 jars of pasta sauce	£1.78
Puff pastry	91p
Spaghetti	39p
Lasagne sheets	32p
Basmati rice	84p
4–6 burger baps	65p
Total	**£37.78**

Week 2

Sunday: Leek and Quorn Pie (page 144), Sweet Potato Mash (page 162), 2 seasonal vegetables
You have the oven on for the Leek and Quorn Pie and you have used half a packet of puff pastry. Use the rest to make something else, sweet or savoury.

Monday: Veggie Mince Lasagne (page 108), Salad (pages 194–207) and Chunky Chips (page 76)
Using last week's spaghetti bolognese base when you prepared two and froze one, you can prepare the lasagne.

You will need to turn on the oven to cook the lasagne and the chunky chips so make use of the heat and cook something extra.

Tuesday: Spicy Rice (page 158)
This can be cooked on a hob so no need to use your oven.

Wednesday: Mushroom en Croûte (page 000) and salad (pages 194–207)
This was prepared when you baked your Mushroom and Cashew Nut Roast in Week 1.

Serve with delicious salad for a filling meal.

Thursday: Broccoli and Cheese Bake (page 139), mini new potato roasts (page 22) and seasonal vegetables
Remember, fill the oven! Look for other items to bake – cakes, dessert or pastry dishes.

Friday: Curry and Rice
Remember to take the leftover curry from last week's curry night out of your freezer before you leave for work.

Cook some rice and serve with yoghurt and mint dip, poppadoms and naan bread.

Saturday: Asparagus and Cherry Tomato Tagliatelle (page 176)
A very quick and easy recipe that can be cooked on the hob – no need to use your oven!

Shopping List

1 bag of Quorn chunks	£1.79
5 onions	57p
1 bulb of garlic	39p (for 2 bulbs)*
2 leeks	£1
1 bag of carrots	89p
Chilli	56p
Ginger	62p
Seasonal salad (enough for 2 meals)	£3.97
2 peppers	£1.48 (for 3)*
Sweet potato	£1.58 (for 1kg bag)*
Broccoli	83p
2.5kg potatoes	£1.98
Asparagus	£1.50 (350g)
Cherry tomatoes	£2.18 (2 punnets)
2kg new potatoes	£1.56
Puff pastry	91p
Quark	59p
Greek yoghurt	99p
Crème fraiche	98p
Mature Cheddar	£3.75 (for 500g)
Parmesan cheese	£2
Red lentils	£0.00
(you should have some left from last week)	
Basmati rice	£0.00
(you should have some left from last week)	
Lasagne sheets	32p
Tagliatelle	95p
Total	**£31.39**

Week 3

Sunday: Stilton, Leek and Mushroom Filo Parcels (page 227), 2 seasonal veg and roast potatoes (page 21)

You have the oven on for the Filo Parcels and you have used half a packet of filo pastry, so use the rest to make something else, sweet or savoury.

Monday: Carrot, Tomato and Lentil Soup (page 52), crusty rolls and hummus (page 186)

Hummus takes only minutes to make, but allow it to rest before serving for the flavours to develop.

You can prepare the soup in the morning before work; it's ideal for the slow cooker. Make more and you will have a wonderful filling soup for lunch.

Tuesday: Spicy Tofu Burgers (73), Chunky Chips (page 76) and salad (pages 194–207)

The burgers were prepared and frozen in Week 1. Defrost and cook as before.

Remember to use your oil spray when preparing the chunky chips

Wednesday: Mushroom Risotto (page 155)

A simple but impressive dish cooked on the hob.

Thursday: Spinach and Ricotta Lasagne (page 174), salad (pages 194–207) and Potato Wedges (page 85)

Take the lasagne you made in Week 1 out of the freezer in the morning to allow time to defrost.

Friday: Goats' Cheese and Red Onion Tart (page 221) and green salad

Remember, you are using your oven, so fill it up. Think of cakes, desserts or pastries.

Saturday: Broccoli and Red Pepper Linguine (page 177)

A simple dish cooked on the hob.

Shopping List

Stilton/blue cheese	£1.29
Hummus	75p
Goats' cheese	£1.30
Crème fraiche	98p
Parmesan cheese	£2
Red onions	76p
Mushrooms	89p (400g)
2.5kg potatoes	£1.98
Seasonal vegetables (enough for 3 meals)	£2.60
Seasonal salad (enough for 2 meals)	£3.97
1 bag of carrots	89p
Broccoli	83p
1 bulb of garlic	39p (for 2 bulbs)*
Tomatoes	96p (for 6)
Lemon	23p
Red lentils	£1.02
Risotto rice	95p
Porcini dried mushrooms	£1.75
Linguine pasta	59p
Crusty rolls	50p
Puff pastry	91p
Filo pastry	£1.22
Total	**£19.68**

Week 4

Sunday: Stuffed Peppers with Goats' Cheese (page 147) and salad (pages 194–207)
Again, remember to make the most of your oven and fill it up.

Monday: Ratatouille (page 148)
A real favourite – if you want to add more bulk, mix with some pasta or serve with crusty bread.

Tuesday: Thai Bean Cakes (page 137) and Green Snap Salad (page 204)
This can be cooked on a hob so no need to use your oven.

Wednesday: Spicy Rice (page 158)
This can be prepared on a hob so no need to use your oven.

Thursday: Veggie Spaghetti Bolognese (page 107, substitute vegetarian mince) (double up)
Double up the recipe and store half in the freezer ready to make another bolognese or a lasagne for another week.

Friday: Black-Eyed Bean Chilli (page 152) and Rice
This can be cooked on a hob or in a slow cooker so no need to use your oven.

Saturday: Tofu Quiche (page 220), salad (pages 194–207) and new potatoes (double up)
Make two quiches and freeze one for another meal.

Shopping List

Goats' cheese	£1.30
Veggie mince	£3.56
2 packs of peppers	£2.96 (2 packs of 3)
Seasonal vegetables (enough for 3 Meals)	£2.60
Seasonal salad (enough for 2 meals)	£3.97
6–8 onions	75p (for 1.5kg)*
Celery (you will use 4–6 sticks)	78p (bunch)
1kg new potatoes	79p
Spring onions	68p
1 bulb of garlic	39p (for 2 bulbs)*
2 courgettes	39p
1 aubergine	£1.18
3 tins of tomatoes	£1.05
Tofu	£1.59
Tin of cannellini beans	48p
Red Thai Paste	£1.39
Lime	20p
Lemon	23p
Chilli	56p
Ginger	62p
Apple juice	56p
Red lentils	£1.02
Basmati rice	84p
Spaghetti	39p
Tin of black-eyed beans	48p
Total	**£28.76**

Index